Theorizing World Cinema

Edited by Lúcia Nagib
Chris Perriam and Rajinder Dudrah

I.B. TAURIS

LONDON · NEW YORK

Published in 2012 by I.B.Tauris & Co. Ltd
6 Salem Road, London W2 4BU
175 Fifth Avenue, New York NY 10010
www.ibtauris.com

Distributed in the United States and Canada Exclusively by Palgrave Macmillan
175 Fifth Avenue, New York NY 10010

ISBN: 978 1 84885 492 5 (HB)
      978 1 84885 493 2 (PB)

A full CIP record for this book is available from the British Library
A full CIP record is available from the Library of Congress

Library of Congress Catalog Card Number: available

Designed and typeset by 4word Ltd, Bristol, UK
Printed and bound in Great Britain by TJ International Ltd, Padstow, Cornwall, UK

Contents

Illustrations

Contributors

John Caughie is Emeritus Professor of Film & Television Studies, University of Glasgow. He is an active researcher in the field of film and television, with interests in British television drama and British and Scottish cinema. He is a member of the editorial board of *Screen*. His major publications are *Theories of Authorship* (ed.) (1981), *Companion to British and Irish Cinema* (ed.) (1996), *Television Drama: Realism, Modernism and British Culture* (2000) and *Edge of Darkness* (2007).

Felicia Chan is RCUK Fellow in Film, Media and Transnational Cultures, University of Manchester. Her main areas of research are: cross-cultural, transnational and 'world' cinemas (mainly East and Southeast Asian cinemas and British Chinese cinema), film festival cultures, culture and technology, theories of intertextuality, diaspora and identity politics, and modernism and modernity in film, literature and culture. She has published recently in *New Cinemas: Journal of Contemporary Film*, *Inter-Asia Cultural Studies* and in *Chinese Films in Focus II*, edited by Chris Berry. She is co-editor of *Genre in Asian Film and Television* (Palgrave Macmillan, 2011).

Rajinder Dudrah is Senior Lecturer and Director of the Centre for Screen Studies at the University of Manchester, where he was also Head of Department of Drama (2007–10). He has researched and published widely in film, media and cultural studies. His books include: *Bollywood Sociology Goes to the Movies* (SAGE, 2006), *Bhangra: Birmingham and Beyond* (Punch Records, 2007) and *The Bollywood Reader* (OUP, 2008). He is the founder and co-editor of the international peer-reviewed journal *South Asian Popular Culture* (Routledge), and is also a regular film commentator for the BBC and other international media.

Song Hwee Lim is Senior Lecturer in Film Studies at the University of Exeter. He is the author of *Celluloid Comrades: Representations of Male Homosexuality in*

Contemporary Chinese Cinemas (University of Hawaii Press, 2006), co-editor of *Remapping World Cinema: Identity, Culture and Politics in Film* (Wallflower Press, 2006) and founding editor of the *Journal of Chinese Cinemas*. He recently completed a book manuscript entitled *Tsai Ming-liang and a Cinema of Slowness*, and a co-edited volume, *The Chinese Cinema Book* (BFI/Palgrave Macmillan, 2011).

Tiago de Luca has recently obtained his PhD degree from the University of Leeds, with a thesis on new realisms in contemporary world cinema. He has published articles in *Senses of Cinema* and *New Cinemas: Journal of Contemporary Film*. He is currently conducting research on digital cinema and realism.

Laura Mulvey is Professor of Film and Media Studies at Birkbeck, University of London. She has been writing about film and film theory since the mid-1970s. In the late 1970s and early 1980s, she co-directed six films with Peter Wollen, including *Riddles of the Sphinx* (BFI, 1978), and *Frida Kahlo and Tina Modotti* (Arts Council, 1980). In 1994 she co-directed the documentary *Disgraced Monuments* with artist/filmmaker Mark Lewis. Her books include *Visual and Other Pleasures* (Palgrave Macmillan, 1989), *Fetishism and Curiosity* (Indiana University Press, 1996) and *Death Twenty-four Times a Second: Stillness and the Moving Image* (Reaktion Books, 2006).

Lúcia Nagib is Centenary Professor of World Cinemas at the University of Leeds. Her single-authored books include: *World Cinema and the Ethics of Realism* (Continuum, 2011), *Brazil on Screen: Cinema Novo, New Cinema, Utopia* (I.B.Tauris, 2007), *The Brazilian Film Revival: Interviews with 90 Filmmakers of the 90s* (Editora 34, 2002), *Born of the Ashes: The Auteur and the Individual in Oshima's Films* (Edusp, 1995), *Around the Japanese Nouvelle Vague* (Editora da Unicamp, 1993) and *Werner Herzog: Film as Reality* (Estação Liberdade, 1991). She is the editor of *Realism and the Audiovisual Media* (with Cecília Mello, Palgrave, 2009), *The New Brazilian Cinema* (I.B.Tauris, 2003), *Master Mizoguchi* (Navegar, 1990) and *Ozu* (Marco Zero, 1990).

Geoffrey Nowell-Smith is Honorary Professorial Fellow at Queen Mary, University of London. He has just completed an AHRC-funded research project into the history of the British Film Institute (BFI), and its relations with government and film culture, from its foundation in 1933 to close to the present day. His publications include: *Making Waves: New Cinemas of the 1960s* (Continuum, 2008), *Luchino Visconti* (BFI, 2003), *Roberto Rossellini: Magician of the Real* (co-editor and contributor) (BFI, 2000), *Hollywood and Europe: Economics, Culture, National Identity* (co-editor and contributor) (BFI, 1998), *L'avventura* (BFI Film Classics series, 1997) and *The Oxford History of World*

Cinema (OUP, 1996). He is co-editor of Antonio Gramsci, *Selections from the Cultural Writings* (Lawrence & Wishart, 1985), and co-editor and translator of Antonio Gramsci, *Selections from the Prison Notebooks* (Lawrence & Wishart, 1971).

Chris Perriam is Professor of Hispanic Studies at the University of Manchester. His research interests are in contemporary Spanish Cinema, Latin American and Spanish poetry, and queer popular writing in Spain. His publications include studies on Spanish film stars, Sara Montiel, Antonio Banderas and Penélope Cruz. He has published recently in the *Journal of Spanish Cultural Studies* and has chapters in *Burning Darkness: A Half Century of Spanish Cinema*, edited by Joan Ramon Resina, and *Spain on Screen: Developments in Contemporary Spanish Cinema*, edited by Ann Davies.

Ashish Rajadhyaksha is Senior Fellow at the Centre for the Study of Culture and Society in India. He has edited numerous books, including: *Ritwik Ghatak: A Return to the Epic* (Screen Unit, 1982); *Encyclopaedia of Indian Cinema* (British Film Institute and OUP, 1994); *The Sad and Glad of Kishore Kumar* (Research Centre for Cinema Studies, 1988); with Amrit Gangar, *Ghatak: Arguments/Stories* (Screen Unit/Research Centre for Cinema Studies, 1987); with Marco Muller, *L'Avventurose Storie del Cinema Indiano* (2 vols, in Italian) (Mostra Internazionale del Nuovo Cinema, 1985); and with Rani Burra, *Looking Back, 1896–1960* (Directorate of Film Festivals/Film India Retrospective of Indian Cinema, 1981). He is currently coordinating the Media Archive of CSCS and working on a two-volume book entitled *Cinema in the Time of Celluloid*.

Paul Julian Smith is Distinguished Professor of Hispanic and Luso-Brazilian Literatures and Languages at CUNY Graduate Center, New York. He was elected a fellow of the British Academy in 2008 for his interdisciplinary work in Hispanic film, television, cultural, and in literary and cultural theory, on which he has published extensively. His recent books include *Spanish Visual Culture: Cinema, Television, Internet* (Manchester University Press, 2007) and *Spanish Screen Fiction: Between Cinema and Television* (Liverpool University Press, 2009). He is a regular contributor to *Sight and Sound* and *Film Quarterly*, and is one of the founding editors of the *Journal of Spanish Cultural Studies*.

Ismail Xavier is Professor of Film at the University of São Paulo. He is the author of, among other books, *Allegories of Underdevelopment: Aesthetics and Politics in Modern Brazilian Cinema* (London/Minneapolis, University of Minnesota Press, 1997), *O olhar e a cena: Hollywood, melodrama, Cinema Novo, Nelson Rodrigues* (São Paulo, CosacNaify, 2003) and *Sertão mar – Glauber Rocha* *e a estética da fome* (São Paulo, CosacNaify, 2007, 3rd edn). He has contributed to *Brazilian Cinema*, edited by Randal Johnson and Robert Stam (New York, Columbia University Press, 1995), *A Companion to Film Theory*, edited by Toby Miller and Robert Stam (Oxford, Blackwell Publishing, 1999), *The New Brazilian Cinema*, edited by Lúcia Nagib (London/New York, I.B.Tauris, 2003), and *Realism and the Audiovisual Media*, edited by Lúcia Nagib and Cecília Mello (Basingstoke, Palgrave, 2009).

Acknowledgements

This book originated from two workshops, Theorizing World Cinema I & II, organized by the Centre for World Cinemas, University of Leeds, in 2006 and 2007, in collaboration with the University of Manchester, and funded by the Fund for International Research Collaboration from the Worldwide Universities Network (WUN). We are indebted to WUN both for this award and for their practical support to many seminal events in the past five years, including the seminar series 'Film, Screen and the Real' (2006–08, co-organized by CWC-Leeds and Manchester), from which we drew two contributions for this book. Special thanks are due to WUN staff Constanze Vageler, Anoushka Kulikowski and Kirsty Mattinson, as well as the technical staff who helped us connect via videolink with other universities in the UK and abroad.

Thanks are also due to the Leeds School of Modern Languages and Cultures, and the Faculty of Arts, represented respectively by the Head of School, Mark Williams, and the Dean, Frank Finlay, for their decisive financial and intellectual support. The Centre for World Cinemas' administrative staff, in particular Paddy Power, also gave us tremendous organizational help.

Finally, the editors would like to thank Philippa Brewster, at I.B. Tauris, for her enthusiasm for our world cinema project and insightful suggestions for this book.

Introduction

Lúcia Nagib, Chris Perriam and Rajinder Dudrah

This is a book about the place of world cinema in the cultural imaginary. Inevitably, too, it is about repositioning world cinema, and placing it in a more open discursive space than traditionally has been the case. As an initiative, it is part of concerted efforts to combine the focus on world cinema as an academic discipline with its development as a research subject, a project which is also at the core of the I.B.Tauris World Cinema Series. Being the first outspokenly theoretical approach to the theme within the Series, this book acknowledges contributions made to the subject under various perspectives, suggests ways of organizing it and proposes steps forward.

As Chaudhuri points out: 'film now belongs to an enormous multinational system consisting of TV networks, new technologies of production and distribution, and international co-production' (2005: 2), which not only justifies, but makes unavoidable, an examination of cinema through its global articulations. As a high-profile cultural industry, transferring images and their makers across borders and technological platforms, and as the site for contestations over identity and visual representation, cinema both shapes and responds to the philosophical, cultural and political effects of transnationalism and cosmopolitanism in the age of the moving image with peculiar intensity. By exploring the interconnectedness of films produced worldwide, the links between cinema and other visual cultural forms, between histories (which may be individual and embodied, or collective and abstracted) and modes of expression, between genres and formations of taste, this book relocates some of the meanings which film theory and film history risk having fixed. It traces a genealogy of the term and its metadiscourses; it intervenes in debates about, and contributes new understandings to, our formulation of the local, national and the transnational in contemporary film studies; and it remaps, carrying forward the work proposed in 2006 by Dennison and Lim.

As we hope the parts and chapters in this collection will demonstrate, world cinema is a reason to believe in the potential of further film theorizing, despite the discredit that has been brought upon film theory as we knew it. The fall from grace of psychoanalytic approaches to cinema from the early 1990s left a whole generation of scholars struggling to find a coherent epistemology to compete with or replace the 'end of theory' as proclaimed by Bordwell and Carroll in their collection *Post-Theory: Reconstructing Film Studies* (1996), echoing the postmodern, nihilistic slogan of the 'end of history'. Applying themselves to the demolition of 'Grand Theory' as represented by 'subject-position theory and culturalism' (Bordwell 1996: 26), they proposed instead middle-brow, in-depth research. Carroll defined this as 'piecemeal theorizing', through which he meant the breaking down of 'some of the presiding questions of the Theory into more manageable questions' (Carroll 1996: 58). Striking a similar note, Bordwell defended 'middle-level research', which he explained as 'empirical studies of filmmakers, genres, and national cinemas', enriched by 'gay/lesbian, feminist, minority, and postcolonialist perspectives' (Bordwell 1996: 27). By an intriguing coincidence, the object of this middle-level research, and the one which particularly called for 'piecemeal theorizing', would be precisely those cinemas often ranged in our day under the category of world cinema; that is, 'Third World Cinemas', 'African films' and 'indigenous traditions' (Bordwell 1996: 27).

Needless to say, the safeguards offered by such fenced-off realms for intellectual work on film did little to prevent the freefall of most film theories for more than a decade, before their gradual and rather discrete resurgence under various guises in recent years. This resurgence responded to the need to reassess central issues in film studies, most notably the experience of film viewing itself, after the demise of the Lacanian spectator, imprisoned in its mirror-stage infancy. The 1990s saw, in its place, the rise of the embodied spectator, whose subjective experience of film was described in the light of Foucault and Deleuze, the former for his sexual politics and the latter for his emphasis on sensory modes of communication. Since Shaviro's groundbreaking book *The Cinematic Body*, first published in 1993, a significant strand in film studies has evolved on the basis of a physical fusion between film and viewer (Marks 2002: xiii–xv), through which the object and subject of film theory became an 'irreducible ensemble' (Sobchack 2004: 4), only apprehensible through a self-questioning, 'haptic' (or tactile) criticism. Embodied though it might be, this criticism is, nonetheless, a theory.

The Diachronic Obsession

Although many film studies' publications have now boldly ventured into the theoretical realm, as exemplified by the volume *Theorising National Cinema*

(Vitali and Willemen 2006) – and the first part of our book is also devoted to the reassessment of the national project – recent world-cinema undertakings have still adopted a cautious approach to master narratives, carefully circumventing the term 'theory'. Dennison and Lim, in their edited collection *Remapping World Cinema*, went as far as qualifying world cinema as 'a theoretical problem', all the while remarking on the variety of cinemas it encompasses and the 'situatedness of each discourse' it elicits (2006: 1). They say:

> To situate World Cinema as a theoretical problem is to question not just what world cinema is but also to/for whom it is a problem, in what contexts, how and why; to interrogate to what purposes does it serve, under what kinds of mechanisms of power does it operate, and what audiences does it seek to address or perhaps empower. Indeed, why theorise, problematise, or even promote World Cinema as a theoretical concept? (2006: 9)

Indeed, the 'problems' with world cinema start with the name itself, whose rise as a commercial label in tandem with 'world music' has given origin to a highly questionable, though enduringly popular, opposition between the American mainstream and the rest of the world. Although this fact alone would have sufficed to strip the term of scholarly interest, the exact opposite is observed in current academia, at least in the UK, where world cinema, as a discipline, has been enthusiastically embraced, in particular in cultural studies' syllabi, as a territory of political resistance. This does not mean, as Kuhn and Grant have observed, a complete disregard for its commercial potential; on the contrary, if the brand 'endows cultural and commercial endeavours, such as film festivals and DVD collections, with a degree of scholarly respectability', 'it also lends a commercial edge to a range of educational and academic initiatives' (Kuhn and Grant 2006: 1).

   It would be misleading, however, to define the world view of cinema as a new or recent phenomenon. As Dennison and Lim also remind us, literature was the artistic field where the globalizing impetus first made an appearance, more precisely in Goethe's formulation of *Weltliteratur* (Dennison and Lim 2006: 2), which expresses the author's fascination with alien literatures placed against the backdrop of those of the West. Such a *Weltanschauung* is at the base of a tradition in comparative literary studies, drawing on the opposition between the West and its others, which has spread through all other arts and continues to thrive almost unchanged up to this day. Andrew's historically and geographically informed 'Atlas of World Cinema', for example, makes no secret of its literary sources. It is in fact an adaptation to cinema of Franco Moretti's 'Atlas of World Literature', proposed in his essay 'Conjectures on World Literature', which draws on a dialectic between centre and periphery imported from political economy (Moretti 2000). Being fully aware of the oversimplification entailed by binary schemes, Moretti identifies a third element in non-European writing, which he calls the 'local narrative voice', whose function is to appropriate and subvert the imported, dominant model. Andrew follows the cue as regards cinema, shifting the emphasis on Hollywood to 'the regional interaction that is particularly visible when storytelling traditions are in focus' (Andrew 2006: 24; see also Nagib 2006: 33).

In effect, finding an alternative or 'third' way has been a favourite response, in film studies, to the vastly predominant binary divisions of the world, drawing on Eurocentric, or US-centred, if not colonial and/or imperial, premises and points of view. An eloquent example of the 'third' approach is given by Guneratne, who, in his co-edited *Rethinking Third Cinema* (2003), turns his back entirely on so-called First and Second Cinemas – those produced respectively in the United States and Europe – proposing instead Third Cinema as a 'theory' in its own right, capable of accounting for 'the majority of the world's films' (Guneratne 2003: 1), despite Third Cinema outputs being limited in time and space to 1960s Latin America. The reason for this choice is his conviction that:

> part of the project of Third Cinema was to challenge this Hegelian notion of a 'philosophy of history' that distinguished the then regnant epoch of 'the German world' from its predecessors, what the anthropologist Claude Lévi-Strauss characterized in another context as the Western obsession with diachronicity. (2003: 5)

Guneratne's assessment is certainly accurate, at least in so far as the 'obsession with diachronicity' is concerned, as this has informed, and continues to inform, not only world-cinema studies, but film theory as whole. If we just think about Bazin's late-1940s' periodization of film history in terms of 'classical' and 'modern', could it not be seen as a direct predecessor of the Hollywood-world cinema binary? Bazin's differential and unique insight into this problem was of course his definition of cinema in terms of Bergsonian duration, which he called 'realism', a style best exemplified by Rossellini and Italian neo-realism, as opposed to the fast-paced, manipulative montage cinema, as represented by the Soviet and most of the American production. Bazin's identification of realism (i.e. spatio-temporal continuity) as the time-space dividing line in global cinema has proved an inexhaustible source of scholarly thought (see Nowell-Smith's chapter), extending its applicability even to the long-take based digital cinema of today (see de Luca's chapter), and this is why we devote the last part of this volume to the reappraisal of the realist project.

Deleuze's highly influential film philosophy, which has inspired so many lines of current film scholarship, builds entirely on the Bazinian scheme. His

binary 'movement-image' versus 'time-image' – which almost literally translates Bazin's 'montage' versus 'realism' – opposes action cinema, as produced by
Hollywood and its avatars, to observational world cinemas, drawing, yet again,
on Bergsonian duration. The French lineage of philosophical thought on film
finds its most distinguished representative in our day in the figure of Jacques
Rancière, who once again goes back (tacitly) to Bazin and (avowedly) to
Deleuze to formulate his own conception of artistic modernity in terms of a
binary division between the 'representative regime' and the 'aesthetic regime'
of art, which he defends in his book on cinema, *Film Fables*, thus:

> The representative regime understands artistic activity on the model of
> an active form that imposes itself upon inert matter and subjects it to its
> representational ends. The aesthetic regime of art rejects the idea of
> form wilfully imposing itself on matter and instead identifies the power
> of the work with the identity of contraries: the identity of active and
> passive, of thought and non-thought, of intentional and unintentional.
> (2006: 117)

It is not difficult to see how such a 'representative regime' would be applicable
to action (Hollywood) cinema, as opposed to realist world cinemas, whose
objectivity, in the best Bazinian ontological tradition, bears 'no traces of the
author's intervention and displays instead only the absolute indifference and
passivity of things with neither will nor meaning' (Rancière 2006: 117).

The list of (often diachronic) binaries which have populated film studies
across history could be extended indefinitely. Its best expression in American
film studies is Bordwell's own concept of the 'classical Hollywood cinema',
celebrated in his co-authored book *The Classical Hollywood Cinema: film style &
mode of production to 1960* (Bordwell, Staiger and Thompson 1988), universally
adopted in academic film syllabi to this day. That this 'classical' in America
opposes the 'modern' elsewhere is made clear, for example, by Miriam Hansen
and her theory of 'vernacular modernisms' (2000), according to
which Hollywood's classical mode gave rise to modern cinemas in countries
such as China and Russia, in the early twentieth century. Similar dual schemes
include the polemic around narrative realism (Hollywood) and political anti-
realism (Godard and Brecht-inspired experimental and avant-garde cinemas),
as represented by Colin MacCabe (1974) and the *Screen* theory of the 1970s
(Mulvey and Nagib revisit these ideas in their chapters). Noël Burch's
(1990) opposition between the Institutional Mode of Representation (IMR),
introduced by American 'bourgeois' cinema, and the Primitive Mode of
Representation (PMR), as seen in early cinema, would be another interesting
example hinging on the centre-periphery dialectics (see Rajadhyaksha's
chapter). Dual organizational modes continue to inspire, often excellent, film

scholarship, as, for example, the recent *Cinema at the Periphery* (Iordanova et al. 2010) and *The Cinema of Small Nations* (Hjört and Petrie 2007). However, in this book, we propose to escape entirely from the dual model, not just by suggesting an alternative or third way, but by proposing a polycentric approach to film studies.

The Polycentric Approach to Film Studies

Binaries posited as a stance of resistance to oppressive powers have been, and will continue to be, indispensable to film studies, both as political and organizational tools. However, in this volume, we have attempted a different approach, which, drawing on Shohat and Stam (1994), we call 'polycentric'. The characterization of this approach as 'theoretical' aims, on the one hand, to avoid the light touch of 'surveys' or 'overviews' that convey a 'world in a nutshell' by compressing whole countries and even continents in a few chapters, in order to fulfil the ultimately impossible task of defining uniform modes of address, distribution and reception across thousands of the most varied and contrasting outputs. Our understanding of 'theory', on the other hand, follows Bordwell and Carroll's suggestion of in-depth research on representative cases, which we combine with a set of theoretical projects, whose usefulness for the assessment of world cinemas' mutual relations and interconnectedness has proved unquestionable as they evolved through time. They are the national, the transnational, the diasporic and the realist projects, as expressed in the division in parts of this volume.

Shohat and Stam's defence of a 'polycentric multiculturalism', in their groundbreaking book *Unthinking Eurocentrism: Multiculturalism and the Media* (1994), is the moment in film theory that allows us to move away from the uniformizing, oppositional and negative understanding of world cinema, and a starting point to question Eurocentric versions of the world and of cinema's place within it. While dismissing as unnecessary and ultimately wrong the world division between 'us' and the 'other', 'centre and periphery', 'the West and the Rest' (1994: 2), Stam and Shohat also warn against the 'inverted European narcissism that posits Europe as the source of all social evils in the world', resulting in a 'victimology' that 'reduces non-European life to a pathological response to Western penetration' (1994: 3). Indeed, in our view, the greatest danger of defining world cinema negatively, as 'non-Hollywood cinema', is to perpetuate the patronizing attitude which sees all other cinemas as victims; that is, purely reactive manifestations incapable of eliciting independent theory (Nagib 2006: 32). Instead, we adopt a positive and inclusive approach to film studies, which defines world cinema as a polycentric phenomenon with peaks of creation in different places and periods. Once notions of a single centre, primacies and diachronicities are discarded, everything can be put on the world cinema map on an equal footing, even Hollywood, which instead of a threat becomes a cinema among others (Nagib 2006: 34; see also chapters by Xavier, Rajadhyaksha, Lim and Mulvey). At the core of this proposal is the belief that different cinemas of the world can generate their own, original theories. They do not depend on paradigms set by the so-called Hollywood classical narrative style, and in most cases are misunderstood if seen in this light. In multicultural, multi-ethnic societies like ours, cinematic expressions from various origins cannot be seen as 'the other', for the simple reason that they are us. More interesting than their difference is, in most cases, their interconnectedness.

Evidence that escaping binarisms is a safe path for original theorizing abounds in this volume. A good example is Caughie's proposal of a new concept of art cinema on the basis of experimentalism in Scottish cinema, which privileges subjectivity over nationality, while turning away from the usual oppositions between art and popular cinemas. Or Xavier's celebrated thesis on 'national allegories', which he applies to American and Italian monumental cinemas. In both cases, contextual knowledge offers solid backing for theoretical ventures, as also seen in Lim's analysis of Ang Lee's 'multiple tongues', which questions notions of national, transnational and accented cinemas. Detailed analysis equally underpins the theory of 'corporeal realism' developed by Nagib on the basis of Nagisa Oshima's erotic masterpiece *The Realm of the Senses* (*Ai no koriida*, 1976), whereas Perriam explores a range of polycentric constructs of feeling and identity in relation to the work of a single actor, the Spanish Eduardo Noriega, within a multilocational network of representations.

Between Transnational Cinema and World Cinema

The prominence of the transnational question across all chapters in this book is such that world cinema often sounds synonymous with it, and for this reason deserves some further reflection. In a newly launched, decidedly theoretical world-cinema collection, entitled *World Cinema: Transnational Perspectives* (Durovicova and Newman 2010), changes in film industries and film style are understood 'not merely to be a response to national conditions and pressures, but also to have, most always, multiple, international determinants' (2010: 4). Part of the work, then, of theorizing world cinema must surely be to attempt to see how its own trajectories coincide with, slide over and slip behind those of transnational cinema (Paul Julian Smith, in his chapter, makes a complementary point in relation to 'globalization', 'transnational cinema' and academic discourse). Sometimes one gives infrastructural support to the other, sometimes the situation is reversed.

Recent conceptualizations of transnational cinema have tended to play up its roles as a cinema of difference or even resistance, and may situate it in radical, unfixed spaces – as hybrid, transcendent of national paradigms and interstitial (Ezra and Rowden 2006). However, the most readily recognized values and mechanisms of the category and set of critiques known as world cinema might be said to have sprung up in reaction, precisely, to a pre-existing conservative transnationalism in cinema inasmuch as it had been based historically on popular, hegemonic filmmaking and star-making industries. That is to say that Los Angeles, Mexico City, Bombay and Hong Kong might at their different apogees be sites and sources of transnational filmmaking and activity, but they almost certainly have not been consistently interstitial, alternative, resistant or troubling of the status quo. An important part of the conversation between transnational and world cinema, then, is the restitution to the former of a radical potential that the latter embodies, but whose negative definition in opposition to the mainstream has all too often elided.

The transnational in its first phases (commencing asynchronously in different territories) is roughly speaking complicit with a homogenizing globalization, producing a rich and popular output whose socio-political and economic inclusivity is an illusion, and whose range of treatment is narrow. The resistant values and mechanisms of world cinema in its own first phase – let us say, with Cowie (2004), in the 1960s – are, of course, generic range, openness in subject matter, aesthetic distinctiveness, a perceived integrity, the building-up of auteurs or elite teams for art-house consumption, festival distribution, and the satisfaction of national cultural politics. Working transnationally in constituting itself as a category and a practice, world cinema attempts, in this particular phase or version, to overcome one hegemony by replacing it (predictably enough) with another, and its self-marking as art cinema produces the assumption that filmmaking in and across different regions has a 'shared cultural sphere', an 'affinity' (Choudhuri 2005: 6). However, if 'The study of world cinema enables us to re-perceive our own cultural positioning, as well as discovering "alternatives"' (2005: 7), through a sense of dynamic relationality and interplay (2005: 5–6, 11–12), the first phase, or version, gets stuck on that cultural positioning while sidelining the sense of difference, remaining (through the effects of critical discourse and commercial concerns) no more and no less than 'those limited forms of difference that can easily be marketed to an international audience' (Badley and Palmer 2006: 11).

However, as the processes of transnationalism move on through their own successive phases, world cinema increasingly includes and takes forward radical elements in filmmaking and film critique, including the questioning of imposed ideas of national cinema. There is, for example, a utopian transnationalism which informs world cinema, one whereby a socio-politically centrifugal 'nostalgia for the periphery' (Cook 2010: 24), 'in the context of transnational flow', enables filmmaking to 'destabilize the field of cultural production and displace the hegemony of the centre' (2010: 10). Or, as Hess and Zimmermann (2006: 99–100) argue in relation to documentary film production, forms of adversarial transnationalism have more recently emerged which can 'wrench the transnational away from its corporatist location', and from its homogenizing project of turning all bodies and images into 'sites and discourses of consumption' (2006: 99). Adversarial transnationalism can make for:

> A re-imaging of relations among media, politics and the economy … a constant shuttle between domination and resistance, between hegemonic power and multi-oppositional alliances … refigur[ing] the relationship between the local, regional, national and global as one of endless mediation, integration and negotiation rather than separation. (Hess and Zeimmermann 2006: 100)

Just such an adversarial transnationalism (which Higbee and Lim would suggest refuses to see itself 'taking place uniquely between national cinemas', 2010: 18) informs the contributions in the present volume, notably in the chapters by Lim, Chan and Smith.

It is interesting that the new – or, rather, renewed – globalization of cinema production, coupled with the deployment of complex mediatic networks, has in some ways favoured a return to prominence of the 'transnational' term in its older guise. Its conventional, primary connections with economics and socio-political dynamics make it a useful analytical tool for present times, especially when combined with the semi-empirical turn in academic film criticism of the past 20 years. It can be used, as Ezra and Rowden argue (2006), to link the economic and socio-political to a consideration of 'aesthetic and narrative dynamics' and 'modes of emotional identification' in the context of an 'increasingly interconnected world system' and, crucially, to discussions of the dissolution of the 'national' as a regulatory force or as a category for thinking cinema (2006: 1). However, world cinema theorized goes further than the connective fix which the transnational term in its older guise facilitates. Placing form in the contexts of the social, economic, political or commercial content of film history is an old skill. Indeed, a new Transnational Cinema Studies is positioning itself more properly and subtly to explore the shifting relationships between the various parts of the global filmmaking enterprise, its users and promoters. As Higbee and Lim have argued (2010), a 'critical transnationalism' can, precisely, take account of otherwise obscured questions relating to power imbalances, exclusion and marginalization (2010: 9, 17–18). Earlier versions of transnational film criticism – focusing on a national/transnational binary, on regional and shared cultural values, or on diasporic and exilic cinemas (2010:

9) – had played their part in obscuring these questions and in over-simplifying the dynamics of transnational exchange. As do Higbee and Lim of 'trans-nationalism in films', we and our contributors shall be arguing for a world cinema that cannot 'be taken as a given or for granted' (2010: 18), or as a 'shorthand for an international or supranational mode of film production ... without any real consideration of ... aesthetic, political or economic implications' (2010: 10). We intend here to recalibrate our understanding of the ways in which world cinema theory might work by including transnational cinema studies' accounts of the shifts and myriad flows in the global distribution and reception of international films (Chan, Dudrah, Perriam), while rethinking film language and form, genres and their permeability under pressure of mediatic change (as does Smith) and materiality (as do Nowell-Smith, Mulvey, Nagib and de Luca).

As a conceptual purchase on our use of the transnational, diaspora cinema in this collection (Dudrah, Chan and Lim) also illustrates some of the contours of transnational movements and identities through the audiovisual medium of film. Used widely in the arts, humanities and social sciences, the notion of diaspora helps reconfigure fixed ideas about ethnicity, race, nation and culture by considering social identities and texts that move simultaneously between a number of locations, helping to shape new global forms of sensibilities. In our interrogation of world cinema, diaspora cinema and its attendant representations not only offer a space for critically theorizing and elaborating the polycentric possibilities of the diasporic subject in his or her varied and fluid modern identities, but also to illuminate and contemplate how world cinema itself has been rejuvenated and made cosmopolitan by the contribution of diaspora aesthetics.

World Cinema Projects

As a result of the application of the polycentric method, and as a means to account for the fundamental world-cinema debates described above around questions of national, transnational and diasporic cinemas, as well as diachronic realism, we have structured this book according to what we call the National, the Transnational, the Diasporic and the Realist Projects.

Part I, on the National Project, comprises meditations within and beyond the national realm. In Chapter One, John Caughie addresses issues of film in post-devolution Scotland, arguing that an idea of art cinema and experiment is more appropriate to the conditional nature of devolution than the issues of heritage and national identity which have obsessed much of the critical writing about Scottish – and British – cinema. Focusing on Lynne Ramsay's 2001 film, *Morvern Callar*, Caughie traces the complexities of its language and its adaptation of Alan Warner's novel which, particularly but not exclusively in Scotland, might loosen the grip of a critical language underpinned by assumptions about the stability of representation and identity.

As part of a concern that has marked his theoretical work as a whole, Ismail Xavier, in Chapter Two, discusses national allegories with respect to *Good Morning, Babylon* (Paolo and Vittorio Taviani 1987), which he describes as a modern film that allows for a comprehensive discussion of classical allegories, as it looks back to the first monumental spectacles in cinema: Pastrone's *Cabiria* (1914) and Griffith's *Intolerance* (1916). The fact that the Tavianis concentrate on empirical and symbolic relations, modern nations (Italy and the United States) and classical filmmakers gives Xavier the opportunity to discuss the ways in which the directors understand the interaction between art, memory and war, and allegorize the continuity of the aesthetic impulse, despite all the discontinuities in history entailed by national conflicts and international catastrophes.

In search of a film theory that can account for Indian Cinema, Ashish Rajadhyaksha, in Chapter Three, contends that crucial components of this cinema are actually narrative self-justifications. These are not isolationist, nor do they take recourse to cultural exceptionalism. Instead, they emerge mainly from a tension-ridden relationship with the Indian state, which is often – uniquely, for a postcolonial state – embarrassed rather than gratified at having inherited the world's largest, and most diverse, film production base. Such a tension allows an important link between textual excess and political instability. Rajadhyaksha argues that textual excess is itself not a new concept to film theorists, but takes on specific meanings in India. This is exemplified in the way Indian cinema finds use for what film theorists call the 'Hollywood Mode of Production', a kind of narrative economy perfected in Hollywood cinema but which becomes the textual location for Indian cinema to play out its crisis of legitimacy.

Part II addresses the Transnational Project on the basis of multinational relations in film production, *mise-en-scène* and stardom. Paul Julian Smith, in Chapter Four, sketches three recent theoretical models of transnational cinema (by Robert Stam, Néstor García Canclini and Chris Berry), arguing that, given the dispersal of production and the nomadism of creative personnel, the 'national presumption' no longer holds as an analytical category. Addressing the distinct cases of Mexico, Argentina and Brazil (and analysing in detail one recent film from each country), he argues for a more flexible understanding of what constitutes 'Latin American Cinema', which goes beyond geographic, economic and political criteria to address questions of cultural participation and creative clusters.

In Chapter Five, Chris Perriam examines a small but representative range of polycentric constructs of feeling and identity in relation to the work of, and to

responses to, a single actor caught up in a multilocational network of representations. The chapter is an exploratory case study of the Spanish actor Eduardo
Noriega, whose international career posits him as an actor in transit between
languages and audiences. By looking at his first bilingual and transnational
role, and by tracing some of the history of his Internet presence through his
official website, it brings together two established conceptualizations of the
idea of motion: movement away as a paradoxical consolidator of cultural
expression (in an anthropological sense of deterritorialization); and the 'transport' of desire.

Finally, Felicia Chan, in Chapter Six, focuses on Wong Kar-wai's *Ashes of
Time* (*Dongxie xidu*, 1994) and its later version, *Ashes of Time Redux* (2008), as
representatives of different stages of the transnational cinema phenomenon.
On the basis of these films, she contends that there is, in a sense, the world
cinema that exists because the films exist, and there is the 'World Cinema' that
is made, through a process of canonization that includes awards ceremonies,
reviews and international distribution deals. *Ashes of Time Redux*, in its new,
improved state, acquires what Chan describes as a global style that has come to
characterize transnational Chinese cinemas, a style that embodies a conscious
look and feel of sumptuousness, of high production values, yet one that also
seems to eschew commercialism and aspire towards 'art'.

As continuation to (and partly consequence of) the Transnational Project,
Part III is devoted to the Diasporic Project, discussing both the ways in
which polycentrism and diasporas can (or cannot) be articulated. Focusing on
Black British Cinema, Rajinder Dudrah, in Chapter Seven, asks: how best
might we theorize and analyse diasporic cinema as part of world cinema? Is it
best considered part of, or beyond, the discourses that have thus far attempted
to map out world cinema? How can we usefully articulate the relationships
between the conceptual categories of 'world cinema' and 'diasporic cinema'? In
order to provide answers to these questions, he analyses the means of production and diegetic possibilities that recent and select post-1990s Black British
diasporic cinema (of combined British, African, Caribbean and South Asian
heritages) might engender.

In Chapter Eight, Song Hwee Lim argues that, in an age of globalization that
has witnessed massive migration of people, capital, cultures and ideologies, the
national (and national cinema) can no longer sustain its myth of unity, coherence and purity. To illustrate this assumption, he focuses on Ang Lee, whose
career has been based in the United States, from the very beginning and who
can variously be claimed as a national (Taiwanese) director, a transnational
Chinese director, a world-cinema director and an accented (diasporic) director.
Lim contends that all these categories cannot be fully accounted for unless we
also consider Lee's career in the United States where he has directed films in a
globally dominant mode of production. Via the example of Ang Lee's career

and 'multiple tongues', he re-evaluates the notion of accented cinema which, in Hamid Naficy's construction, only concerns itself with filmmaking activities situated in an exilic or diasporic condition, emerging from migratory routes from Third World and postcolonial societies to Western cosmopolitan centres.

Part IV is devoted to a reassessment of the Realist Project which, as explained above, was at the very origin of the diachronic idea of world cinema, identified as the 'modern' as opposed to the 'classical' mainstream. Geoffrey Nowell-Smith, in Chapter Nine, goes back to the immediate postwar period, where Bazin had located the beginning of modern cinema, to observe a sudden surge of realist filmmaking in many parts of the world, beginning most famously with Italian neo-realism but soon spreading throughout Europe and beyond. He asks: was this a return to values which had always been latent in the cinema, or was it something completely new and without precedent in film history? In particular, what was the 'neo' in neo-realism? His chapter argues that neo-realism was every bit as new as Bazin held it to be at the time and that its legacy continues to inspire – and haunt – filmmakers today.

In Chapter Ten, Nagib's take on 'corporeal realism' aims to demonstrate the advantages of a polycentric approach to film studies, drawing on local context and traditions, over the arbitrary application of alien (usually Hollywood-based) paradigms to films produced across the globe. To that end, she looks at *The Realm of the Senses* (*Ai no koriida*, Nagisa Oshima 1976) as a rare and fully accomplished example of how cinema can elicit continuity between terms normally seen as antagonistic in film studies: staged representation and presentation of reality, exhibitionism and voyeurism, critical and cathartic spectatorship. In so doing, she attempts to redress perceptions of this film which have systematically resorted to Brecht-inspired body-mind dualisms in order to deny the infectious power of its hard-core eroticism.

In Chapter Eleven, Tiago de Luca argues that in the last decades a number of art-house directors, from different corners of the globe, have consistently resorted to a meditative and minimalist style of filmmaking, notable examples being Abbas Kiarostami (Iran), Apichatpong Weerasethakul (Thailand), Carlos Reygadas (Mexico), Béla Tarr (Hungary) and Tsai Ming-liang (Taiwan), among many others. For de Luca, their work can be grouped under the rubric of cinematic realism insofar as they adhere to devices Bazin had defined, over 50 years ago, as essentially realist, such as location shooting, non-professional actors, deep-focus cinematography and, in particular, the long take. One way of theorizing this contemporary realist trend in world cinema, de Luca suggests, is to consider its stress on the material world as a reaction to simulation processes enabled and disseminated by digital technology. In order to prove his hypothesis, he resorts to Deleuze's concepts of time-image and 'cinema of the seer' to underpin the analysis of what he considers the most distinctive aspect of this cinema: a contemplative attitude, through which the perceptual qualities of the audiovisual components are enhanced and narrative deflated.

Finally, in Chapter 12, Laura Mulvey discusses rear-projection in so-called 'classical Hollywood cinema' as a device that offered solutions to some practical problems of star-system filming, but also, if only incidentally, produced images that were at odds with the principles of transparency and associated realism to which Hollywood cinema generally aspired. She argues that, as it was almost impossible to conceal completely the mechanics of the device, the discordance between studio and setting tended to become visible, affecting narrative coherence and threatening the transparency of the classical cinema. Consciously or unconsciously, rear-projection inserted into movies another cinematic realism, one that foregrounded the 'reality' of process and material. Mulvey's consideration of this paradox brings to light the contradictory perspectives of modernity and modernism in the cinema.

As a whole, the theoretical approaches to a varied plethora of world cinema contained in this book, though far from covering all the epistemological possibilities suggested by the enormous richness of current and past world-cinema outputs, testify to the advantages of the polycentric method, not least its democratic inclusiveness in a multi-ethnic, multipolar world.

References

Andrew, Dudley (2006) 'An Atlas of World Cinema', in Dennison and Lim (eds), pp.19–29.

Badley, Linda and R. Barton Palmer (2006) *Traditions in World Cinema* (Edinburgh, Edinburgh University Press).

Bordwell, David (1996) 'Contemporary Film Studies and the Vicissitudes of Grand Theory', in Bordwell and Carroll (eds), pp.3–36.

Bordwell, David and Noël Carroll (eds) (1996) *Post-Theory: Reconstructing Film Studies* (Madison, University of Wisconsin Press).

Bordwell, David, Janet Staiger and Kristin Thompson (1988) *The Classical Hollywood Cinema: film style & mode of production to 1960* (London, Routledge).

Burch, Noël (1990) *Life to Those Shadows*, ed. and trans. Ben Brewster (Berkeley, University of California Press).

Carroll, Noël (1996) 'Prospects for Film Theory: A Personal Assessment', in Bordwell and Carroll (eds), pp.37–68.

Chaudhuri, Shohini (2005) *Contemporary World Cinema* (Edinburgh, Edinburgh University Press).

Cook, Pam (2010) 'Transnational Utopias: Baz Luhrmann and Australian Cinema', *Transnational Cinemas* 1:1, pp.23–36.

Cowie, Peter (2004) *Revolution!: The Explosion of World Cinema in the Sixties* (New York, Faber & Faber).

Dennison, Stephanie and Song Hwee Lim (2006) 'Situating World Cinema as a Theoretical Problem', in Dennison and Lim (eds), pp.1–15.

Dennison, Stephanie and Song Hwee Lim (eds) (2006) *Remapping World Cinema: Identity, Culture and Politics in Film* (London and New York, Wallflower Press).

Durovicova, Natasa and Kathleen Newman (eds) (2007) *World Cinemas: Transnational Perspectives* (London and New York, Routledge).

Ezra, Elizabeth and Terry Rowden (2006) 'General Introduction: What Is Transnational Cinema?', in Ezra and Rowden (eds) *Transnational Cinema: The Film Reader* (London and New York, Routledge), pp.1–12.

Grant, Catherine and Annette Kuhn (eds) (2006) *Screening World Cinema: A Screen Reader* (London, Routledge).

Guneratne, Anthony R., Wimal Dissanayake and Sumita S. Chakravarty (eds) (2003) *Rethinking Third Cinema* (London and New York, Routledge).

Hansen, Miriam B. (2000) 'The mass production of senses: classical cinema as vernacular modernism', in C. Gledhill and L. Williams (eds) *Reinventing Film Studies* (London, Arnold), pp.332–50.

Hess, John and Patricia R. Zimmermann (2006) 'Transnational Documentaries: A Manifesto', in Ezra and Rowden (eds) *Transnational Cinema: The Film Reader* (London and New York, Routledge), pp.97–108.

Higbee, Will and Song Wee Lim (2010) 'Concepts of Transnational Cinema: Towards a Critical Transnationalism in Film Studies', *Transnational Cinemas* 1(1), pp.7–21.

Hjört, Mette and Duncan Petrie (2007) *The Cinema of Small Nations* (Edinburgh, Edinburgh University Press).

Iordanova, Dina, David Martin-Jones and Belén Vidal (eds) (2010) *Cinema at the Periphery* (Detroit, Wayne State University Press).

MacCabe, Colin (1974) 'Realism and the Cinema: Notes on Some Brechtian Theses', *Screen* 15:2, Summer, pp.7–27.

Marks, Laura U. (2002) *Touch: Sensuous Theory and Multisensory Media* (Minneapolis/London, University of Minnesota Press).

Moretti, Franco (2000) 'Conjectures on World Literature', *New Left Review* 1 (Jan/Feb), pp.54–68.

Nagib, Lúcia (2006) 'Towards a Positive Definition of World Cinema', in Dennison and Lim (eds), pp.30–7.

Rancière, Jacques (2006) *Film Fables*, trans. Emiliano Battista (Oxford, Berg).

Shaviro, Steven (1993) *The Cinematic Body* (Minneapolis, University of Minnesota Press).

Shohat, Ella and Robert Stam (1994) *Unthinking Eurocentrism: Multiculturalism and the Media* (London, Routledge).

Sobchack, Vivian (2004) *Carnal Thoughts: Embodiment and Moving Image Culture* (Berkeley/London, University of California Press).
Vitali, Valentina and Paul Willemen (eds) (2006) *Theorising National Cinema* (London, BFI).

PART I

THE NATIONAL PROJECT

Chapter One

Morvern Callar, Art Cinema and the 'Monstrous Archive'[1]

John Caughie

On the cover of his book of short stories, *Unlikely Stories Mostly*, embossed in gilt lettering above an intricate pattern of thistles but hidden behind the dust jacket, Alasdair Gray has concealed the motto 'Work as if you were living in the early days of a better nation' (Gray 1983). In *Cinema 2: The Time-image*, Gilles Deleuze instructs us:

> Art, and especially cinematographic art, must take part in this task: not that of addressing a people, which is presupposed already there, but of contributing to the invention of a people. (Deleuze 2000: 217)

'Not the myth of a past people', he adds, 'but the story-telling of the people to come' (2000: 223).

Deleuze's book was first published in 1985, and its reference point is the movements in 'Third Cinema', the radical cinema of the developing and marginalized 'third world' in the 1970s and 1980s, away from what he calls 'Rocha's Guevarism, Chahine's Nasserism, black American cinema's black-powerism' towards a more complex realization of a people which is not always already there waiting for the spark of liberation, but is yet to be invented, glimpsed only in the conditional tense: working *as if* in the early days of a better nation. 'After the 1970s', he says:

> Black American cinema makes a return to the ghettos, returns to this side of a consciousness, and, instead of replacing a negative image of the black with a positive one, multiplies types and 'characters', and each

time creates or re-creates only a small part of the image which no longer
corresponds to a linkage of actions, but to shattered states of emotions
or drives, expressible in pure images and sounds: the specificity of black
cinema is now defined by a new form, 'the struggle that must bear on
the medium itself'... (2000: 220)

For Deleuze, and, in their work on Kafka and minor literatures written a year
later, for Deleuze and Guattari (2003), the people as an already constituted
identity – the people which was available to Eisenstein or Capra – is now missing. This for them is the given condition of a modern political cinema.

Alasdair Gray, whose conjunction with Deleuze and Guattari, Kafka and
minor literature may be less unlikely than at first it seems, wrote his *Unlikely
Stories Mostly* in 1983. The context of its motto is the disappointment surrounding the muddle of a 1979 referendum which failed, on a technicality, to
produce Scottish political devolution, a disappointment which for many was
both rational and emotional, inscribed on both our institutions and our psyche.
Devolution finally came in 1999, the Scottish Parliament now inhabits its
iconic building, and we might now indeed be living in the early days of a better
nation. Devolved power, however, is still a delegated authority, a conditional
state, constitutionally assigned to the territory of 'as if': in Deleuze and
Guattari's sense, perhaps, politically we still inhabit a deterritorialized territory,[2] a nation without the full territorial powers of a state. Such a conditionality is the context for this chapter. Rather than longing for the certainties of
statehood, however, the securities of territory or the authority of achieved identity, I would argue that this provisional, deferred, uncertain nationality, this
constitutional 'as if', is much to be preferred to rising and being a nation again,
with all the grotesque self-assertions and aggressions which that has so often
implied in the new world order.

Both Duncan Petrie and David Martin-Jones have spoken of Scottish
cinema in the context of devolution. For Petrie, the process of becoming
devolved can be found in a 'growing sense of cultural self-determination' and
the forging over the last quarter-century of 'a new culture of possibility' which
has enabled Scottish film to enter the new millennium with 'unprecedented
levels of confidence, achievement and ambition' (Petrie 2000: 226). David
Martin-Jones draws directly on Deleuze in his discussion of Peter Mullan's
Orphans (1997) as an expression of a minor cinema: 'Deleuze's theory', he says:

illustrates how Mullan's film performs a minor action on an aesthetic
which has previously been used to create an Anglo-centric, consensual
view of British national identity, and how, in doing so, it aids the recre-
ation of Scottish national identity after devolution. Thus *Orphans'* textual renegotiation of social realism parallels the nation's, and the film

industry's, attempts to recreate a sense of Scottish national identity in
relation to the vestiges of 'Britain'. (Martin-Jones 2004: 226–41)

Both Petrie and Martin-Jones appeal to a notion of post-devolution national
identity. My own view of devolution, reflecting on the experience of the past
11 years in Scotland, would place the emphasis much less on a new sense of
identity than on a sense of experiment, of operating from time to time without
the safety net of precedent. Frequently derided for immaturity by a Scottish
press which has seen it all and has grown weary, we may also be witnessing a
gauche politics, the wobbly steps of a political class which has not yet fully settled into being politicians. Immaturity may be the cynic's name for playing on
the edges of possibility. Who would have thought that Scotland would be the
first in the UK to introduce a smoking ban, and who would have thought it
might be a success? Who would have thought of a Scottish Cultural
Commission speaking the language of cultural entitlements, and cutting through
the fragmented bureaucracies of cultural patronage? And who would have
thought of a Scottish National Theatre without a building, resisting the model
of the national museum and breaking up the nation into its living and lived in
localities? And if architecture, after modernism and postmodernism, is the first
green shoot of a paradigm shift, who would have thought of a Cancer Care
Centre in Dundee built by the American, Frank Gehry, or a garden in Dumfries
landscaped by his friend and compatriot, Charles Jencks, or a museum of transport by the Iraqi-born Zaha Hadid, or a Scottish Parliament by the Catalan,
Enric Miralles? Rather than stabilizing a post-devolution identity, this experimentalism seems to me to pose the challenge to identity. The tentative conditionality of devolution has the potential to defer solidification and the settled
assumptions of an ineluctable 'us', opening a space for difference, a disassem-
blage of unity into an assemblage of disunities, not just trying on national identities but imagining not having one. It is in the nature of experiments, of
course, that the result is not already determined and experiments fail as often
as they succeed – even successes (the smoking ban) contain their own absurdi-
ties (the ban on the representation of smoking on stage). The experience of
Scotland in the last 11 years has not been without its embarrassments. For the
purposes of this chapter, however, I want to hold onto this notion of
experimentalism for the mark it leaves on the possibility of an art cinema – an
art cinema which may be thought of as a sensibility rather than simply as an
industrial category – and on the privileging of subjectivity over identity.

In his essay, 'Revisiting the national', Paul Willemen distinguishes between
identity and subjectivity thus:

> ... there is a diametrical opposition between identity and subjectivity.
> The former, being what the institutionally orchestrated practices of

address seek to impose, constitutes a never-quite-fitting straitjacket; the latter is an ambiguous term designating individuals as the crossroads or condensation points of multiple sets of institutionally organised discursive practices. As such, subjectivity delineates a 'space' where the plethora of grammatical subjects activated in language fold into and over each other to form what any of us might call his or her 'subjective world'. Subjectivity always exceeds identity, since identity formation consists of trying to pin 'us' to a specific, selected sub-set of the many diverse clusters of discourse we traverse in our lifetimes, and that stick to us to varying degrees. Subjectivity, then, relates to what we may think and feel to be the case regarding 'our' sexuality, kinship relations, our understanding of social-historical dynamics acquired through (self)education, work experience and so on. Some aspects of our subjectivity may be occupied or hijacked by the national identity modes of address, but there are always dimensions within our sense of 'subjective individuality' that escape and exceed any such identity straitjacket. (2006: 30–1)

For Willemen, following Tom Nairn, national identity 'is a question of address, not of origin or genes' (2006: 30). Identity is constructed, or recognizes itself, in the discourses which are addressed to it. Subjectivity exceeds identity, slipping the security of its moorings, resisting the fixity of representation and the interpretation which binds it. Subjectivity is never always already defined; it is experimental, trying it out and trying it on. Identity, on the other hand, finds itself in the already there, recognizing itself in the discursive formations which history has distilled and congealed out of the pandemonium of past experiences and possibilities. It is the 'necessary fiction' which enables collective action and social interaction, but it must constantly be checked for a hardening of the national arteries and the mistaking of a necessary fiction for an essential truth. For my argument, with a simplification which acts as a provocation, subjectivity in the cinema is the proper subject of art and an art cinema; identity is the object of what has come to be known as a European quality cinema, a cinema which occupies the middle ground between art (what Adorno haughtily and flagrantly calls 'genuine art') and the popular. In the present context, the difficult, yet-to-be-fixed subjectivities of an art cinema seem to me particularly attuned to the experimentalism, the conditionality, the 'as-if-ness' of devolution.

It will be apparent that by 'art cinema' I do not just mean a market niche within the production and exhibition of cinema (though it is, of course, also that), nor am I convinced that the art cinema I am imagining (an imaginary art cinema, perhaps rather than an achieved reality) can usefully be confined within the regulatory framework of nation or of genre. If the experimentalism

– and the difficulties, the possibilities of failure – in devolution provide particular conditions of existence for an art cinema, then an art cinema, with its experimental, avant-garde sensibility, has particular contributions to make in the early days of a better nation.

In *The Man without Content*, Giorgio Agamben projects a 'traditional society' in which there is an immediacy, an 'unmediatedness', between the act of transmission and the thing transmitted. When this immediacy is broken, as it is in all 'modern societies', he speaks of an 'accumulation of culture', culture as a thing to be valued in itself independently of its means of transmission: there is 'an inadequation, a gap between the act of transmission and the thing to be transmitted, and a valuing of the latter independently of the former' (Agamben 1999: 107). 'When a culture loses its means of transmission', he says:

> man is deprived of reference points and finds himself wedged between, on the one hand, a past that incessantly accumulates behind him and oppresses him with the multiplicity of its now-indecipherable contents, and on the other hand a future that he does not yet possess and that does not throw any light on his struggle with the past. (1999: 107)

The alternative he proposes to what he calls 'the infinite accumulation of the old in a sort of monstrous archive' (1999: 107) – a formulation which seems familiar in the context of British heritage cinema and from a whole tradition of Scottish cinema – is a re-engagement with the means of transmission, with the form of the content, with the elusive difficulty of art which has been subjected to the alienation of non-traditional societies. 'History', he says, 'is not a bus you can get off …' (1999: 46). The art cinema which I am imagining, then, a cinema which has confronted the difficulty of alienation and can no longer believe in the transparency of representation, is one which offers the possibility of founding the present, as Agamben says, 'as the relationship between past and future' (1999: 107), situating ourselves as complex subjects in the present rather than confirming our identities in the monstrous archive.

Morvern Callar

My interest in Lynne Ramsay's 2001 film, *Morvern Callar*, is in the extent to which it seems to me to confound the received notion of national cinemas and confuses the desire for a national identity expressed through cinema. It puts in play subjectivities which resist any attempt to contain them within the familiar contours of a national identity. It experiments instead with ways of being and behaving, seeing and representing, which never quite congeal into the acceptable or resolve into closure.

Morvern Callar was developed by BBC Scotland, and was funded by the National Lottery in association with the Film Council, Scottish Screen and the Glasgow Film Fund. So far so good: this is the familiar institutional lineage – or patronage – of a national cinema whose claims on public funding rely less on a return on investment than on a desire for a national cinema of quality. The involvement of the BBC is a reminder of the curiously British alignment of independence and public service which has characterized British cinema and broadcasting since Grierson and Reith.

Better still, *Morvern Callar*, like so much quality film and television in Britain, is an adaptation, adapted from the book of the same title by the Scottish author Alan Warner (1995). Its legitimacy is guaranteed not by its status as an established literary classic, but rather by a certain cult fascination with its strangeness: the legitimacy of a select readership. Although it does not command the breadth of the market for adaptations which Forster or Austen might reach, it nevertheless inscribes the film in a culturally elite niche market attractive to public patronage – a market which it shares, for instance, with the adaptation of Trocchi's *Young Adam* (David MacKenzie, 2003), and a market whose economic driver may be the international success of yet another Scottish adaptation: the adaptation of Irving Walsh's *Trainspotting* (Danny Boyle, 1995).

It is filmed on location in Oban and the surrounding West Highlands, and in a Spanish resort and its very different surrounding wilderness; and of the two principal actors, one is a non-actor ('a trainee hairdresser plucked off the Glasgow streets', according to one review). The use of location and non-actors places the film in a recognizable British tradition of social realism, one which can trace its cultural links back to neo-realism and the very beginnings of post-war European art cinema.

So far, so good indeed. In these selective lineaments, *Morvern Callar* seems to fit the bill, to resonate with the recognizable tones of a British, or Scottish, quality cinema.

At every stage, however, there are complications and discords. The involvement of the Glasgow Film Fund, for example, reminds us of that new and slightly disorienting economic alignment of enterprise, employment and inward investment on the one hand, with culture and – sometimes – art on the other. The Glasgow Film Fund was administered by the Glasgow Film Office, whose current website describes itself thus:

> Creating businesses of scale is essential for the sustainable growth and development of the sector. GFO will work with local production companies and facilities & service companies to help develop more businesses of scale within the city, working with businesses that have demonstrated high growth potential whatever their size.

Not much about Scottish culture and identity there. And yet in funding local production companies as part of an 'enterprise culture' or as a way of stimulating business growth, agencies may stray into funding a local imagination and a local imaginary. Thinking only of facilities, services and capacity for growth, rather than the big, defining issues of culture and identity which preoccupy the desire for a national cinema, agencies may end up – even if only occasionally – supporting the creativity and individual talent through which difference leaks and on which an experimental art cinema depends.

And, yes, it is an adaptation, but an adaptation which seems to confound rather than confirm the familiarities and recognitions of cultural identity. Like the book, the film bears the traces of a Scottish gothic or an anti-Kailyard, but one in which the connections to the familiar topographies have become attenuated. The usual visual markers of Scottish landscape fail to carry their usual significance: a sequence of snow-capped mountains, sharp in winter sunlight, is the setting for Morvern's disposal of the bits of her dead boyfriend (Figure 1). The lyrical landscape of the scene ends in an oily peat-pool, squirming with beetles, bugs and the insect life of our nightmares (Figure 2). *Morvern Callar* is Scottish gothic filtered through the sensibility of a small-town supermarket shelf-stacker and pill-popper, who drinks Remy Martin while cutting up her boyfriend's dead body to the Walkman accompaniment of John Cale and the Velvet Underground. As the blood spatters her, their odd ballad, 'I'm Sticking with You' ('I'm sticky with you'?), plays on the soundtrack and on her Walkman.

Perhaps the most scandalous transgression of all in the adaptation from novel to film is the translation of Morvern Callar herself, emphatically Scottish in speech and lineage in the novel, into an English interloper: Samantha Morton, an outstanding English actress, quite capable of mastering a Scottish accent, is not asked to be anything other than a migrant worker in the West Highlands. Her cultural otherness, potentially meaningful for a national cinema, is given no more significance than any other young English woman who happens to have family connections in Scotland, and finds work in a supermarket for lack of anything better to do or any better place to be. Her 'Englishness' is not an issue for the film: it is not the explanation for anything, nor is it explained.

It is worth pausing on this. Scotland in the cinema, and particularly the West Highlands of Scotland, have traditionally had the same kind of transformative effect on outsiders as the American West. Like the West, it is a mythic landscape. From Scott and young Waverley to John Buchan and Richard Hannay, the Scottish Highlands, the last wilderness on the western edge of Europe, have tested the values of modernity and found them wanting. In a series of iconic films, from *Brigadoon* (Vincente Minelli, 1954) and *The Maggie* (Alexander McKendrick, 1953), through to *Local Hero* (Bill Forsyth, 1983),

American values have foundered on the waywardness of the natives, while from I Know Where I'm Going (Michael Powell and Emeric Pressburger, 1945), to Mrs Brown (John Madden, 1997), English women – even English monarchs – have been enriched and restored to full humanity by their encounters with their wilder northern neighbours. In this context, the casting of an identifiably English actress with no attempt to impersonate Scottishness, and the apparently casual translation of Morvern Callar from local girl to incomer, cannot be innocent. It refuses a tradition of the 'Scottishing' of the outsider, the mystic Celticization of the Anglo-Saxon, the magical transformation of the other through exposure to the mythic landscape. In Morvern Callar, no one seems to come from Oban or the West Highlands; they have just arrived there – literally, at the end of the line. She – Morvern Callar/Samantha Morton – just happens to be from Nottingham.

In these fairly apparent ways, Morvern Callar throws difficulties in the way of the reductiveness which often seems to characterize attempts to identify and define – and sometimes celebrate – a national cinema. What is perhaps more interesting and intricate is the way in which the film's cinematic language also resists the quest for identity.

Adaptation

In the familiar terms of adaptation and origins, the film adaptation follows the story of the novel: Morvern, in Oban, finds her boyfriend dead in the kitchen doorway having killed himself by slitting his wrists. She steps round him and over him for a few days, and continues her life, going to the pub and partying, winning sympathy from her friends who believe her boyfriend has walked out on her. On his computer is the manuscript of a novel, 'A NOVEL by James Gillespie', and a suicide note asking her to send the manuscript to a publisher. She does so, but first changes the author's name on the title page from his name to hers. Then she cuts him up and takes him out to the hills in a rucksack to dispose of the body. She draws money from his account and she and her friend, Lana, go off to a Spanish resort for all the reasons that young British tourists go to Spanish resorts – sun, sex, sangria and chemical ecstasy. Morvern tires of partying and drags Lana off to the Spanish wilderness, which Lana hates but in which Morvern seems to find some contentment – but not enough to constitute a mythic transformation. Back at the resort, she is contacted by the publishers, who fly out to meet her and offer her a £100,000 advance (an unlikely story, indeed) for the novel which she did not write. She does the deal without qualms, returns briefly to Oban before heading again for Spain, and seems destined to use the advance to support her clubbing lifestyle.

My interest is not in the fidelity of the film to its origins, but in the ways in which literary language is refigured in cinematic language, in what we may learn about the cinematic and the literary from the differences between them, and in what we may learn about an art cinema from the singularity of this film. Novel and film share the sense of a central character who does not grow, who is not worked on by the narrative to achieve identity, carrying us with her on a voyage of self-discovery. Instead, things happen to Morvern; she acts without the narrative logic of motivation, quest or morality. In the novel, however, Morvern is held together in a first person narrative, a consistent voice which does not tell us directly how her actions feel to her or how we should feel about them – how it feels, for example, to cut up her boyfriend's body – but it does tell us, indirectly, by recounting what track she listened to on her Walkman while she was doing it. In the film, on the other hand, without voiceover we are denied that consistent, guiding, interior monologue. In the sequence identified above, for example, in which she buries the remains of her boyfriend, her sub-sequent moment of release, wheeling and running on the hillside, is explained in the novel by the fact that she is listening to the Cocteau Twins on her Walkman (an explanation which may be amoral, but is at least interiorized). In the film, uncharacteristically, the music soundtrack which might accompany or explain her release is withheld; the action is left in a limbo without motivation or interiority; the moment resists our desire for interpretation or psychological meaning.

In terms of adaptation, then, the most surprising feature of the screenplay is the absence of the voiceover which the first-person narrative of the novel seemed to demand. Without its help, we see the image and hear the soundtrack of her Walkman, sound shifting between apparently diegetic and apparently non-diegetic as we move from inside Morvern to outside, from Morvern as a subject listening, to Morvern as an object of the image. Subjectivity shifts, is left unstable, unfixed by the narrative logic. The perversity of the adaptation is the withdrawal of the logos from a narrative which, in the novel, is told by a logorrhaeic in whose verbal rush the suicide of her boyfriend carries the same weight – or lack of it – as a Christmas Eve party or the subsequent hangover. In the film, the withdrawal of the voiceover and interior monologue which might have given us an edge on motivation or affect, produces a kind of weightless-ness, a flatness of significance and signification.

One of the problems which distinguish the analysis of films from the analy-sis of literature is the problem of quotation: how do you illustrate an argument with the evidence of a referent which can only ever be an awkward translation, trying and failing to entrap the visual in the verbal? How can the force of the moving image be rendered in words and sentences? More particularly, in a novel such as this which is so literary, so dependent on a writing whose colloquialism masks its condensations and estrangements, what resources does visual narrative have to match the experimental elusiveness of literary language? What I am attempting to illustrate is not the basis of an interpretation, but a sense of the tones and forms and shifts of the film, entering the film somewhat arbitrarily, as Deleuze and Guattari recommend for the rhizome 'by any point whatsoever'. 'Only the principle of multiple entrances', they say, 'prevents the introduction of the enemy, the Signifier, and those attempts to interpret a work that is actually only open to experimentation' (2003: 3). So it is the experimentation of the film that I am trying to illustrate rather than its interpretation, recognizing the ways in which that experimentation is common to novel and film, but specific to each.

There is a sequence in which Morvern enters the supermarket to a languid country soundtrack by Lee Hazlewood, 'Some Velvet Morning'. The camera shifts between expressionless subjectivity to expressive objectivity: in the first, the butcher waves directly to Morvern from behind his counter, and, consequently, to the camera which is identified precisely and subjectively with her point of view; in the second, the camera, shooting from waist level, projects Morvern from below, representing her 'walking tall' against the ceiling, and the hanging cut-outs of fruit and vegetables (Figure 3). The shift from subjective to objective is marked and dramatic, and leaves us in no doubt where we are looking from. At the same time, the 'objectivity' is not neutral, not really objective, but is marked by a dramatic expressiveness through the angle of the shot: it does not just show Morvern, it shows how it feels to be Morvern at this moment, with that soundtrack. The soundtrack itself could have any of three sources: it could be extra-diegetic, the film's soundtrack simply the conventional accompaniment located nowhere in the narrative space; it could be diegetic and objective, the musak of the supermarket (and this is indeed anticipated precisely by the opening strings); it could be diegetic and subjective, the interior sound of Morvern's Walkman, the opening strings bridging smoothly into Lee Hazlewood's country voice reverberating inside her head, determining her mood, replicating and interiorizing the feeling of walking tall: 'Some velvet morning when I'm straight / I'm going to open up your gate...' The scene is incidental in terms of plot or story, but it is exemplary in signalling the shifting points of view and positionings which undermine any desires for fixed subjectivities and identifications. The constant shifting between objectivity and subjectivity, expressiveness and flatness, stasis and movement create an instability. The unstable perspective and point of view which deprive us of the security of identification are properties of camera placement and camera movement: that is to say, they are properties of the image and the cinematic. It is these which we have to analyse and understand, if we are to understand the relationship between the literary and the cinematic as a relationship of language systems rather than simply of plot elements.

Warner's prose in this novel is also characterized by a certain weightlessness. He gives to Morvern a voice which describes every action from the same perspective, without seeming to inhabit any of them or confer value on them. He follows precisely the rhythms and nuances of Morvern's speech, refusing the drama of events or the differentiation of moment. Nevertheless, the position which the reader occupies, however deprived of the point of judgement, is a consistent position, always shadowing Morvern's distance from the events which she describes. Throughout the film, on the other hand, there is a felt movement between interiority, exteriority and points between; the spectator's position, his or her identification with character and camera, is constantly modulated; any stability of perception is unsettled; the look and point of view themselves are put in play, mirroring the weightlessness in Warner's prose, but without the 'guide' of a first-person narrative. At the end of the sequence above, in the movements of the soundtrack between non-diegetic and diegetic, subjective and objective, we reread the narrative space retrospectively at the point at which Morvern switches off her Walkman. It is only at that point that we properly know which space we have been occupying: the space inside Morvern's head. This constant play of retrospection and anticipation is the play of subjectivities – our subjectivities as readers echoing the fluidity and weightlessness of Morvern's subjectivity as a protagonist.

There is a scene towards the end of the film, and still in Spain, when Morvern, having posed successfully as an author and having sold 'her' manuscript to the publishers over several glasses of wine, takes them to a Spanish graveyard at dawn. In a single remarkable shot, starting from a mid-shot of Morvern, with a red carnation, standing beside a memorial plaque set into the wall, facing screen right, the camera tracks along the wall, past other memorial plaques, to find Morvern at the other end of the same shot, beside another plaque set into the wall, now facing screen left, still holding the red carnation, which she finally places in a small memorial vase (Figures 4–6). Within the conventions of narrative space, it is an impossible shot, placing Morvern in two places at once within a single tracking shot, the red carnation marking out a narrative time within the shot in which the end is the mirror image of the beginning. If Warner's language marks out the 'literariness' of his writing – in Roman Jakobson's sense of 'literariness' as 'language calling attention to itself', where 'the emphasis is placed on the form of the utterance rather than on its referential capacity' (see Vidal 2002: 8) – Lynne Ramsay's camera marks, again and again, an equivalent consciousness of cinematic language 'calling attention to itself', a 're-engagement', as Agamben suggests, with the 'means of transmission'.

Endings are always telling when one comes to compare films and the novels which provoke them. In its closing lines, Warner's novel brings with it the hint of a new life, a kind of renewal, a promise of redemption which is unanticipated and out of the blue:

I placed both hands on my tummy at the life there, the life growing right in there. The child of the raves.

I put my head down and closed my mouth. I started the walking forward into that night. (Warner 1995: 229)

More open and ambiguous, Lynne Ramsay's film tries out a number of endings. At the end of the scenes in Spain, there is a two-shot sequence which seems to offer the possibility of a redemption, a conventionally romantic transformation through encounter with the wilderness. In an almost excessively bucolic image, Morvern is found sitting on arid earth, her back to a tree, a rustic farmhouse behind her, goats feeding nearby, and the sea in the distance (Figure 7). The soundscape is not a Walkman but goats' bells. This idyll of rural tranquility, however, is cut into by a close-up of her hand splayed out on the earth, with an ant crawling over it (Figure 8). Insect life is one of the motifs which run through the film, a perturbation in benign nature, threatening ripeness with corruption. There is a quick cut to the damp, dark streets of Oban, the goats' bells segueing into the mewling of gulls (Figure 9). The image of redemption is there only to be refused, the romance of renewal held open in one image only to be closed off in the next. Not for this film the glimpse of easy resolution or achieved identity.

In the end she escapes the small town, but maybe Lana is right: 'There's nothing wrong wi' here. It's just the same crap as everywhere.' The Oban sequence ends with Morvern sitting by an empty railway as a dawn chorus of birds marks the soundtrack (Figure 10); the scene fades to black and opens onto an extended, strobe-lit club scene, geographically unlocated and played out to the non-diegetic and somewhat anachronistic soundtrack of the Mamas and the Papas, from a more innocent age: 'This is Dedicated to the One I Love'. The escape is not to the stillness of the Spanish wilderness in which a stable identity might be found, but to the flat ecstasy of clubbing, the fragmentation of the image and the dissolution of identity. The closing credits roll (Figures 11 and 12).

It would be absurd to suggest from this that the film *Morvern Callar* is somehow better than the novel *Morvern Callar* because it is more open in its ending, a claim which would simply reverse and refresh the wearisome claim that films can never be as good as novels, or adaptations can never be as good as their originals. What interests me, however, is a certain experimental consistency in the film which refuses to return the instabilities of perception that have characterized it to the possibility of stability and renewal at the end. The novel follows the logic of speech: a first-person narrative which, however weightless, disconnected, however much a 'language torn from sense, conquering sense' (Deleuze and Guattari 2003: 21), has a single sensibility and a speech behind it which in the end finds some hint of stability and achieved identity, some possibility of renewal, even if 'out of the blue'. The film, on the other hand, follows the logic of a camera which moves constantly between points of view and perspectives – now, Morvern seeing; now, seeing Morvern – a play of subjectivities and objectivities which need not or cannot be brought back to a unified sensibility, to identity. These seem to me to be the experimental logics which are at work. The particular 'difficulty' of an art cinema – the reason why this film by Lynne Ramsay was much less favourably received than her previous film, *Ratcatcher* (1999) – lies in its refusal to offer the footholds of identity in the play of subjectivity. In return, its achievement – the achievement of the great European art cinemas – is to keep faith with alienation.

But this may be too neat to capture the intricacies of language, whether literary or cinematic. Consider again the last sentence of the novel:

I started the walking forwards into that night (Warner 1995: 229)

The use of the definite article 'the' and the demonstrative adjective 'that' follows a pattern of acutely observed colloquial speech which is distinctive in the novel, placing it in an oral tradition of language which is often remarked as a characteristic of Scottish writing. Here, however, the colloquialisms are not simply part of the redundancy of casual speech, but introduce a sense, an allusiveness, which darkens the possibility of resolution and closure: 'the walking' and 'that night' seem to make us complicit in an understanding of a particularity which eludes explanation, like characters in an Edward Hopper painting standing on the edge of a forest which recedes into darkness, or echoing Dylan Thomas' injunction not to go gentle. Or, in the film, consider the blank stare of Morvern fading up from and out of the strobe in the final clubbing scene: a blank stare which invites us to put meaning on it – despair? realization? awakening? – without giving us the means of determining which meaning to put. It is not that, between novel and film, one closes down on meaning and the other does not, but that each uses the resources of its language to hold open the ambiguities, experimenting to the end with the play of subjectivities and identities, and their uncertain realization in language.

The Erotics of Art

So one of the reasons I wanted to think about and write about Lynne Ramsay's film is precisely because of the confusion it creates: because of the complexities of its language, but also because of the way, particularly in Scotland, it might loosen the grip of a critical language which seems to be underpinned by assumptions about a certain stability of representation and identity, by a barely suppressed belief that representations – discursive formations – really do identify us. In British film studies, the category of the 'national' seems to have supplanted the traditional categories of genre and authorship; and the category of the national in British film criticism, as John Ellis told us in an article in *Screen* in 1978, is founded on the postwar desire for a 'quality' cinema which 'projects' Britain and the British character (Ellis 1978). It is precisely the awkwardness of an art cinema which is experimental in its sensibility, its 'lack of fit' within any of the generic or national categories, which makes it both critically and culturally valuable – particularly valuable in the context of a cultural and political nation which is itself still conditional. And yet, for historically and politically explicable reasons, film studies have a long history of neglect and embarrassment around the terms of an art cinema.

'Real art', Susan Sontag told us 40 years ago in 'Against interpretation', 'has the capacity to make us nervous. By reducing the work of art to its content and then interpreting *that*, one tames the work of art. Interpretation makes art manageable, conformable' (Sontag 1970: 17). 'The introduction of the enemy, the Signifier' say Deleuze and Guattari, resisting the rush to interpretation as the way of unmasking what the work is *really* about. In thinking about films as exemplars of national cinemas and in seeking interpretations which reveal in them the identities that they are really about, we have to be alert to the danger of turning the work of criticism into a work of taming; of making art manageable; of a reductivism which is effective not because it is adequate, but because it is teachable. 'In place of a hermeneutics', Sontag tells us, 'we need an erotics of art' (1970: 23).

Or Agamben again:

> Wherever the critic encounters art, he brings it back to its opposite, dissolving it in non-art; wherever he exercises his reflection, he brings with him non-being and shadow, as though he had no other means to worship art than the celebration of a kind of black mass in honor of the *deus inversus*, the inverted god, of non-art. (Agamben 1999: 46)

Agamben acknowledges the role of the critic in exercising aesthetic judgement, understanding how art works in an age when it has been freed from its subjugation to the divine. Clearly, to write about a film is to put it in a frame, and the work of critical analysis cannot escape the tension between pinning it down and releasing it. What may be read in Agamben's critique, however, is the desire for a criticism which hesitates before rushing to judgement and assigning works to the regulatory frameworks of genre and nation – a criticism which instead considers the work in its irregularity, freeing it into its real unruly creativity; approaching art, he proposes, from the point of view of the artist rather than that of the reader, viewer or consumer. In his recent book, *The*

Singularity of Literature, Derek Attridge similarly argues for a mode of criticism which approaches the singular work of literature as an event in itself, rather than as a symptom of something else which must be hunted down by interpretation. 'I am suggesting', he says in his conclusion:

> that the attempt to do justice to literary works as *events*, welcoming alterity, countersigning the singular signature of the artist, inventively responding to invention, combined with a suspicion of all those terms that constitute the work as an object, is the best way to enhance the chances of achieving a vital critical practice.

'Literature', he says, 'may be a cultural product, but it is never simply contained by a culture' (Attridge 2004: 6).

Of course, we can find a critical approach which will tame *Morvern Callar* and bring it into the order of representation and national culture. When I started thinking about the film, I began from the position that it floated free from Scottish culture, but the more I watched it and re-read the novel, the more clearly it became saturated with the gothic sensibility of Hogg, Stevenson and the anti-Kailyard novels, *The House of the Green Shutters* and *Gillespie*, or with a similar sensibility in the Scottish filmmaker, Bill Douglas. These are the critical landmarks which might allow us to situate the film as a Scottish film; and, certainly, to cut the film off entirely from the tradition which gives meaning to its difference would be to diminish its significance. And yet, to leave it there, enclosed in a national tradition and a national system of meanings, rather than opened up to its distinctive alterity, its confusion of the tradition, is, equally, to diminish its real creativity: its 'difficulty'.

Even more, within the politics of culture, it is important to recognize Lynne Ramsay as a *Scottish* filmmaker, expanding the range of creative practices within Scotland, opening up a repertoire of creativity in film which has historically been quite limited, making it a little more difficult to seek shelter in a poverty of creative imagination. To close off questions of authorship and creativity is to remove the film from its history and locality, and to lose the strategic, tactical and imaginative value which the film brings to the possibilities of being creative in Scotland.

These debates about identity are important for a Scottish cinema which should be working as if it lived in the early days of a better nation, and they are debates with which criticism should quite rightly engage. In the traditions of cultural criticism, however, they are issues which remain within the comfort zone of critical language, a language which, as Agamben says, deals with the non-art in the work more comfortably than with art; or, as Attridge suggests, treats art as a symptom of something else. What the critical language, which aspires to describe or bring into being a British or Scottish national cinema, so often seems to miss in its search for the traces of identity is that erotics of the image which Sontag speaks of – it misses it so much that the conjunction of national cinema and Eros seems trivial or perverse. The singularity of *Morvern Callar* lies not in what links it to everything else or in the patterns of identity which it informs and which inform it, but in the effect of the language and its refusal to conform to the closure of interpretation. Its awkward beauty, whether novel or film but in each differently; the experience of watching it or reading it and being held by its duration, by the flatness of its expression, by its ambiguity, by the play of its languages, by the image and its movement – its movingness – and by the twistings and turnings of its subjectivities: these are the bits which slip away from, or – worse – are simply contained by a critical language attuned only to identities and their fixing in interpretation.

References

Agamben, Giorgio (1999) *The Man Without Content*, trans. Georgia Albert (Stanford, Stanford University Press).

Attridge, Derek (2004) *The Singularity of Literature* (London, Routledge).

Deleuze, Gilles (2000) *Cinema 2: The Time-Image*, trans. Hugh Tomlinson and Robert Galeta (London, Athlone Press).

Deleuze, Gilles and Félix Guattari (2003) *Kafka: Toward a minor literature*, trans. Dana Polan (Minneapolis/London, University of Minnesota Press).

Ellis, John (1978) 'Art, culture and quality: terms for a cinema in the 1940s and 1970s', *Screen* 19:3, Autumn, pp. 9–50.

Glasgow Film Office: http://www.glasgowfilm.org.uk. Accessed 14 September 2006.

Gray, Alasdair (1983) *Unlikely Stories, Mostly* (Edinburgh, Cannongate).

Martin-Jones, David (2004) '*Orphans*, a work of minor cinema from post-devolutionary Scotland', *Journal of British Cinema and Television* 1:2, pp.226–41.

Petrie, Duncan (2000) *Screening Scotland* (London, BFI).

Sontag, Susan (1970) 'Against interpretation', in *Against Interpretation and Other Essays* (New York, Dell Publishing).

Vidal, Belén Villasur (2002) 'Classic adaptations, modern reinventions: reading the image in the contemporary literary film', *Screen* 43:1, pp.5–18.

Warner, Alan (1995) *Morvern Callar* (London, Jonathan Cape).

Willemen, Paul (2006) 'The National revisited', in Valentina Vitali and Paul Willemen (eds) *Theorising National Cinema* (London, BFI Publishing), pp.30–1.

Notes

1 An earlier version of this article appeared in *Scottish Studies Review* 8:1 (2007). I am grateful to the publisher and editors for permission to reprint.

2 See, for example, Deleuze and Guattari (2003: 16), for deterritorialization as a characteristic of minor literatures.

Chapter Two

On Film and Cathedrals: Monumental Art, National Allegories and Cultural Warfare

Ismail Xavier

Films resorting to allegories as a means to assess their national histories abound in world cinema. Notable examples are Rainer Werner Fassbinder's *The Marriage of Maria Braun* (*Die Ehe der Maria Braun*, 1979), Glauber Rocha's *The Age of the Earth* (*A idade da terra*, 1980), Theo Angelopoulos' *Voyage to Cythera* (*Taxidi sta Kythira*, 1984), Fernando Solanas' *Tangos, the Exile of Gardel* (*Tagos, l'exil de Gardel*, 1985), Manoel de Oliveira's *Non, or the Vain Glory of Command* (*'Non', ou a vã glória de mandar*, 1990), Emir Kusturica's *Time of the Gypsies* (*Dom za vesange*, 1988), the Paolo and Vittorio Taviani's *Good Morning, Babylon* (1987). Each has its own formal choices, which may include an ironic dialogue with an established film genre. Their narratives are quite different in scope, and show the diversity of strategies available for allegorical storytelling, which for this reason lend themselves to comparative study. As part of my concern with the general question of historical allegories in European and Latin American cinemas, I will focus here on *Good Morning, Babylon*, a modern film that allows for a comprehensive discussion of classical allegories, given that it looks back to the historical time in which the first monumental spectacles were made in the cinema.

The Tavianis concentrate on empirical and symbolic relations involving films (Pastrone's *Cabiria*, 1914, and Griffith's *Intolerance*, 1916), modern nations (Italy and the United States) and filmmakers. My purpose is to discuss the ways in which they understand the interaction between art, memory and war, and allegorize the continuity of the aesthetic impulse, despite all the discontinuities in history, entailed by national conflicts and international catastrophes. In this film, they celebrate art as monument, raising the question of what is politically implied in this particular celebration. I see their work as an example of how the impulse to represent a previous moment of history comes to grips with a sense of crisis and radical separation from the past, a question I will focus on by reference to Walter Benjamin's understanding of the interplay of continuities (progress) and discontinuities (disaster) of human experience in time.

The Banquet: Philosophy at the Table, as in Ancient Times

We are situated on the celebrated stage set of *Intolerance* representing the Babylonian staircase, with its plaster elephant columns and the monumental décor usually seen in still photographs of the film. In a succession of shots, this set is repeatedly shown from a frontal perspective, as was the case in Griffith's film. On the lower part of the construction, formerly packed with extras hired by the lavish production, and where women danced in honour of the god of love, there are now but a few people. A small group of actors move around to compose a different scene, shot in 1986, as part of a modern film which tells the story of two Italian immigrants, the brothers Nicola and Andrea, involved in the production of Griffith's classic. They are on the set of *Intolerance* during a shooting interval, laying the table for their wedding banquet, for which, rather symbolically, this place and its notable make-believe architecture have been chosen as a venue.

As spectators of *Good Morning, Babylon*, we have no trouble accepting the monumental character of this construction of wood and stucco, for this is how it became renowned as an image. The solemnity which accompanies this perception is purposely provoked by the Taviani Brothers, who seize this moment of the narrative to highlight concepts previously only hinted at, as the story of the two young Italian immigrants in America unfolds. Following a series of misfortunes in the country, they end up in California, playing an important role in the creation of the Babylonian stage set, in which they now have their wedding party (Figure 1).

This party has a host: the young men's boss, D.W. Griffith, already seen in the film on various occasions, acting in an overly theatrical manner. The character is a good-humoured gentleman, endowed with nobility and an understanding of various different values and rivalries. He had already been seen praising the film *Cabiria*, made by Giovanni Pastrone in 1914, a moment staged by the Taviani brothers to show us that the American director's admiration for the Italian filmmaker had been the main inspirational force for his conception of the greatest of spectacles, the one he now prepares, and whose set, where his assistants will get married, has become emblematic. As far as the two immigrants are

Figure 1 The wedding banquet in Good Morning, Babylon

concerned, he had helped them financially and protected them whenever possible, for he had immediately recognized their talent. They had been forced to leave Italy following the closure of their father's beloved firm, which had specialized in the restoration of cathedrals, during an economic crisis.

A meeting has been arranged and will take place on the set. For the first time, the old father-master (*padre padrone*), Bonanno, honours his sons with a visit to the New World, bringing from Italy his pride as well as his jealousy. He comes not only as a father, but also as a representative of an honourable tradition. He is an artist dedicated to the preservation of Europe's cultural heritage, and he comes to the heart of the new artistic trade to give it his patriarchal blessing. His affected manners and authority are purposely displayed so as to preserve his aura in his sons' eyes. This scene confirms the success of the young men in America, but the promise of a stable life alongside their wives is still uncertain, since the inevitable confrontation between the old father who has just arrived and the new symbolic father may never reach the desired resolution. Mutual acceptance and the recognition of values shared between the two forms of patriarchy are far from guaranteed.

This is hence an allegorical scene. Cinema, architecture, religion, art, family, Europe the United States are all conflated here. The confrontation takes shape, solemnly, alternating long shots as reminders of where we are – the stage set of *Intolerance* – and closer shots which scrutinize the faces, and confirms the status of both paternal figures, as well as what can be expected of them. Gestures and phrases are rehearsed, composing a self-conscious theatre in which a duel is acted out, leading to a final resolution. The state of tension, though short-lived, is visible on the faces of the insecure youngsters and their brides, and their drama is amusing. We have been prepared by the Taviani brothers to admire Griffith's sense of performance and good disposition towards the Italians. He does not let us down and, in a key moment, challenged by the father to defend the new world, he rhetorically praises cinema for its power to give continuity to the past. This had already been suggested at the beginning of the film, which shows Father Bonanno, a master artisan, placed right in the middle of the construction site, sitting in a chair similar to the well-known film director's chair. Likewise, the scene showing the end of the cathedral's restoration is staged as a spectacle: a huge cloth in the shape of a curtain covers the front of the church and all stands still, waiting for the removal of this cover to expose the façade. Griffith then pays homage to the Italian cathedrals and Bonanno's work of restoration, explaining that cinema is the new version of what fascinates us in the history of art. His words please the guests, soothe the father and change Griffith himself into the herald of the central idea in *Good Morning, Babylon,* namely that the old collective spirit behind the building of cathedrals corresponds to the mass spectacle of film. The theatricality with which he develops this idea charges it with ambivalence and bestows upon the images the look of 'cinema for exportation'.

Griffith's act of legitimating tradition, typical of Hollywood from its early days, are certainly not meant to be taken too seriously. However, the most ironic moments in *Good Morning, Babylon* are not related to Griffith, but to the film's historical context. The film is set in the period of the First World War, in which the hegemonic control of film production is transferred from Europe to the United States. American cinema between 1908 and 1914, in its turn, had shown repeated signs of fascination with the images of Antiquity, and especially with the archaeological, sentimental and dramatic heritage of the Roman Empire. Spectacular Italian films such as *Quo Vadis* (Enrico Guazzoni, 1913) and *The Last Days of Pompeii* (*Gli ultimi giorni di Pompeii,* Luigi Maggi and Arturo Ambrosio, 1908) were well received and admired, paving the way for *Cabiria*'s much greater impact in the United States.

Not accidentally, it is Griffith who, in the banquet scene, draws attention to the aesthetic affinity between the new world of cinema, and the old world of Bonanno's and his sons' craft. Although in itself Griffith's point falls short of being a theory of cinema, it recalls how, in 1922, art historian Élie Faure had praised what he called *cinéplastique,* the formal and expressive force of moving images or, in his words, 'moving architecture', as seen in Tintoretto's monumental paintings (1953a: 11–13). Although not always in tune with early twentieth-century avant-garde critics and artists, Faure's celebration of cinema demonstrated his perception of cinema's essentially visual nature. He countered the hegemony of banal dramas imposed by the imperatives of the growing film industry; however, unlike those who attacked the new technological age for its supposed 'lack of soul', he insisted on its spiritual virtues and saw cinema as a powerful vehicle for the expression of an ecumenical sense of the oneness of life and cosmos, thanks to its aesthetic magnificence, emotional power and collective scope. In short, he saw cinema as the modern correlative of medieval cathedrals. Film and the church, for Faure, contained a rich assortment of community values because they were sites of shared rituals and monuments to the human creative power. *Cinéplastique*, a combination of visual spectacles, plastic poems, new rhythms and new spaces, was made for the masses; that is, all human beings. Faure magnified its social function to a cosmic scale, encompassing the whole of humankind, talking of cinema as church, mosque and pagoda (1953b: 21–45, 61–85). His idea of film as a place for communion set against individualism and private interests is explained in universalist terms, and its specific relation to socio-historical context remains unclear. Although inscribed in the erudite discourse of the outstanding art historian, it has an archaic flavour which, curiously, is not far from Griffith's popular philosophy, or from other voices which, across film history, have expressed a utopian view of cinema as a universal language, and cinemas as church-like venues meant to elicit human reconciliation and the realization of a collective dream.

Inscribed in a more specific historical context, the Taviani brothers formulate a similar idea of a collective dream which is inflected by the cultural background of the Italian Left and a Gramscian respect for the national popular culture. Italian left-wing intellectuals were certainly more specific than Élie Faure in their reflexion upon early twentieth-century cinema. However, the way in which they paid homage to cinema as a monumental spectacle is more akin to Faure's understanding of the same phenomenon than one might expect. *Good Morning, Babylon* highlights the power of a millenarian knowledge imputed to cinema by this Italian tradition. Griffith is seen as a great master, and the United States as the birthplace of mass culture as we know it. However, Griffith's most daring work confirms that he had drawn inspiration from *Cabiria*. The Americans had been fascinated by Italian mastery and by the spectacular Italian pavilion at the 1915 San Francisco World Fair, shown in the film as the venue where Griffith saw *Cabiria*. The two youngsters, upon their arrival in Hollywood, indeed had themselves worked on the Italian pavilion, and developed their talent and craft sculpting the details of cathedral décors displayed there. It all culminates when they conceive of and make the spectacular plaster elephants for the set of *Intolerance*.

Cabiria was the finest example at the time of the sort of great spectacle known as 'quality cinema' in Italy and as 'art film' in France, a tendency which critics opposed to the American traditional narrative style, characterized by dynamic editing (*découpage*) and an effective dramatic structure. *Intolerance* consolidated Griffith's international prestige, both for his daring editing technique and versatility in employing, in a single film, a number of different styles representing rival strands in filmmaking across the world, and, in so doing, defining the paths for cinema as a spectacle in the 1920s. *Good Morning, Babylon* is not concerned so much with virtuosity as with its relation to *Intolerance*; that is to say, with the incorporation of architecture as a mediator between art history and cinema, and, more specifically, the incorporation of elements of the Italian tradition by the increasingly hegemonic American industry.

Pastrone and Griffith are indeed the first outstanding cinematic heirs of the operatic spectacle. Pastrone formally epitomizes the first stages of European cinema, which privileged the *cadre* (frame composition and depth of field).[1] Griffith, in turn, expanded on the American tradition to incorporate European influences. Miriam Hansen's analysis of *Intolerance* (1991: 129–62) and Silvio Alovisio's essay on the Italian cinema of the 1910s (1998) look at American and Italian films as exemplary works of a transitional period in the formation of classical cinema. In them, the principle of analytical editing and continuity still includes passages organized around exhibitionist gestures and visual attractions; that is to say, action is interrupted in order to make room for the contemplation of the architectural scenery. Both *Intolerance* and *Cabiria*, each in its own way, are seen by these critics as 'hybrids' for conveying an idea of cinema as a spectacle related to a new universal language, whose basic rhetoric of bodies in space and dramatic action they were contributing to shape on a monumental scale.[2]

As admirers of *Intolerance*'s aesthetic innovation, monumental scale and, above all, popular appeal, the Taviani brothers project their concern for the national-popular element onto D.W. Griffith's persona, albeit with a shade of self-irony. Thus, the film ends up conjuring up an image of a heroic filmmaker which would have corresponded to Griffith's own dreams. He embodies an epic version of the emergence of cinema based on the principle of continuity and reconciliation, as celebrated in the wedding scene. This is the climactic moment in the brothers' story, a time in which they hope to celebrate their integration and the success of their emigration from Italy to the United States, from the building of cathedrals to that of film sets. However, troubles will intervene and change their achievements into tragedy.

In *Good Morning, Babylon*, nationalistic cultural rivalry, with the exception of Griffith's chivalrous emulation of Pastrone, has unwanted consequences for the lives of the young protagonists. Despite being deprived immigrants who have to fight for a job, they demand respect by invoking on more than one occasion their condition as heirs of an aesthetic tradition going back to Raphael and Michelangelo. They are also indignant about the prejudices inherent in American society. Granted, Americans cultivate the classical tradition, as expressed in monuments dedicated to the new republic and 'founding fathers', such as Thomas Jefferson. However, they look down on Italian worker immigrants, thus evidencing a radical discontinuity between Italy as archaeological site, including antiquity as incorporated into cinema as a 'great spectacle', and the living Italy as represented by the immigrants. Provisionally redeemed by their success in the new world and in the eyes of their own kin, the young-sters will only savour it for a short time. Once their contribution is completed as a fraternal personification of the bridge between the world of cathedrals and the world of cinema (Italy and the USA), the outbreak of the first World War I precipitates their fall. Their story is thus an allegory not only of cinema, but also of the nation – with repercussions across Europe.

In order to discuss the connection between monumental allegories and national experiences, I will resort to other examples dating back to the 1920s. I will focus on the interaction of art and politics, aesthetics and pragmatics, moving my argument radically away from Élie Faure's ecumenical concept of the film-cathedral. This will hopefully shed a better light on the Taviani brothers' mode of representation of what they see as cinema's age of innocence.

Film-Cathedrals: Nation, Religion and Aesthetic Singularities

Cabiria and Intolerance are film-cathedrals at a time when Christianity was no longer the only unifying force in European and American societies. Modernity had ushered in other cultural paradigms, social values and conceptions of state for the legitimization of political systems. Throughout the twentieth century, films were to have the function of collective rituals celebrating common values in lavish dramas and iconographic displays. Increasingly, however, such rituals, whose dynamics and values were akin to religion, would acquire a secular meaning, most of the time connected to the idea of national and cultural unity.

In the 1910s and 1920s, the great historical spectacle on screen became the locus of competition involving the world's great powers, the Soviet Union among them. Major investments in ambitious super-productions expressed the rivalry among countries such as the United States, France, Germany and Italy. Ingenious technical effects and tales of epic scale were privileged as a nation's showcase. Architecture functioned as the base for cinematic creation, not only as regards set design, but also as the very subject matter of the fable in question.[3] Emphasis was also given to the cultural effect of the film as a national monument by creating strong images of a nation in the face of polit-ical and economic competition on the international scene. Here, following Jacques Le Goff, I oppose the idea of monument to that of document, in order to highlight the strategic use of intensity and the spectacular for posterity (1984: 95–103).

Monumental films were the nation's showcase of technical competence and artistic talent, but they also enabled the rational organization of a complex industrial task. The ability to project orchestrated masses and ambitious archi-tectural scenery onto the screen was an achievement which secured for the producing nation a pre-eminent and pioneering position in the industry.

Miriam Hansen (1991: 173–98) identifies a kind of hegemonic claim in Griffith's mixture of styles as he interweaves four epochs in *Intolerance*. For her, Griffith's historical teleology is reflected on his own conception of cinema. Based on a graphic technique of reproduction, the new art brought with it the possibility of a universal visual language, a promise which, for Griffith, was present in Babylon but was destroyed with the city's fall. Thus, for him, cinema is an instance of return and his own work is the great moment in which the promise is fulfilled, confirming the United States' leading role in the development of cinema. He responds to *Cabiria* in order to surpass it in its depiction of the Ancient World. *Intolerance*'s representation of the Night of Saint Bartholomew dialogues with and aims to supplant the French *film d'art* tradition, and its re-enactment of The Passion of Christ celebrates one of the most renowned cinematic themes to have recurred since the early twentieth century. In the modern story of *Intolerance*, Griffith further develops what is identified as his style *par excellence*; that is, the classical narrative he had begun to experiment with at Biograph. In the general architecture of his film's composition, he dares to employ a type of editing which attempts to express modes of historical interpretation typical of Christianity. The editing style turns out to be more grandiose than the architectural prodigy of the stage sets. In short, he builds a monument, an allegory of history which allows us to see his cinema as the restitution of old promises.

Given their formal design and the epic-historical dimension of their subject matter, films like *Birth of a Nation* (1915) and *Intolerance*, or Abel Gance's *Napoleon* (*Napoléon*, 1927) found in the category of nation a privileged sphere within which to thrive, since they could explore the monumental and collective scale of the experience in many directions. As historians and political scientists have taught us, nation is not a substance, or a natural way of subsuming a conglomerate of people under the same category. Nation is a product of modern times, of a market culture and of industrialization, a social and cultural construct which elicits a sense of totality. It is a cohesive entity involving heterogeneous groups of a complex society at a time when the experience of a homogenous community is out of reach (Gellner 1983; Hobsbawm 1990; Habermas 1995). This is what is implied in Benedict Anderson's notion of nation as an 'imagined community', the collective entity which, in modern times, offers guiding principles and a narrative paradigm that coordinates collective experiences in time (1983: 11–31). The sense of belonging to a single cultural and social body can be based on cultural-aesthetic foundations, as was the case of German Nationalism from the eighteenth century; or it can be more directly political, when related to a sense of collective union drawing on a social contract and republican citizenship, as established by the ideals of the French Revolution. In the latter case, the nation forms a collective union that does not derive from a common religion, contrary to what contemporary fundamentalists believe; or a common language or ethnic background, contrary to what Griffith's *Birth of a Nation* strongly enunciates.

Despite the nation's secular roots in modern history, problematic ideas such as 'national destiny' or 'national character' had found their dramatic embodiment in monumental films since the 1910s. These featured heroic figures shaped as allegorical personifications of values, in narratives that suggested affinities between national iconographies and the sense of the Sacred. In the 1930s there was a radicalization of national mythologies of the fascist kind.

Cinema, as a new locus of competition, lived side by side with other phenomena dating back to the nineteenth century, such as exhibitions in international fairs. Indeed, through the life of the two immigrant brothers, *Good Morning, Babylon*'s plot incorporates a network of symbolic cultural elements dating back to the Belle Époque, which historians connect with cinema's own development, including the importance of fairs such as the 1915 San Francisco World Fair, where different countries paraded their level of development on the basis of architectural spectacle and advanced technology. It was a friendly competition, which concealed a more sinister side. These fairs celebrated a notion of spectacle linked to progress. They ended up including cinema and defining the parameters of the first form of screen spectatorship. However, they also celebrated the importance of nationalism as a political force that fuelled competition among different countries in the period which immediately preceded the firstWorld War, 'the Age of Empire' (Hobsbawm 1989). This was marked by the emergence of the United States and the consolidation of cinema as an international merchandise, meant to circulate through organized webs.

The film-cathedral involved not only different conceptions of history and nation in the form of political statements with religious overtones, but also the search for different aesthetic innovations that blurred the boundaries between visual spectacle and an architecture of monumental scale. *Cabiria* and *Intolerance*, *Napoleon* and Fritz Lang's *Metropolis* (1926) feature a combination of aesthetic ambition, political engagement and celebration of national values.[4] These are singular works in film history because of their stylistic excess, as epitomized by the display of monumental architecture and their dynamic, geometric treatment of masses. Excess is indeed what distinguishes Griffith's editing strategies based on the principle of continuity; Gance's frame composition, camera movements and superimposition of images (Leblanc 1999); Pastrone's depth of field; and Lang's experiments with light and geometric formations, especially the cone and the triangle (Xavier 2007).

Griffith experimented with parallel editing on a new scale, interweaving four storylines taking place in different historical periods. Combined through cross-cutting, they elicit a kind of teleology, coming to paroxysm in the final sequence. Gance created audacious camera movements in radical explorations of simultaneity through multiple screens, in an attempt to produce an altered state of spectatorship close to hypnosis or a quasi-religious immersion in Napoleon's adventure. These directors testify to a faith in the virtues of hyperbolic forms. The idea is to create a spectacle which is highly revealing of its material resources and the filmmakers' artistic talent, while reasserting film's status as a showcase of national values and creative power.

Allegory as Foundational Fiction of Redemption

National allegories presenting a totalizing view of history, combining private dramas and public affairs, create what Doris Sommer calls 'foundational fictions' (1993: 30–51). These may or may not be directly engaged with a political debate, but they are always in tune with a more or less dominant conception of national formation and identity, albeit on the basis of different values. The first canonical example is still Griffith's *Birth of a Nation*, where the criterion for the legitimate belonging to the collective body of the nation is whiteness, with the exclusion of any post-slavery sense of integration: those who were brought from Africa as slaves are portrayed as agents of discord. *Napoleon* changes the political sense of the nation based on citizenship and sovereignty, as affirmed by the French Revolution, into the celebration of the great historical hero. Gance presents Napoleon as the predestined leader with the mission to correct the course of a revolution which was descending into disorder and chaos. To protect their new political values, the French people should be conducted to military conquest and establish an Empire.

In different ways, the celebration of the new medium and its potential as a collective ritual aims to combine the ideas of progress and civilization, as embodied in the new Nation, in Revolution or in the consolidation of the Roman Empire, with the reaffirmation of traditional and religious values. Historical forces are embodied in individual life stories seen as exemplary journeys inflected by a cosmic order, monumental warfare and providential denouements. As allegories, foundational fictions effect the condensation of a complex set of events and agents, a schematization of time and space able to provide the *Gestalt* of human experience of history (or of an ancient mythic time) which incorporates specific models drawn from traditional or mythological narratives, such as the Bible, or from modern genre formulas, such as melodrama.

Pastrone's central plot concerns Cabiria's convoluted life story, which begins with the eruption of the volcano Etna that destroys her family house. A little child, she is saved by servants that who end up selling her to Phoenician merchants who take her to Carthage. There, she is twice providentially saved from being immolated in Moloch's mouth of fire by the two heroes: the patrician Fulvio Axilla and his slave Maciste. After the canonically conventional ordeal of the unprotected innocent facing threat and exile, Cabiria, in love, is taken back home by Fulvio, exactly when the Romans win the Punic Wars.[5] The apotheosis is her election as the child whose destiny parallels the Roman victory, celebrated in classical, kitschy style, with garlands in the sky and Maciste playing the Pan pipes on the ship, keeping his 'appropriate' position as a slave. The lovers' happiness is similar in meaning to the triumphal parade performed by the young couple at the end of *Birth of a Nation*. *Cabiria*, as foundational fiction, refers to the consolidation of the Roman Empire and the celebration of the Mediterranean as 'Mare nostrum'. This is a historical experience that modern Italy turns into a myth projected onto its own colonial conquests in the twentieth-century world, something which functions in 1914 as a prelude to the more political Fascist shaping of a national mythology based on the glories of Ancient Rome.[6]

Gance's film is a hyperbolic construction of myth following the paradigm of teleological biographies in which every moment of life is seen as a stage in the super-hero's ascent to glory. Each of the hero's private events is narrated as the anticipation of a great public action. Every scene marks the unfolding of the hero's special virtues since childhood: his clear-sightedness, courage, endurance of solitude, self-control, laconicism and powerful hypnotic eyes repeatedly emphasized by the figure of the Eagle that follows his career, up to his consecration in the Italian campaign. The daring camera movements and editing strategies highlight the hero's eagle eyes, contrasting his totalizing view and self-assurance with the desperate agitation of the masses lost in the whirlwind of battles.[7] The idea of a fundamental affinity between the moving image, the liquid essence of the world and the animism of nature, as advanced by Jean Epstein (1974: 131–7) in the 1920s, is here replaced with the exaltation of the strong hero controlling the fluid waves of history. Epstein's key concept of *photogénie* (1974: 137–52) is by these means linked to the idea of excess, great power and magnificence. Modern cinematic techniques shape the rhythm and energy of the masses led by the Eagle, who has received his sacred mandate from the dead leaders of the Revolution. Without Napoleon and his enlightened pragmatism, revolution would only be an uncontrolled energy, driving passionate human beings towards the abyss and chaos. This movement had already been compared to a 'storm' by Griffith in his interpretation of the French Revolution in *Orphans of the Storm* (1923). Fritz Lang's *Metropolis* will also make the workers' rebellion march towards chaos by means of a similar metaphor, that of deluge.

The fluid masses' uncontrolled overflow leading to chaos and death is a recurrent motif in all those narratives, reaching emblematic expression in *Metropolis* and pointing to an uneasiness with the time of their own production.

This visual rhetoric seems to have a common substratum of instability and fear of disaster, configured as natural and organic phenomena (such as Etna's eruption in *Cabiria* and the passionate human crowds in *Napoleon*), but also as cultural artefacts and man-made machines representing inimical forces. Indeed, machines are represented as Moloch, the savage god of infant Cabiria's nightmares, or as a threatening Other, such as women, foreigners, different races and the rise of masses in public life (Figures 2–3).

In a framework of radical opposition between collective damnation and salvation, these configurations and recurrent waves of fire, or huge, liquid, crowds, suggest how, quite apart from the optimistic teleological framework in which the past is represented through the winners' view of history, these grand statements about universal history and human destiny touch upon specific problems involving the powers and limits of human beings. Monumental allegories hint at a strong sense of instability in the same way that the rise of melodrama as a popular genre from the early 1800s was related to the uncertainties of economic life during the rise of capitalism and the political turmoil entailed by the French Revolution. Intensity is inherent to both.

Cabiria is a symphony of fire: Etna's lava is a 'river of fire'; Moloch demands human sacrifice in his mouth of fire, as he will do in the underground factory of

Figure 2   Moloch in Cabiria

Figure 3   Moloch in Metropolis

Metropolis. Napoleon is the titanic figure who mimics Prometheus (nominally quoted in Gance's film), stealing fire from the gods and making it useful to a people freed from blindness under his leadership. *Intolerance* expresses Griffith's patriarchal concern for domesticity and maternity in response to the rise of women in public life and the workforce (Rogin 1989: 510–55). In his essay on *Metropolis*, Andreas Huyssen reads the 'vamp-machine' (Maria) as the embodiment of a threat ushered in by technology out of control, associated with the unruly feminine sexuality which disrupts labour discipline and industrial order (Huyssen 1986: 65–81). Maria the robot embodies all evil: she seduces the father (the primal scene, from his son Freder's point of view), leads the masses to rebellion and institutes the cult of the woman as fetish (1986: 78–81).

If the representation of the past (or the future, in science-fiction) carries an allegorical reference to the fears of the present, *Metropolis* emphasizes a particular aspect of the new industrial society. Industry and urban life mean labour discipline, bureaucratic organization of life, and the primacy of rational calculation and planning, entailing a corresponding decline in religious values. In short, the film performs a critique of the 'disenchantment of the world', a central feature of modernity, as explained by Max Weber (1946: 129–56). In response to the traumas of modern life and the need for reassurance, Lang's allegory incorporates traditional narratives and mythic figures, promoting a re-enchantment of the world.

As is well known, *Metropolis* opens with the description of a world marked by regularity and repetition, robot-like gestures, a vertical social hierarchy dominated by instrumental reason and the time of the clock. The disruptive factor has to be someone alien to this electro-mechanical order. Maria's invasion of the upper level of the city triggers the magic plot and takes us from the futuristic city to a gothic scenery. A more traditional form of allegory is thus brought to life, making room for prophecies and their fulfilment, as well as for personifications such as Rotwang, the daemonic agent par excellence representing death itself (in the cathedral and in Freder's nightmare).[8] Rotwang's obsessive genius chimes with the Faustian paradigm. Freder, the Saviour, in his turn, undertakes the mythic hero's paradigmatic journey: he visits hell, confronts the deluge and is compared to Christ. In the city of the future there is room for witchhunt, magic causation and a melodramatic denouement. The overall social conflict opposes two historical emblems of time: the clock rules over labour and everyday discipline; but the church bells call the people's attention to the church roof, where good Maria is under attack. The film-cathedral, in Élie Faure's sense, finds here literal expression in the medieval architecture and references to fundamental values. The Christian temple takes centre stage when the city-machine redeems itself from its vocation for disaster.

Denouements like this are intended to neutralize the sense of imminent catastrophe. In the film-ritual, the liquid dynamism requires domestication through the comforting revival of the myth of certainty. However, its major attraction and seductive power lies in the spectacular description of present threats and dangers. The allegory of hope – which comes at the very end – has to defeat the allegory of disaster. In this pendular movement between the figures of chaos and progress, the allegories display their structural tension as discourses impelled by a dialectic of fragmentation and totalization (Xavier 1999): fragmentation, because they are discourses marked by discontinuity, excess and the thematization of disaster; totalization, because they are engaged in the construction of a path to salvation on which every hindrance is a necessary stage for the redemptive teleology. The impressive visual apparatus put in place to describe the dehumanization of work in *Metropolis*, the revolutionary excesses enacted in *Napoleon*, and the violence generated by intolerance in *Intolerance*, are more powerful, in terms of plastic values and plot, than the climactic scene of the final promise of happiness in which the protagonists come together to lead the procession of the redeemed.[9]

The sense of balance and organic perfection is not the aim of these works devoted to excess, discontinuity, spectacular reversals and monumental decor. An epitome of excess, *Metropolis* incorporates so many mythological and iconographic references that it has become a polemical work, generating an enormous variety of readings. Its seductive power survives to this day, thanks to its achievements and contradictions.[10]

Cultural Monuments, Civilization and Barbarism

I will now focus on Lang's monumental allegories as an expression of the competition among nations alluded to above. The aesthetic impulse inherent to film-cathedrals will be considered here in connection with the opposition between the pious monuments dedicated to God and the self-aggrandizing monuments dedicated to men.

In Lang, the aesthetic impulse becomes a central issue due to the way the allegory of Babel is presented and reworked throughout the film. The idea of building the Tower with no practical purpose except man's glory is the original sin. At the same time, Metropolis seems to be a city in which all work is done simply to sustain its monumental structure, a place in which the cult of visual appearance plays a key role in the power struggle. Evil shows its face through the robot, embodying sexual fetishism and illusionism, and the Babel theme of the misunderstanding among men is displaced from the sphere of the Verb to that of the Image. Emotions and drives are expressed in the relationship between the gaze and the object, spectator and spectacle. Cinema is what determines this choice.

In response to the centrality of the aesthetic impulse, Lang's allegory establishes a mirroring relationship between the building of the Tower and the production of the monumental film, implying that both come to existence through an autarchic decision free from any exterior mediation. The relationship between the creator (man) and the image (the Tower) dispenses with a third term. Not only is the biblical God absent, but also the reference to any Other – another city, another people – that could be placed on the same level of power and operate as a contender or rival. What is repressed in this imaginary construction is the fact that making the best monumental film (the highest tower) is not just a gesture derived from pure will, but something inscribed in the battlefield of modern society based on market competition.

Worthy of note here is the centrality of the impulse to assert hegemony (or resist it) within a field of competition between nations, not only as narration but as practical structures of wealth and power. It has been said that the 'mediation of the heart' between the brain and the hands – performed by Freder, the Saviour – expresses the nationalist face of the film's conception of the malaise of modernity and its remedy. According to this view, Metropolis provides a German response to the American Way by asserting that the 'lack of spirit' dehumanizes a modernity dominated by vulgar pragmatism.[11] However, the usual competitive character of monumental films is simply not represented within the allegorical autarchic space of Metropolis. There is a blind spot, a repressed knot in this enterprise. The allegory of Babel, as told in the film, expresses an acute sense of the ambivalence of cultural forms within a context of class conflicts and exploitation of labour, but it leaves no room for another form of conflict relating to the national rivalries of the period, which was central to the very conception of *Metropolis* as a high-tech monumental film. The Babel sequence stresses the Tower project as a gesture of construction and oppression that establishes a necessary connection between teleology (for the winners) and disaster (for the losers), a dialectic leading to ruin. By going beyond the biblical text, *Metropolis'* allegory of Babel resonates with Walter Benjamin's famous formula: 'There is no document of civilization which is not at the same time a document of barbarism' (1976: 256). However, its version of Babel is framed by Maria's prophetic words to the workers: 'Wait for him; he will surely come'; that is, the future redemption to be granted by the mediator between the brain and the hand. This prophecy will be confirmed at the end of the film when the announced mediator acts. One could say that this ending contradicts the acute perception of catastrophe embedded in the allegorical Babel sequence. *Metropolis*, like *Intolerance*, focuses on Babel and Babylon as the paradigm of hubris, followed by catastrophe. Ironically, both films, on a pragmatic level, produced a similar combination of great (aesthetic) achievement and (economic) disaster. On the level of the fable, however, both stage something that is common to the film-cathedrals: 'mythic regression', in Benjamin's words, or a denouement reinforcing a false totality. In *Metropolis*, the major faults highlighted by the images of Babel as the mirror of the futuristic factory-city are redressed when the film completes its teleology in the final sequence, which redeems the spirit, the aesthetic impulse and cinema itself. This dialectic of disaster and redemption is precisely what is at play in *Good Morning Babylon*.

Modern National Allegories and the Taviani Brothers' Melancholy Eulogy to Innocence

National allegories, based on the dialectics of totalization and fragmentation, progress and disaster, still feature in modern cinema, even though filmmakers tend to problematize rather than celebrate their recent national past. Rainer Werner Fassbinder's *The Marriage of Maria Braun* (1980), for instance, is a caustic deconstruction of national allegories, with its narrative of progress as disaster. In the critical context of the Balkans, a major example is Theo Angelopoulos, whose national allegories recapitulate a problematic twentieth-century Greek history, always avoiding mythic regressions. Different geopolitical contexts favour distinct ways of dealing with the questions raised by foundational narratives, as the case of the Taviani brothers' film illustrates. The Third World experience fuelled ambitious historical retrospectives with allegorical overtones in Brazil, Mexico, Cuba and Argentina, alongside post-colonial foundational narratives in Algeria, Egypt and Senegal. More recently,

European filmmakers have faced a new historical conjuncture in which the nation has lost status in the dynamics of world power. The phenomenon of globalization has created a new context for this discussion.

Made in 1987, in a difficult moment for Italian cinema (Spagnoletti 1998), *Good Morning, Babylon* revisits the 1910s by means of an elegiac discourse on the continuity of art in history, an allegory which encapsulates the European crisis entailed by the eruption of the First World War, the emblematic ending of the Age of Empire. This allegory, however, keeps a distance from any totalizing prophecy of messianic salvation. Acknowledging the European vicissitudes in the twentieth century, the film is dominated by a melancholy tone clearly expressed in its musical score, which accompanies the Italian immigrants' rise and fall, until their pathetic death in the battlefield.

After the wedding scene described at the beginning of this chapter, the Italian brothers achieve a moment of consecration at the premiere of *Intolerance*. However, the campaign launched by pro-war 'patriots' against the film announces a decisive turn in their life. The violence in the streets upsets Nicola and Andrea's pregnant wives, who are taken to hospital; their babies are born well, but Nicola's wife dies on delivery. He does not accept this tragedy and decides to fight in the war. Later, Andrea will follow in his brother's fatal footsteps in European territory.

The brothers' deaths epitomize the film's melancholy, carefully developed in its homage to the innocence typical of the early monumental cinemaspectacle. At its base is the crisis of current Italian cinema, now far from the famed vigour of the period between 1945 and 1970. It also reflects the alienation of Italian cinema from its popular genres, including the *peplum*.[12] There are, thus, interesting parallels to be drawn between the moment in which the film was made and the past being represented in it, a past in which, according to the Tavianis' view, it was still possible – within Hollywood's incipient 'little community' – to carry out heroic and praiseworthy actions. The creative outburst at the heart of Hollywood is, in the film, isolated from the larger historical context in which the war erupted. The Taviani brothers articulate the issue of national rivalry in a mythic key and exempt cinema from any connection with the bloodshed of 1914–18. The latter is abruptly introduced in *Good Morning, Babylon* as an intervening factor coming from an alien realm, distanced from the characters' sealed-off world. The news of the American declaration of war represents the victory of the bellicose spirit over the pacifist inclination symbolized in the film by Griffith himself. Once its presence is felt, the war cancels out all the accomplishments and cultural dynamism represented in the film. Griffith disappears, and the studios with him, as if Hollywood had no connection with the war. Cinema will only reappear as a humble camera, abandoned by a cameraman killed on the battlefield, and it is used by the dying brothers as a farewell gesture. They take the camera in their hands and take their portraits, fixing images addressed to future viewing as part of family rituals, and hoping that their smiling faces will reach their newborn children. The radical discontinuity between the elegiac vision of Hollywood, pictured as the upcoming artists' 'little community', their home town and the tragic image of war is finally sealed, making room for the film's final symbolic twist.

Griffith and the Italian artisan family had gathered to celebrate the idea of continuity in the arts, an idea ritualized in the wedding scene in the Hollywoodian Babylon. The set features the famous elephants, a symbol of continuity which presides over the film, stemming as it does from the *Cabiria* settings, which influenced Griffith's *Intolerance*, and it is now a reason of pride for both father figures, Bonanno and Griffith. *Good Morning, Babylon* finishes with an evocation of this craftsmanship. Focusing yet again on the elephant sculptures, it reasserts the endurance of the monument in history amidst suffering and calamity. The final image of the film, which repeats the first, brings back the restoration work in its plenitude, precisely when the spectator's emotion is activated by the protagonists' death in the European landscape. The value of continuity in art is celebrated by cutting back to the image of the shining, newly restored cathedral which overshadows the decomposition of forms in the battlefield, where death and destruction prevail. The repetition of the image reaffirms a wholeness that supersedes the landscape of ruins. Andrea and Nicola die, Europe suffers the disasters of war, but the editing drives the architectural monument away from the vicissitudes of time, raising it instead to a symbol of permanence – the sculpted elephant.

By privileging the monumental works which reaffirm the enduring continuity of art in the face of historical disasters, *Good Morning, Babylon* highlights the Italian contribution to cinema as grand spectacle. But the epic moment of its accolade is obstructed by the abrupt rupture caused by the war, a traumatic experience that affected culture and film production in equal measures. Although quite distinct from the sombre historical period of the World Wars and fascism, the 1980s were a very difficult time in Italy, in which production seemed to have come to a halt, confronting filmmakers with the dilemma of 'to film or not to film in Hollywood'. This sort of migratory dream or nightmare echoes Andrea and Nicola's fable, and also the story of the Taviani brothers themselves. At this moment of crisis, the homage to the origins of cinema was articulated as a eulogy to something which was long gone and was never to return.

This eulogy draws on a strong idealization of the Hollywood world, particularly evident in the gentlemanly image of the father-filmmaker, monumentalized alongside the architectural constructions celebrated in the film. The world of artists is radically isolated from the world of values where war is bred. This sublimation of material history is also present in the abstract connection between cinematographic production and the medieval-style craft guilds, implicit in the identity of the two father-masters. They are portrayed in the film as priests of an artistic religion purveying moments of beauty and hope, amidst a practical world in which artists are irrevocably alien. In other words, the separation between art as an institution and the realm of real conflicts, upon which monumentalization is grounded, preserves the innocence of the 'provincial' Hollywood.

The Taviani brothers chose to emphasize those elements which make *Intolerance* a monument to the art of cinema, frequently idealized as the swansong of the age of innocence which preceded North American hegemony. And they refrain from questioning the way the great Griffithian spectacle strove to build a self-image able to celebrate the complicity between cinema and American national pride, as part of a general movement which left its mark on Hollywood history, notably in classic genres such as the western and the war film. The *Birth of a Nation* was a national foundational fiction structured as a racist melodrama of exclusion; *Intolerance* announces hegemony using a teleological ordering of time, based on figural realism (Auerbach 1974: 73–6, 156–72) and establishing a historical (divine) plan in successive stages: the pre-Christian World, the Passion, European Christian civilization until its decline (through corruption and the Wars of Religion), and the rise of Christianity in the New World. These pave the way for the advent of the new nation and its universal mission. Within this overall design, Babylon is the object of homage as a realm of love devoted to Ishtar – the goddess of fertility – and the birthplace of writing, but Griffith's view of its defeat requires a further comment on his conception of war (reality principle) and peace (utopian desire).

Starting with the latter, Hollywood, as seen by the Taviani brothers, echoes Griffith's conception of Babylon, a place of idyllic experiences whose promises were cut short by alien violence and invasion. By providing the filmmaker with the image he himself wished for, the Tavianis are actually giving him back something of what he had projected onto the character of Belshazzar, an allegory of the noble pacifist symbolizing the separation between the efforts of the artist and the realm of social conflicts and war. However, the allegorical design of *Intolerance* brings, side by side with its eulogy to Babylon, an admonitory dimension in that it suggests that history teaches 'eternal vigilance'. Babylon is the instance of an irreparable mistake. Belshazzar lives in peace and love and is not ready for war, and for this reason he has to face death and the destruction of his values. *Intolerance* calls our attention to his blindness to such threats and to his inebriation which, although based on good principles, is also prone to condemnable excess as love slithers into hedonism, being fatally insensible to the reality principle: as the ancient maxim goes: 'if you want peace, prepare for war'. The filmmaker is not only engaged in the acclamation of monuments of the past, but also in the defence of their hegemony in the present, as representative of the power of the nation.[13]

Despite idealizing the figure of Griffith, the allegory articulated by the Tavianis has its own admonitory dimension implicit in the father's words when he prophesies that the brothers' union is a precondition for their success. This is an allusion to the European disaster, correlated to North American hegemony as celebrated in *Intolerance*. Following this lead, *Good Morning, Babylon* gives closure to its historical commentary and reaffirms the principle of unity as a condition for efficacy, both within the family and in the more general sphere of political struggle. In fact, the idea of unity and of an essential connection with the popular has always been dear to the Italian Communist Party. In 1987, this idea became relevant to cinema itself, which was in need of a common effort from the European nations (or the European Community) to boost a revival which would ultimately stop its filmmakers from going to Hollywood. This notwithstanding, the Tavianis reaffirm in their film a ceremonial conception of art which privileges monumental heritage and spiritual continuity. Under this continuity principle, akin to the foundational fiction of popular cinema as opera, spectacle and cathedral, the film builds a teleology of the 'collective dream' that demands the construction of an idealized image of cinema for posterity.

Here, it is worth recalling Walter Benjamin's comment on the antagonistic ideas of history as teleology, constructed from the winners' point of view; and history as violence and disaster, as seen from the losers' point of view. He reminds us that the former is implicated in the latter in a way that is not expressed in the Taviani brothers' remarkable film. Although made by filmmakers concerned with the unresolved tensions between culture and violence, it remains excessively reliant on the uncritical celebration of art as a monument. Benjamin recommends that we look at 'cultural treasures' with 'cautious detachment', rather than full empathy:

> for without exception the cultural treasures he [the historian] surveys have an origin which he cannot contemplate without horror. They owe their existence not only to the efforts of great minds and talents who have created them, but also to the anonymous toil of their contemporaries. There is no document of civilization which is not at the same time a document of barbarism. And just as such a document is not free from barbarism, barbarism taints also the manner in which it was transmitted from one owner to another. (Benjamin 1976: 256)

In *Good Morning, Babylon*, the debate on art focuses on monumental works which attest to the human effort to overcome the corrosive effect of time. The filmmakers understand those ambitious works as social products and project on them the democratic horizon of a 'collective dream'. This, however, remains a ceremonial approach that confirms what is typical of monuments; that is to say, to offer to posterity the self-image that a system of power at a given time defines as the mark of civilization. The aim of their film is not to celebrate a national myth or a foundational fiction. The Taviani brothers' political view and critical approach to Italian history would not allow such an approach. But the way they historically construe their eulogy to monumental art testifies to an unexpected idealization of the aesthetic; this is particularly remarkable for those familiar with their other brilliant political films.

References

Alovisio, Silvio (1998) 'L'Itala Film nei primi anni dieci: ipotesi per un'analisi stilistica', in Paolo Bertetto and Gianni Rondolino (eds) *Cabiria e il suo tempo* (Turin, Museo Nazionale del Cinema, Editrice Il Castoro).

Anderson, Benedict (1983) Imagined Communities: Reflections on the Origin and Spread of Nationalism (London, Verso).

Auerbach, Erich (1974) *Mimesis: the Representation of Reality in Western Literature* (Princeton, Princeton University Press).

Benjamin, Walter (1976) 'Theses on the Philosophy of History', in Hanna Arendt (ed.) *Illuminations* (New York, Schocken Books).

Bernardini, Aldo and Jean Gili (1986) *Le Cinéma italien de la prise de Rome (1905) à Rome, ville ouverte (1945)* (Paris, Centre Georges Pompidou).

Dagrada, Elena, André Gaudreault and Tom Gunning (2000) 'Regard oblique, bifurcation et ricochet, ou de l'inquiétante étrangeté du carrello', *Cinémas: Journal of Film Studies* 10:2–3, Spring.

Daney, Serge (1986) *Ciné journal 1981–1986* (Paris, Éditions Cahiers du cinéma).

Dimendberg, Edward, Martin Jay and Anton Kaes (1994) *The Weimar Republic Source Book* (Berkeley, University of California Press).

Epstein, Jean (1974) *Ecrits sur le cinéma, tome 1: 1921–1947* (Paris, Seghers).

Faure, Élie (1953a) 'La prescience du Tintoret' (1922), in *Fonctions du cinéma: de la cinésplastique et son destin social (1921–1937)*, Preface by Charles Chaplin (Paris, Librairie Plon).

Faure, Élie (1953b) 'De la cinéplastique' (1922), 'Introduction à la mystique du cinéma' (1934) and 'Vocation du cinéma' (1937), in *Fonctions du cinéma: de la cinésplastie et son destin social* (Paris, Librairie Plon).

Fletcher, Angus (1970) *Allegory: The Theory of a Symbolic Mode* (Ithaca, Cornell University Press).

Gellner, Ernst (1983) *Nations and Nationalism* (Ithaca, Cornell University Press).

Greenfeld, Laih (1992) *Nationalism; Five Roads to Modernity* (Cambridge, Harvard University Press).

Gunning, Tom (2000) *The Films of Fritz Lang: Allegories of Vision and Modernity* (London, BFI Publishing).

Habermas, Jürgen (1995) 'Citizenship and National Identity', in Micheline Ishay and Omar Dahbour (eds) *The Nationalism Reader* (New Jersey, Humanities Press).

Hansen, Miriam (1991) *Babel & Babylon: Spectatorship in American Silent Film* (Cambridge, Harvard University Press).

Hobsbawm, Eric (1989) *The Age of Empire 1875–1914* (New York, Vintage Books).

Hobsbawm, Eric (1990) *Nations and Nationalism since 1780: programme, myth, reality* (Cambridge, Cambridge University Press).

Huyssen, Andreas (1986) 'The Vamp and the Machine: Fritz Lang's *Metropolis*', in *After the Great Divide: Modernism, Mass Culture, Postmodernism* (Bloomington, Indiana University Press).

Icart, Roger (1983) *Abel Gance ou le Prométhée foudroyé* (Lausanne, Éditions L'Age de l'Homme).

Landy, Marcia (2000) *Italian Cinema* (Cambridge, Cambridge University Press).

Leblanc, Gérard (1999) 'Gance et le regard de l'aigle', in *Champs Visuels: Revue interdiciplinaire de recherches sur l'image*, 12–13 January.

Le Goff, Jacques (1984) 'Documento/Monumento', in *Memória/História – Enciclopédia Einaudi* vol. 1 (Lisbon, Imprensa Nacional-Casa da Moeda).

Rogin, Michael (1989) 'The Great Mother Domesticated: Sexual Difference and Sexual Indifference in D.W. Griffith's *Intolerance*', in *Critical Inquiry* 15:3, Spring.

Sommer, Doris (1993) 'Love and Country: an Allegorical Speculation', in *Foundational Fictions: the National Romances of Latin America* (Berkeley, University of California Press).

Spagnoletti, Giovanni (1998) 'Îles, 1976–1998, ou Que s'est passé dans le cinéma italien?', in Sergio Toffetti (ed.) *Un'altra Itália: pour une histoire du cinéma italien* (Paris–Milan, Cinémathèque Française–Mazzotta).

Weber, Max (1946) *Essays in Sociology* (New York, Oxford University Press).

Xavier, Ismail (1999) 'Historical Allegories', in Toby Miller and Robert Stam (eds) *A Companion to Film Theory* (Oxford, Blackwell).

Xavier, Ismail (2007) 'A alegoria langiana e o monumental: a figura de Babel em *Metropolis*', in Capelato, Morettin, Napoliano and Saliba (eds) *História e cinema* (São Paulo, Alameda Casa Editorial).

Notes

1 Elena Dagrada, André Gaudreault and Tom Gunning comment on this formal feature of European cinema, and point out the singularity of Pastrone's camera movement, the *carrello*, a variation of the tracking shot as seen in the classical film (Dagrada, Gaudreault and Gunning 2000: 207–23).

2 In fact, this mixture of 'principles' involving classical narrative and cinema of attractions has been reiterated in film history, particularly in those moments in which a new technology allows for the creation of new special effects and the renewal of classical genres, such as science-fiction and horror films.

3 Abel Gance's *Napoleon* is an example of how the idea of the monumental is projected from the narrative onto the visual composition, with the help of an enlarged frame provided by multiple screens, camera movements and the editing style.

4 Sergei Eisenstein's *October* (*Oktyabr*, 1927) could be included here, but its main question is not the nation, but the institution of the proletarian state. The foundational fiction related to the national formation will appear in *Alexander Nievsky* (Sergei Eisenstein, 1937) at a time when the defence of national values and Mother Russia had become the central issue in the conception of historical allegories, thanks to the new political conjuncture dominated by Stalinism.

5 There is an interesting analogy involving *Cabiria*'s plot and the way in which, in John Ford's *The Searchers* (1956), Uncle Ethan only succeeds in bringing Debbie back home after she had spent years among the Native Americans who had abducted her as a child, when the US Army arrives to participate in the charge against the natives and to consolidate the nation-state in the western territory.

6 *Scipione l'Africano* (1937), directed by Carmine Gallone, is a good example of this linkage between modern Italy and its colonial adventures in the glorious Imperial past, an analogy that was seen as the representation of 'national history as retrospective illusion' (Landy 2000: 48–71).

7 The most famous metaphor addressed to Napoleon's personal power to control the waves of history appears in the sequence of the alternation of the two tempests: the literal, with Napoleon alone in a small boat lost in the sea; and the metaphorical, with the agitated session of the Convention lost in rhetorical disputes at the time of Terror. The camera movements and editing style provide the visual experience of lack of control and imminent disaster, suggesting the Convention is on a ship adrift. Roger Icart (1983) and Gérard Leblanc (1999) comment on that sequence as inspired by Victor Hugo. Icart's book includes Abel Gance's writings about his notion of cinema as a universal language and his statement to the public at the opening of *Napoleon* in 1927: 'By supporting *Napoleon* you will help to bring our national cinema back to the position it deserves, which should be and will be the top' (Leblanc 1999: 196).

8 For the notion of 'daemonic agent', see Angus Fletcher and his analysis of the obsessed, one-directional agent who acts as if possessed by 'hidden forces', typical of allegories (Fletcher 1970: 25–69).

9 In terms of dramatic effects, *Cabiria* is much more interesting and visually powerful when it deals with Sofonisba's tragic experience, and the way she, as Princess of

Carthage, confronts defeat and death, than when it deals with Cabiria and Fulvio's ascetic love affair. The intense Italia Manzini (Sofonisba) and actor Bartolomeu Pagano (Maciste) are real operatic 'divas' in the film.

10 Tom Gunning's reading of *Metropolis* is the best analysis of this radically inclusive allegorical device. His account makes clear how the film's many references (mythological narratives, fictional genres) and iconographic proliferation elicit different interpretations, including a sense of *kitsch* derived from excess (Gunning 2000: 52–83).

11 For the analysis of the role of nationalism in the late nineteenth and early twentieth centuries, see Greenfeld (1992); for a specific account of the German reaction to the American presence at the time of accelerated modernization in the 1920s, see the documents compiled in the section 'Imagining America: Fordism and Technology', in Dimendberg, Jay and Kaes (eds) (1994: 393–411).

12 This historical genre devoted to the Ancient World was derived from literary and operatic traditions, and found in Pastrone its great master. French critic Serge Daney points out this trace of popular Italian culture in the Tavianis' films. See his review of *The Night of the Shooting Stars* (*La notte di San Lorenzo*, Paolo and Vittorio Taviani, 1982) in *Ciné journal 1981–1986* (1986: 128–31).

13 John Ford, Griffith's greatest disciple, will explicitly develop the idea of a humanist institutional order, structured upon such figures who, at the expenses of democratic premises, guarantee its defence against enemies. The opposition between civilization and barbarism, in the western genre, will have subtler arrangements compared to those found in Griffith, and Ford will hone heroes with tragic faces, whose truculence, employed almost beyond reasonable limits but for the sake of keeping order, will be linked to a dilemma, entailing exile or oblivion, as in *The Searchers* and *The Man Who Shot Liberty Valance* (1962). One of the effects of Ford's allegory is to preserve them against oblivion.

Chapter Three

A Theory of Cinema that Can Account for Indian Cinema[1]

Ashish Rajadhyaksha

This chapter explores a film-theoretical approach to the Indian cinema. Here I contend that crucial components of Indian cinema's 'productions', including but not limited to film productions, are actually narrative self-justifications for why the cinema should exist at all. Contrary to how many see Indian film, this narrative self-justification is not isolationist, nor does it have recourse to cultural exceptionalism. Instead, it emerges mainly from a tension-ridden relationship with the Indian state, which is often – uniquely, for a postcolonial state – embarrassed, rather than gratified, at having inherited the world's largest, and most diverse, film production base. Such a tension allows an important link to be made between textual excess and political instability. This chapter argues that textual excess is itself not a new concept to film theorists, but takes on specific meanings in India. One such specific meaning is the way the Indian cinema finds use for what film theorists call the 'Hollywood Mode of Production', a kind of narrative economy perfected in Hollywood cinema, but which becomes the textual location for Indian cinema to play out its crisis of legitimacy.

The Indian Cinema Conundrum

When the object of research happens to be one of the most elusive cinematic practices in the world, and in a geo-cultural region that is still hard to confront as a whole, I propose that an inevitable consequence is the emergence of a very different, often elusive, register of film production. In this essay I hope to draw attention to Indian cinema's account of itself: its self-description. In doing so, I shall attempt to provide not just one more account of Indian cinema, but rather to generate through the account a theory of cinema itself – one that can, I will propose, most appropriately account for Indian cinema.

Much of the energy of this argument will be derived from my contention that – contrary to many theoretical representations of it – Indian cinema's self-description is not isolationist and does not have recourse to arguing for its own uniqueness. As with any major film industry, Indian cinema is hugely invested into producing explanations of why it exists; indeed, this is a serious and significant enterprise on its part. Some of the enterprise is dedicated to fulfilling an original expectation: that of producing a national cinema, something that it has done poorly, mainly because to do so involves overcoming the often incredibly complex problems posed by what has been described as a 'Delhicentric' national media paradigm[2] and an Indian state that has been more embarrassed than otherwise at having been saddled with the world's most diverse film production base.

Addressing this problem from within the welter of confusion as to whether the cinema exists to serve a *national* purpose has been the business of numerous published accounts provided by agencies designed, officially and otherwise, to administer Indian film: legal material; reports and field studies by inquiry committees; the academic curricula of institutions wanting to teach films (the disciplines of Film Appreciation and Media Studies); and, of course, the theoretical work of spokespersons of various components of the industry, including federal associations representing producers, technicians, actors and other artists. Many of these explanations could validly constitute themselves as the genealogy of film theory in India. The important link for me is between such material and a related – and equally visible – location for the self-descriptive account. I refer to the one embedded in film narratives themselves.

That all film narratives also produce self-validating accounts of why they exist, and what work they do, is a basic film studies truism. Such an umbrella narrative, internalizing various institutionalized explanations, takes on a particular edge in places like India, where a cinematic text is inevitably required to handle several responsibilities in addition to narration proper. Given that the 'narrative account' of a film always (again, especially in India) considerably exceeds the boundaries of plausible storytelling, it is perhaps best to see it as existing on top of the story, shored up with additional surrounding layers that provide an 'instruction manual' for how the film should be read and, even more significantly, used. Amongst the key descriptive functions of any Indian 'story' is an accommodation of several external mechanisms of cinematic regulation. A film narrative includes, at the very least, an argument for industrial self-legitimacy, a second argument (often addressed to the Censor Board) qualifying the film's 'public' address, a possible third providing the pedagogic-instructional aspects guiding spectatorial action, and maybe even a fourth and a fifth. The 'production' of all these narrative registers lies analogous to the economic production of a film. All of these registers have intersected with proto-theoretical discourses on the identity of given categories of production, and their places of belonging or origin, almost from the inception of film in India: as is perhaps most evident in the 'how-to' writings by filmmakers, which incorporate such theory into trade and industry-driven accounts alongside state-driven discourses on regulation.

Avant-garde filmmakers of course participate self-consciously in such crossover actions, and self-consciously avant-garde films are therefore easily accepted as arguments, their narratives possessing theoretical ambition. It is less easy to attribute such theoretical ambition to, say, a mainstream commercial Indian film, and yet I believe that such an attribution can be made. If writing and discussion on Indian cinema has also, for example, historically made it its business on behalf of its film industry to try and elevate mere categorizing justifications into an intellectual argument – admittedly making it difficult sometimes to establish where the publicists leave off and the theorists take over – this should not be seen as a criticism of the process, whatever its limitations. Rather, it should draw our attention to the nature of the self-justificatory arguments we are faced with, and the specific, at times bizarre, responsibilities that 'theory' – the development of discourses on category, identity and belonging, admixed with the process of, as it were, talking up the idea of 'Indian Cinema' – has accepted in this space of film production, in however rough-and-ready a fashion.

My own argument also consciously tries to locate itself at this cusp. On the one hand, I recapitulate and take forward a now long and politicized history of engagement with, and disengagement from, Western film theory by those writing on Indian cinema. However, what concerns me is that after all this is done, there still appears to be something out there that even now seems to need 'an account'. And that something continues with some obstinacy to concern cinema, notwithstanding the obsolescence of its most distinctive technological vehicle, celluloid. It has also to do with India, an equally stubborn presence, despite the changes wrought by globalization. The two terms continue to come together easily enough in a mundane but still worthwhile, and as yet unanswered question: why did India take to the cinema in the way it did?

This enquiry forces a deeper quest. It seems that the Indian state – that complex, gigantic endeavour of the twentieth century, which the social sciences have made it their primary task to comprehend – has something foundational to say to the question, with its own take on why the cinema took root in India the way it did and, even more, on why the state finds itself, even today, so dramatically, and so uncomfortably, implicated in the question of cinema.

The 'Time of Celluloid'

I need to take a small detour here, familiar to professional film theorists. Inquiries into the assembly of 'storytelling' structures in cinema have concentrated on the efficient organization of the intradiegetic system, or the choreographing of spaces, looks, gestures and the paraphernalia of camera, editing and sound, existing at the service of the spectator's look.

If the cinema famously has three 'looks', among the greatest difficulties that the Indian (and generally non-Western) cinema has faced has been the underdevelopment of the third look – the look that characters on screen exchange between themselves, and where the spectator is permitted a transcendent anonymity – that has framed Indian cinema's traditional inability to choreograph its screen action into a storytelling logic, and which constitutes, by many arguments, the primary evidence of its underdevelopment both as text and as industry.

I propose that this textual inadequacy has links with the problem I mentioned in the previous paragraph: the uncomfortable relation of Indian cinema to the Indian state. I further propose that a somewhat specific political problem had a direct textual representation, providing some rather precious material for our argument. In exploring this link, I plan to restrict my argument to the era of celluloid, and therefore on a set of cinematic 'productions' – cinematic effects – that were prototyped on celluloid, but which are increasingly being reprised in sequel technologies. This period to which I refer thus was inaugurated in a way we can define with extraordinary precision: on 28 December 1895 at the Salon Indien of Paris, and on 7 July 1897 by Marius Sestier at Bombay's Watson's Hotel; and ended on dates that, less accurately (and less spectacularly), can be located somewhere around the early 1990s with the first acquisition of Avid editing consoles. This period can, I think, be *globally* bracketed off as determining a particular kind of public engagement with the moving image, one that celluloid not only exemplifies but, in hindsight, may have fabricated, or constructed, more or less on its own, a public narrativized primarily as a mix of text and social action through the twin regulatory mechanisms of containment and excess. 'Containment' is a formal requirement of the film frame and a social requirement of the movie theatre itself. Celluloid's inherent structural instability, notwithstanding – perhaps exacerbated by – the fantasy character of film, has real public consequences that it does not apparently share even with sequel technologies such as video.[3] It is, I think, worth noting the innate tendency of film to create such excess, before we transfer that excess into Indian conditions and track its consequences there.

Numerous institutions of social governance from the early years of the cinema have noted the social and economic consequences of cinematic excess, and how they can spill over into extra-textual social spaces. My proposal to restrict this unstable public engagement to celluloid is additionally substantiated by the distinct presence of both a pre- and a post- to this 'modern' era. Pre-celluloid exhibition practices, evidenced for example in the various *pata* (paper) traditions preceding the invention of the *chitrapat* (literally, picture), can be characterized through what Sudipta Kaviraj (1992: 33) has called 'narrative communities', and their unstable reconfiguration through the splitting up of the narrative/communitarian sequences of storytelling into individually saleable 'units', using technologies such as the oleograph and woodblock printmaking – which also allows us a narrative definition for early capitalist production and exhibition systems that cinematic narratives would inherit. At the other and more familiar end of our era is of course the post-celluloid privatization and domestication of exhibition, with its own political consequences for the public domain. The 'time of celluloid' therefore opens up both retrospective and prospective histories to the many consequences of its structural instability.

Film theory again has shown that the particular kind of public engagement with the moving image became a primary characteristic of the medium in the 'time of celluloid' in the way celluloid film was able to transform its technology into a full apparatus – a transformation that required the literal 'cinema machine' (the basic camera-projector mechanism) to become a 'larger social and/or cultural and/or institutional "machine" for which the former is only a point of convergence of several lines of force in the latter' (Rosen 1986: 282) – presumes that the locus of this transformation is not so much in the technology as in the transformed position of the spectator.

If celluloid did anything at all, it was to perform this astonishingly efficient act of transference, as much in India (and generally Asia) as anywhere else.[4] The abstracted spectator-position reproduces the properties of the apparatus as, continuing with Rosen, a 'conjuncture of determinants and effectivities' (1986: 282), providing one with perhaps the most influential 'nodal point of a social construction of knowledge, desire, pleasure, signifying adequacies, etc.' (1986: 282). In fact, so complete is celluloid's transformative power, and so extreme the welding together in complicity, of *appareil* and *dispositif*, that a real fear arises that 'the investigation of subject-positioning and the specular could get too strongly localized in the machinery' (1986: 281–2), with reductive and 'debilitating' consequences (1986: 282) for the ways in which the purposes of the technology might be understood. While the technologization of a spectatorial subject-position – yesterday's spectation machine sitting today at a videogame terminal with consoles, or at least with a television remote – is a commonplace in the digital era, it is instructive to consider how, in the heyday of celluloid, all the work we do today with zapping or web-browsing was done by the complex-looking mechanisms which allowed the spectatorial senses to negotiate the apparatus.

In my view, the enormous collective desire to keep the unity of the diegesis together, to suture the gap between shots and between the camera's, the characters' and the spectator's gazes, draws attention, first, to the, at the very least dubious and certainly politically contentious, nature of the transaction, and, secondly, to the uncertain role that the authority of the cinematic apparatus plays in underwriting that negotiation.[5] Such diegetic unity is clearly possible despite the fact that even the most untutored film-going experience reiterates that what you see on screen is *not* identical to what the camera saw; that the image has been processed – enhanced, that is, captured on film, edited and mixed with a soundtrack that is reproduced in multitrack arrangements in the auditorium – through interventions that, far from remaining unobtrusive, insistently draw attention to themselves. This performance and the interventionist role of the apparatus have only grown more and more grandiose over time in film-industrial contexts everywhere, with newer screen aspect ratios, increased tracks to the sound and spectacular camera movement. The seeming absence of contradiction between diegetic continuity and technological performance, one that flies in the face of a famous classical principle in the modern medium of film which requires that interventionist narrative modes be rendered invisible, draws our attention to the way the apparatus performs to a spectatorial gaze.[6] Such a smooth, if perennially insecure, transition can only be accounted for by the presence of some mechanism within celluloid systems that allows the spectator's own visibility to become a surrogate of the hypervisible apparatus. Existing in its image, it would appear that as the spectator navigates through the film narrative, s/he also thereby navigates through at least three kinds of transactive change, all reprising the basic processing of the first look into the second. These modes of navigation can be briefly summarized as: first, the transformative role of spectatorship in the visible production of the subjectivity that a 'modern' subject is presumed to possess, now expressed through the capacity for modern-subjective action (including the risks of irrational, immoral and unsafe action); second, the further facilitation of new public spaces for the performance of that subjective action as the fabricated textuality opens up a new fantasy public domain; and third, the ambitions of defining the role and purpose of the visible celluloid apparatus as it layers itself on to a fully fledged apparatus of social organization by naming itself as both representational guarantor of public right and its authorized regulator (and thus permitting a further fantasy of symbolically claiming to govern the national public domain).

The Role of the Modern State

From the inception of the cinema in India, in the colonial period onwards, all three modes were noticed by state agencies who realized that cinema was having an impact on its audiences that was unprecedented. As colonial authorities scrambled to devise new legislation to address the problem, they also inaugurated what would be a long and complicated saga of state intervention in

India, mired in various kinds of administrative and textual chaos. The intrinsic link in the three registers between celluloid systems of shooting and projection, and the 'publicness' of the moving image, can be seen to underpin something of greater significance still: the role and function of the modern *state*.

In fact, so compelling is the link that India throws up for film history itself that we may well periodize the 'time of celluloid', 1895–1990, as precisely the rise and fall of the modern state. (If the Spanish-American war of 1898, that saw the rise of the United States of America as the modern imperial power, coincides historically with the invention of celluloid – and if the most famous twentieth-century version of that celluloid production, Hollywood, is inextricably linked to the economic and political rise of the United States[7] – then the decline and radical transformation of the structure of the modern state with the onset of globalization, for which one marker is surely the collapse of the Soviet Union and the East European economies, coincides eerily with the date of obsolescence of celluloid film.) This is not merely a matter of historical coincidence. From the 'Hollywood/Mosfilm' of the twentieth-century superpowers to the national cinemas of decolonized postwar nations, the centrality of celluloid as a privileged presence within the modern (newly independent, postcolonial) national state apparatus needs to be accounted for at multiple levels. At least one of the levels of film 'production' would then be the public production of the apparatus of cinema, and the mapping of technological storytelling upon systems that validate and authorize modern states. A critical part of the mapping has to be its further capacity to produce appropriate symbolic structures under conditions of spectatorial authorization. We are now looking at narrative as a relay action whose end-result is the production of an enfranchised spectator, with storytelling becoming a means to map the spectatorial presence upon the structures by which modern states produce and authorize their self-image.[8]

An icon of the imaginary associated with the 1955 Bandung conference of non-aligned nations, India is of course a prime instance of postwar decolonization, and is thus frequently presented as most 'typical' of the ambitions and failures of the developmental state in this time. The astonishing, often befuddling, success of the 'world's largest democracy' in ingesting and reproducing the discourses of Western liberalism in its own modes of functioning, equalled only by the failure of the state machinery to see through the 'bourgeois-democratic revolution' – the study of whose failure, as Ranajit Guha (1982: 7) proposes, must form the central problematic of any historiography of colonial India – provides the best example of what I see as the domain of symbolic operation that characterizes several of the Indian state's ex-colonial instruments of governance: instruments often valued for their colonial pedigree rather than their political effectiveness.

Ranajit Guha was among the first to note the need for identifying some special kinds of symbolic mechanisms while theorizing the Indian state, and his argument of colonial India as 'Dominance without Hegemony' is accompanied by his famous chart showing the 'General Configuration of Power' (Guha 1997: 20). While the chart, and its splitting up of Dominance (with its sub-tropes of Coercion and Persuasion) and Subordination (split into Collaboration and Resistance), may appear quaint today, I believe it still contains grains of the following truth. There can be no understanding of the Indian state's deployment of subordination mechanisms within its social functioning without prior comprehension of the dominance of Western liberalism. Contrarily, no dominant Western concept, such as democracy or the legal mechanisms that define its processes, can by itself provide an adequate explanation for its often particular, against-the-grain, usage in India.

Narrative typically brings together normative and functional elements into a particular account that has significant resonances within the domain of state operation in India. It also commonly uses the normative detour simulating western discursive rationality to 'explain itself', even though, as Partha Chatterjee suggests, such an explanation reproducing the 'rational consciousness of the state ... does not exhaust the determinate being of the state' (1994: 207). The difficulty has to do not with definitional insufficiency but, rather, with the need that functioning systems in India apparently have to define themselves through the refracted gaze of the 'West': an old political issue that still cuts to the bone in the cinema. Symbolic production, to my understanding, is the way a system, say, the Indian state (and its cinema), defines its own existence and purpose, and often its problems, through (re)producing another system, say, Western democracy (or, for our purposes, the Hollywood mode, on which more below). As with any symbolic interpretation, a literal reading in such a situation would be a structurally insufficient explanation for what is going on beneath, but understanding a functioning system through a prior understanding of what it 'ought to be' nevertheless seems a necessary detour for the account itself to hold. The cultural difficulty of translating such symbolic attributes into functioning systems has crippled several major initiatives, precisely because their belief in the direct applicability of abstract democratic values does not take the detour into consideration.

Chatterjee once asked if there is something mandatory about modernity's 'universal adoption of western forms of civil society' (2000: 40). If indeed there is something mandatory here – about modern narrative's gesturing towards rationality, for example – can we use this presumption as a springboard to explore the symbolic structure's role of locally deploying Western forms as a means by which to keep profoundly functioning, non-Western systems alive? This appears critical to any understanding of Indian cinema as primarily condensing a spectatorial habit of reading into what is on screen, rather than reading off it – a substantive (mis)representation that puts seemingly familiar concepts to work in extremely unfamiliar arenas and opens up laboratory conditions for understanding several properties of certain mislocated founding concepts.

The Problems with the Hollywood Mode

I conclude with the most classical of cinema's founding concepts, the 'Hollywood mode of production', a much-vaunted category of narrative cinema that would find itself taking a curious detour, and playing a role in Indian cinema during the interwar period and immediately after independence.

The Hollywood mode, it is said, was a specific set of narrative, production and exhibition systems first introduced in the United States in the 1920s, and consolidated, with the introduction of sound technology, through the 1930s and 1940s into an elaborately conceived master text including duration and performance style, camera shooting techniques, editing and sound-recording and mixing conventions, down to specific and largely inviolable conventions of negative processing and printing, and eventually even to projection conditions. The Hollywood mode consciously fuelled its claim to global intelligibility with a claim to unfettered access to audiences across the planet, and, further, by equating such textual access with a democratic free-market ideal as incarnated in the New Information Order (MacBride 1980), and, more controversially, in the GATT (General Agreement on Tariffs and Trade) and WTO (World Trade Organization) negotiations of the Uruguay Round (1994). Recent work on early film, combining theory with film-archival preoccupations, further puts the spotlight on those contemporary film practices – such as Indian cinema – that apparently continue to possess characteristics of performance, camera work, editing and even celluloid-processing that the 'coherent syntax' theory would typically consider extinct, or, if at all, present only in marginal phenomena such as cult movies (including cult-Bollywood).

Sustaining such a view, after the 'coherent syntax' and 'Hollywood mode' theories, is a third formulation: that of the industrial/institutional mode of representation, or the IMR. The task of the IMR is, in a sense, to make the Hollywood mode globally applicable. And so, speaking of an era of cinema constituted in the period 1895–1929 that saw Hollywood define its mechanisms, Noël Burch (1990: 2) identifies a form that for 'fifty years, has been explicitly taught in film schools as the Language of Cinema and which, whoever we are, we all internalize at an early age as a reading competence thanks to an exposure to films ... which is universal among the young in industrial societies'. Burch cuts a swathe through at least three layers of argument. First, he textualizes all Hollywood narrative production as *industrial* – not an easy thing to do; second, he universalizes this textual process into a universal industrial process;[9] and third, he resolutely primitivizes all practices not following the IMR through the concept of PMR or Primitive Mode of Representation, standing for practices not 'yet' compatible with it.

Extrapolating an industrial argument from one driven by textuality has of course this immediate consequence: it renders Indian cinema into a pre-industrial phenomenon, which of course is nonsense. A further consequence of the miraculous discovery of what historian and anthropologist D.D. Kosambi called 'primitive survivals in the superstructure'[10] is the logical accommodation of its enquiry into the domain of visual anthropology[11] rather than economics, which may well have had difficulties with the contradictions within a concept such as a 'pre-industrial cinema'.

Just how such a 'primitive' Indian cinema could exist, leave alone hold out against the global domination of Hollywood, has been a matter of some confusion to film theory. India is the largest filmmaking country in the world. This fact is widely reproduced in film accounts, often with awe. How did it achieve that? One account of how world cinema deals with Hollywood reproduces a common claim: that Indian cinema simply 'ignored' Hollywood ('an accomplishment managed by few'), and that this was possible only because it did not directly compete with Hollywood, but focused instead on 'targeting a distinct, specialized market sector' (Crofts 1993: 45). Sequel common sense then has it that since this sector now includes an increasingly wealthy Indian diaspora, not only does India have a captive home audience, but it can globalize itself without really having to confront the Hollywood juggernaut, which it bypasses primarily through its ability to create new markets as against competing in existing ones.

In fact, Indian cinema did not ignore Hollywood. Although this cannot be proved in a brief essay, I shall nevertheless propose that the Hollywood mode (as distinct from the American cinema) defines a key zone of negotiation in the postwar, independent Indian state's dealings with its several film industries. How does the Hollywood mode become something like the elusive presiding deity arbitrating the tension between a delegitimized film industry, incapable, in the eyes of the Indian state, of becoming a properly national cinema? This detour remains one of the most under-debated themes in world cinema theory, one where I believe Indian cinema shares some common features with Soviet, Brazilian and postwar Japanese efforts, to take the most prominent instances, to deploy Hollywood mode structures under state supervision. In drawing attention to the immense attraction that such a structure of control would have had for independent states seeking to fabricate their own systems of social administration, I am more interested in a slightly different question that has also been a feature of world trade. This has to do with a further intervention into IMR's global operations: one that refashioned the 'textual feint' – the foregrounding of textual intelligibility to open up economic opportunity – for a particular sort of national use.

Such a move is in fact a seminal part of the space-clearing exercise of several postwar nation-states which used Hollywood as a textual rationale for all proto-industrial economies that needed cultural reform. To conclude with one important theoretical example that has yet to be emulated in India, Tom O'Regan (1990) proposes that, since Hollywood produces an 'international product made for domestic and international consumers', 'any simple identification of Hollywood with the USA' should inevitably be rendered 'problematic'. 'To be wholly local' in a pure form in front of and behind the camera is not the natural condition of a national cinema, says O'Regan (1996: 55), even when it looks to be doing precisely that. 'In their choice of actors, locations, production personnel, story and dialogue, local producers routinely take into account the requirements of international circulation', and, therefore, 'Hollywood's role in making, inventing and repairing cinema and in making, shaping and repairing our sense of ourselves reconfigures the Hollywood legacy. We are not outside Hollywood, we are implicated in ongoing negotiations with it' (1996: 139).

In India, Hollywood's reconfigurations of its legacy in local negotiations comprises one of the more complex ways by which Indian cinema textually transformed itself in tension with its own state mechanisms. Its internal negotiations have partly to do with the extraordinarily complicated problems that especially (though not by any means uniquely) Hindi cinema, India's most 'visible' film industry, poses to the Indian state. They have also something to do with this industry's 'grey' economic status, as with its cultural disqualification from the status of a 'national cinema'.

References

Burch, Noël (1990) *Life to Those Shadows*, trans. Ben Brewster (London, British Film Institute).

Chatterjee, Partha (1994) *The Nation and Its Fragments: Colonial and Postcolonial Histories* (New Delhi, Oxford University Press).

Chatterjee, Partha (2000) 'Two Poets and a Death: On Civil and Political Society in the Non-Christian World', in Timothy Mitchell (ed.) *Questions of Modernity* (Minneapolis, University of Minnesota Press), pp.35–48.

Crary, Jonathan (1992) *Techniques of the Observer: On Vision and Modernity in the Nineteenth Century* (Cambridge, MIT Press).

Crofts, Stephen (1993) 'Reconceptualizing National Cinemas', *Quarterly Review of Film and Video* 4:3.

Guha, Ranajit (1982) 'On Some Aspects of the Historiography of Colonial India', in Ranajit Guha (ed.) *Subaltern Studies I: Writings on South Asian History and Society* (New Delhi, Oxford University Press), pp.3–4.

Guha, Ranajit (1997) *Dominance without Hegemony: History and Power in Colonial India* (Cambridge, Harvard University Press).

Hansen, Kathryn (1992) *Grounds for Play: The Nautanki Theatre of North India* (Berkeley, University of California Press).

Jinhua, Dai (2002) *Cinema and Desire: Feminist Marxism and Cultural Politics in the Work of Dai Jinhua*, eds Jin Wang and Tani E. Barlow (London, Verso).

Kaviraj, Sudipta (1992) 'The Imaginary Institution of India', in Partha Chatterjee and Gyanendra Pandey (eds) *Subaltern Studies VII: Writings on South Asian History and Society* (New Delhi, Oxford University Press), pp.1–39.

Kosambi, Damodar Dharmanand (1999) [1956] *An Introduction to the Study of Indian History* (Bombay, Popular Prakashan).

Lelyveld, David (2002) 'Talking the National Language: Hindi/Urdu/ Hindustani in Indian Broadcasting and Cinema', in Sujata Patel, Jasodhara Bagchi and Krishna Raj (eds) *Thinking Social Science in India: Essays in Honour of Alice Thorner* (New Delhi, Sage Publications), pp.355–66.

Lutgendorf, Phillip (1990) 'Ramayan: The Video', *The Drama Review* 34:2, pp.127–75.

MacBride, Sean (1980) *Many Voices, One World: Towards a New More Just and More Efficient World Information and Communication Order* (London/New York/Paris, Kogan Page/Unipub/Unesco).

Metz, Christian (1974) *Film Language: A Semiotics of the Cinema* (New York, Oxford University Press).

Ministry of Information and Broadcasting (1985) *An Indian Personality for Television: Report of the Working Group on Software for Doordarshan* (New Delhi, Ministry of Information and Broadcasting).

Pilar, Santiago A. (1983) 'The Early Movies: From Stage to Screen Was the Only Step', in Rafael M. Guerrero (ed.) *Readings in Philippine Cinema* (Manila, Experimental Cinema of the Philippines and Manila Film Center), pp.8–17.

Rajadhyaksha, Ashish (2003) 'Spilling Out: Nalini Malani's Recent Video Installations', *Third Text* 17:1, pp.53–61.

Rajadhyaksha, Ashish (2009) *Indian Cinema in the Time of Celluloid: From Bollywood to the Emergency* (New Delhi, Tulika/Bloomington, Indiana University Press).

Ray, Satyajit (1993) *Our Films, Their Films* (New Delhi, Orient Longman).

Rosen, Philip (ed.) (1986) *Narrative, Apparatus, Ideology: A Film Theory Reader* (New York, Columbia University Press).

Shaik, N. Meera Anita Jhamtani and D.U.M. Rao (2004) 'Information and Communication Technology in Agricultural Development: A Comparative Analysis of Three Projects from India', AGREN Network paper 135 (Agricultural Research and Extension Network) online at: http://

www.odi.org.uk/work/projects/agren/papers/agrenpaper_135.pdf. Accessed 15 October 2010.

Notes

1 This paper was first given at the workshop Theorizing World Cinema II, organized by the Centre for World Cinemas, University of Leeds, in November 2007. An expanded version of it has been published in Rajadhyaksha (2009). I would like to thank Rajinder Dudrah for his feedback and support, without which this text could never have reached its current state of completion.

2 The term was originally used in national media discourse by the Working Group on Software for Doordarshan, chaired by P.C. Joshi (Ministry of Information and Broadcasting 1985), which attacked India's state television broadcaster, noting with concern its often narrow, Delhi-centric view of India. The transgressive presence of especially Mumbai's Hindi cinema within India's national media policy is significant to my approach.

3 Video deals with the 'public' character of its own excesses rather differently, as I have tried to address with respect to the only significant exploration of this issue that I have come across in India: Nalini Malani's single-evening exhibition of video work, curated by Pooja Sood, at the Apeejay Technopark (see Rajadhyaksha 2003).

4 And perhaps more so in India/Asia than anywhere else. An indicator would be through the discipline of psychoanalysis, arguably the privileged discipline for the analysis of modern consciousness. The International Psychoanalytic Association website (http://www.ipa.org.uk, accessed 24 August 2007) shows only two constituent Asian organizations, in India and Japan, perhaps suggesting the difficulties this continent has posed to the institutionalization of a discipline meant to analyse the modern rational subject. Such resistance is in sharp contrast to the widespread impact of Freud's and, later, Lacan's writings on Asian cultural theory. Film studies, the most visible location for this impact, arguably offers a key location to mediate psychoanalysis theory in its alluring capacity to fabricate an analysable/ pathologizable spectator-subject. Dai Jinhua (2002), for example, uses Lacanian terminology to outline the Fifth Generation's prehistory and social context, suggesting that it is 'the memory of the Cultural Revolution and the era after Cultural Revolution [in which] they recall the act of killing the Father, the Carnival of the Sons, the revolution within the Order against order, the castration of History inherent in the order of Father-Son, and the death and resurrection of the Father of experience' (2002: 31). Speaking of Zhang Yimou's *Red Sorghum*, she says it 'presented a perfect answer to what this country "needed", indeed to everything this era was demanding. With its son-cum-father nationalist hero and the insolent and violent story of patricide, the film completes the coming of age for the Fifth Generation as well as the ritual of entering the symbolic realm' (2002: 33). I am grateful to Sana Das for this suggestion.

5 Such an authority is somewhat graphically in evidence in recent years in the deployment of 'neutral' technology such as computers within e-governance

initiatives, which have, when successful, seen computer-illiterate farmers make wide use of ICT services where they 'do not feel that there is a barrier to their obtaining information', a 'tribute to the grassroots staff and their training', but also to 'faith in the technology' (Shaik, Jhamtani and Rao 2004: 9).

6 Critiquing Chaplin's statement about a camera 'giving a performance' – 'When a camera is placed on the floor and moves about the player's nostrils, it is the camera that is giving a performance, not the actor' – Ray (1993: 178) reiterates the modernist dictum: 'Anyone with a modicum of familiarity with the aesthetics of cinema knows that a camera cannot give a performance. It is the director who expresses himself in a particular manner through a particular use of the camera.' My conclusion here would apparently contradict Ray in its claim that the cinematic apparatus does indeed give a performance (though perhaps I mean the term to mean something slightly different).

7 In some places the link between the birth of American colonialism and the origins of the cinema can be disconcertingly direct. Pilar (1983: 8–9) tracks the origins of the Philippine cinema thus: 'Movies were shown in the Philippines for the first time during the alarming days of the revolution against the Spanish regime. While armed encounters raged between Filipino revolutionaries and Spanish colonial forces in the countryside, Manila followed a leisurely pace or perhaps a false daring, for its theatres had never been as full and as thriving as they were in those tense days.' This lasted just four months – between 31 August 1897, the date of opening of the first movie theatre, and its closure that November, just prior to the cessation of the Philippines to the United States.

8 I am thinking of the kind of inversion of state surveillance mechanisms into the production of spectacle that Crary (1992: 18) also envisages, in his contention that received Foucauldian wisdom opposing surveillance and spectacle fails to acknowledge how these two regimes of power can often coincide, where spectacular action at spectatorial behest can actually take over techniques for the management of attention.

9 So, for example, the initial development of IMR is linked to Great Britain, which was far ahead of both the United States and France in 1903, but then declined. By 1906 'only a move from artisanal to industrial production could have protected [the British] from French and soon American competition' (Burch 1990: 80).

10 This refers to Kosambi's famous assertion that archaeological work on India should happen not only in 'primitive Indian survivals in marginal territories', but also in 'social clusters that survive even in the heart of fully developed areas ... in and around cities' (1999: 7), since these too 'constitute priceless evidence for the interpretation of some ancient record or archaeological find [as] their survival as backward groups also furnishes the real problem for explanation in the light of historical development' (1999: 7–8). 'The survivals mean [either] that no conflict was felt in that particular case, or that primitive instruments of production have endured in spite of imposing, complicated, and often tortuous developments of the superstructure' (1999: 8).

11 A key strand of visual anthropology has explored cinema's derivation of its aesthetic practices from epic structures, as well as from folk origins such as the

nautanki. Kathryn Hansen (1992: 42) claims that nautanki 'reaches audiences more through the electronic media – records, cassettes, films and television – than through the older mode of face-to-face contact'. Lutgendorf (1990: 128) adds: 'To suggest that the making of a TV serial [*The Ramayana*] began several millennia ago may risk mimicking the hype that emanates from the publicity department at Sagar Enterprises, yet it is clear that the success of India's most popular serial derives in large measure from the enduring appeal of the narrative tradition on which it draws.'

PART II

THE TRANSNATIONAL PROJECT

Chapter Four

Transnational Cinemas: The Cases of Mexico, Argentina and Brazil[1]

Paul Julian Smith

A commercial shown in Mexican cinemas in summer 2008 went like this. In the exotic setting of a village in India, mysterious boxes begin to arrive. On opening them, the exotically-clad locals discover that they contain cases of Corona beer. Suddenly India is Mexicanized: the women sport frilly skirts in red, white and green, and the snake charmers turn into mariachis, playing brassy rancheras on their pipes. The tagline follows: 'El espíritu mexicano no conoce fronteras' ('the Mexican spirit knows no boundaries').

In its humorous way, the ad points to two serious themes. On the one hand, Latin American cinema (and especially, perhaps, the Mexican variety) has, like its beer, become transnational, crossing frontiers with ease and winning increasing acceptance abroad. On the other, this abolition of borders raises an anxiety around identity: if, fortified with Corona beer, Indians can be as Mexican as the native-born *chilango*, then how is one to define a national culture? Tellingly, a public service ad playing in Mexican cinemas at the same time supported the current grass-roots campaign against chronic public *inseguridad*, or dangerous crime. Against a background of white ribbons, the symbol of the movement, the exhibitor assures audiences: 'En Cinemex queremos un México seguro' ('In Cinemex we want a safe Mexico'). The confident exporting of national culture abroad thus contrasts with a certain uncertainty around the experience of that culture at home, even within the relative security of a cinema.

This chapter is divided into two halves. In the first, I give an account of three recent models of transnational cinema, the term which seems to have supplanted 'globalization' as the fetish term in academic discourse; in the second, I will discuss three recent films (one each from Mexico, Argentina and Brazil) which offer different and perhaps unexpected examples of transnationalism in Latin American cinema. The films are the supernatural thriller or genre movie *KM 31*, by Mexican Rigoberto Castañeda (premiered at the Morelia festival in 2006, but not distributed until the following year); the enigmatic art movie or, my preferred term, 'festival film' *The Headless Woman* (*La mujer sin cabeza*), by Argentine Lucrecia Martel (2008); and the (mainly) English-language 'prestige picture' (also my coinage) *Blindness*, by Brazilian Fernando Meirelles (also 2008). Curiously, all three of my chosen films begin with what appears to be an everyday traffic accident, but which is later revealed to be more complex and problematic. There could be no clearer sign of the missed or violent encounters between individuals and nationalities explored within them.

Now it is striking that my first film, *KM 31*, casts a Spanish actor as the male lead, as had been the case with the female leads in the two critically acclaimed features associated with the so-called 'New Mexican Wave' at the start of this decade: González Iñárritu's *Amores perros* (2000) and Alfonso Cuarón's *And Your Mother Too* (*Y tu mamá también*, 2001). As we shall see, this phenomenon, which (beyond broader transnationalism) raises the very specific question of the relation between Mexico and Spain, extends beyond auteur and prestige cinema into genre films, such as *KM 31*. If the theory of transnational film is complex and contradictory, then its practice may well be even more so.

Three Models of the Transnational: Stam, García Canclini, Berry

I take my three versions of transnational cinema from plenary papers read at a conference on that same topic, held in Puebla, Mexico, in August 2008, and hosted jointly by a franchise of Nottingham University in China and Mexico's Iberoamericana. While the value of the papers themselves was that they contained at the time the most recent account of the topic offered by major authorities in the field, the great novelty and utility of this conference was its juxtaposition of two geographical regions which are rarely compared: Latin America and East Asia.

The paper by Robert Stam, a well-known Brazilian specialist at New York University, was called 'From Revolution to Resistance: Alternative Aesthetics in Transnational Media' (Stam 2008). As its title indicates, the focus was textual, based on specific sequences of films that were either canonic or little known. While Stam did not explicitly suggest what mode of present-day 'resistance' had replaced the revolutionary trend of the 1960s, he noted that in the context of teaching, students no longer looked kindly on the militant cinema of the past, such as *The Hour of the Furnaces* (*La hora de los hornos*, Octavio Getino and Fernando Solanas, 1968), while they showed more enthusiasm for recent video works by indigenous filmmakers. (Such films constitute an important strand in the International Film Festival of Morelia, which in October 2008 hosted a 'forum' for first peoples' filmmakers.) What remained unclear in Stam's paper was how his approach, which he defined as a 'politicized aesthetics', could address the interconnection between these texts, which he submitted to a minute formal analysis, and extra-textual questions, such as the socioeconomic, which are vital for an understanding of national and transnational cinemas.

This socioeconomic sphere was precisely the focus of another distinguished speaker, Néstor García Canclini of Mexico City's UNAM, who spoke on 'Mexican Cinema as Industry and Culture: Its Transnational Relocation'. García Canclini (who had previously predicted the disappearance of cinema in Latin America: García Canclini 1997) preferred in Puebla to diagnose the medium's current condition in the continent (García Canclini 2008). He began by redefining the notion of 'culture', following in the steps of Appadurai, not as the possession of individuals but as 'a form of articulating the frontiers of difference', as in the case of the intercultural process in which current cinema is now formed. Secondly, García Canclini recognized that traditional values of the autonomy of the aesthetic (to which Stam had implicitly bowed), and the individuality of artistic creation, are no longer necessarily appropriate for the new circumstances in which film and cultural television have drawn closer to commercial cultural industries. (Discreetly, he chose not to cite in this context the three transnational giants of current Mexican cinema, González Iñárritu, Cuarón and del Toro, directors who are clearly exemplary of this trend.)

Thirdly, if even art or auteurist cinema has been contaminated to some extent by design, urban planning, tourism and fashion (fields mentioned by García Canclini), the internationalization of cultural industries (including film) has coincided with the decline of cinemas as the main form of exhibition, reduced as they are to just another element in a multimedia distribution system with many 'windows'. One example, which García Canclini had cited on another occasion (1994: 334), was the classificatory system employed by video stores in Latin America, according to which local features (unlike North American) are defined not by genre (horror, drama), but as 'foreign films' in their country of origin.

For García Canclini, then, globalization still means Americanization. Accordingly, in his rather desolate survey, García Canclini stressed US domination of distribution and the role of NAFTA, which had contributed, in his view, to the collapse in Mexican feature production in the decade that followed its ratification. The existence of Hispanic accords on economic and cultural exchange, such as Ibermedia, apparently positive, was also diminished by an asymmetry, in this case the dominance of Spain, which provides two-thirds of the budget for this organization. On the other hand, said García Canclini, it is only in Madrid (and not in Buenos Aires or Mexico City) that it is possible at any given time to see as many as ten films from different Spanish-speaking countries screened in theatres.

To remedy this panorama, which is so relentlessly bleak for Mexico, García Canclini proposes only a certain distancing from the United States, together with the increased cultivation of still weak cultural exchanges between Mexico and the rest of Latin America. What is more, García Canclini takes for granted that state aid to culture (in its restricted sense) is indispensable for that sector of the audiovisual industries that has not yet completely abandoned aesthetic autonomy and creative individuality.

If Robert Stam does not succeed in contextualizing his 'politicized aesthetics' within the new transnational socioeconomic order, García Canclini, while attempting to address this order, still relies on concepts that have already been called into question by his own analysis. For example, although García Canclini suggests we should expand the frontiers of the category of 'culture' to embrace new media and forms of production, he does not question the primacy of the fiction feature film. Hence when he laments that 'we [Latin Americans] do not see ourselves represented' on screen, he seems not to take seriously the contribution of shorts or documentaries to that national project or, indeed, the role of the ubiquitous and powerful Mexican television sector that holds up a media mirror to local audiences.

In a rather similar way, although García Canclini recognizes in theory that current production of feature films cannot fail to be globalizing, crossing national frontiers as it does artistic borders, in practice he focuses on the number of 'domestic' features produced each year, defining them according to the classical criteria of finance or geography. He seems willing neither to value nor to theorize the unprecedented ascent of Mexican globalizing directors (González Iñárritu, Cuarón and del Toro, once more), who are rivalled only by their Brazilian equivalents (Fernando Meirelles and perhaps Walter Salles). It thus follows that the films by del Toro shot in Spain – *The Devil's Backbone* (*El espinazo del diablo*, 2001) and *Pan's Labyrinth* (*El laberinto del fauno*, 2006) – count for nothing in his analysis. The Mexican cultural contribution these films have made to Spanish cinema does nothing to help make up for the socioeconomic deficit caused by the decline of fiction features shot within Mexican borders; the only ones, it would appear, to qualify as 'national'.

Finally, García Canclini does not call into question the problematic role of the Mexican state, which he believes to be still the only salvation for an audiovisual industry threatened by US cultural imperialism. Although current first-time directors have indeed been helped by article number 226, a recent reform to promote investment in so-called 'national films' (Senado de la República 2008), it scarcely needs mentioning that the three established filmmakers mentioned above, who are globally celebrated, have offered harsh criticisms of the cultural policy and artistic control wielded by government organizations such as CONACULTA and IMCINE in Mexico. González Iñárritu and his then producer Martha Sosa were proud to claim that they made the privately-funded *Amores perros* in 2000, a film that staked a claim to embody a 'change' that was both political and artistic, without accepting any state funding (Smith 2005: 15).

I would like to conclude this theoretical survey with the paper from the Puebla conference, which seemed to me to be the most convincing and fruitful for the analysis of Latin American film – ironically, perhaps, the one by Chris Berry, a Professor of Film and Television Studies with a specialism in Chinese cinema, at Goldsmiths College, University of London. As we shall see, there are certain parallels between the case of film in Chinese (i.e. shared by the People's Republic, Taiwan and Hong Kong) and that of the Spanish-speaking countries.

Berry's title (2008) was 'Transnational Chinese Cinema as a Transborder Cinema'. Coinciding with the earlier speakers, Berry noted that it was clearly no longer possible to take for granted the existence of any national cinema. (In parentheses here, it is telling that two recent British books on national cinema in Spain and Mexico, by Nuria Triana-Toribio (2003) and Andrea Noble (2005), respectively, were dedicated to questioning the concept stated in their own titles.) Berry cited some figures showing the apparent collapse of film production in Taiwan, figures which looked very similar to those mentioned by García Canclini in the case of Mexico. But for Berry, the focus on the brute numbers of features produced, based on financial and geographic criteria, is short-sighted, since it is founded on a 'national presumption' which has been overtaken by current circumstances. In fact, Taiwanese production has been 'dispersed', taking advantage of the perceived comparative advantages provided by each Chinese-speaking territory: the People's Republic's cheap labour, Taiwan's expertise in screenwriting, and Hong Kong's financial and legal sophistication. Given these circumstances, we need criteria that value more accurately the contributions and creative participation of each territory in specific projects: economic or geopolitical factors, although still necessary, are no longer sufficient.

This new model, then, takes for granted that the transnational has supplanted the national, a flexible post-Fordism the rigid Fordism of the past, and discrete production 'packages' the studio system previously dominant in China, as in Mexico and (in an earlier era) the United States. Nonetheless, this initial revision does not break with two traditional premises: it fails to question the ideology of globalization and the definition of 'cinema' as fiction feature films. Hence, following (he says) in the steps of Anna Tsing, Berry proposes a new paradigm for the transnational, differentiating it clearly from the globalizing (a term which remains nonetheless significant): if the latter relies on an ideology in which capitalism is a quasi-natural 'flow' impeded only by commercial barriers, the former is rather a social practice manifest in concrete projects which may or may not promote global capital, as the case may be. For example, it is noticeable that Chinese-speaking transnational directors rarely choose to work in Hollywood, but rather, taking advantage of cultural affinities and local creative nuclei, they rely on neighbouring territories with whom they share a language, if not a history or, much less, a political system.

Berry concluded, in rather more abstract terms, by suggesting that the terminology of Foucault or Deleuze and Guattari might be more appropriate than that of political economy for the investigation of a new cinematic topology that is so flexible and changing. Within such a Foucauldian context, power would not be seen as exclusive to the unitary state, but rather as circulating through multipolar relations; practices would be seen not as independent of power, but rather as constituted by it; and finally, the reduction of state power would result not in the unimpeded flow of globalization, but rather in the appearance of new forces that would seek to canalize that flow. Transborder cinema, the term which Berry finally prefers to 'transnational', is thus not so much a network or system, as a Deleuzian 'assemblage' of multiple plateaux that are interconnected and mutually affecting. This may well be a model that could be developed to analyse the current situation of transborder Hispanic and Lusan cinemas, as for the Chinese.

One specific observation by Berry is especially relevant for the case of Mexico and Spain. It is the following. Although there are so many rich examples of creative cooperation between Chinese-speaking territories, only one kind of film has been massively popular across all markets: the historical epic set in distant Imperial China and employing the skilled martial arts choreographers based in Hong Kong, as exemplified by Zhang Yimou's *Hero* (*Ying xiong*, 2002) and *The Curse of the Golden Flower* (*Man cheng jin dai huang jin jia*, 2006). In contrast, films set in the present are rarely exported with any success, as audiences in Taipei, Beijing and Hong Kong display a mutual lack of interest in the everyday contemporary reality of their neighbours. It might not be surprising, then, to find that Spanish-speaking countries might also reject contemporaneity and rely on historical references that are, if not shared, at least recognizable to the diverse and dispersed audiences of transnational feature films.

Three Genres of the Transnational: Genre Movies, 'Festival Films', 'Prestige Pictures'

In the second half of this chapter, I go on to examine the three films I mentioned at the start. Although they are of different nationalities, they occupy positions in their respective cultural fields that often (but not always) have parallels in each country: *KM 31* (2006) as commercial genre film; *The Headless Woman* as unrepentant art movie or 'festival film'; and *Blindness* as the middle-brow super-production or 'prestige picture' that seeks the box office of the former, even as it aspires to the auteurist status of the latter. What is striking about *KM 31*, however, is that although it is set quite precisely in the present, beginning with an apparent car accident at the point in a suburban highway to which the title refers, it relies on broad references to the colonial past shared between Mexico and Spain, in order to connect with popular audiences in both countries.

KM 31 was a resounding commercial success in Mexico, attracting an audience of over 3 million; moreover, boasting production values that were unusually accomplished by Latin American standards, it won Ariels (Mexican Oscars) in the technical categories of special effects, wardrobe and sound (see Smith 2007). Director Rigoberto Castañeda claimed himself in his press notes that he had wanted to make a horror movie as effective as a genre film in 'any continent' (Castañeda 2006); and the casting of the young Catalan actor Adrià Collado as the male lead, the habitual sign of a Mexican-Spanish co-production such as this one (made by Lemon Films and Filmax, respectively), ensured theatrical distribution would follow in Spain. Since Collado was then known above all in his home country for his role as a sympathetic gay man in the farcical flatshare sitcom *No-one Could Live Here* (*Aquí no hay quien viva*, Antena 3, 2003–06), *KM 31* took advantage of the intimate familiarity of the Spanish audience with his persona, even as it subverted it (as we shall see) by having him play finally against type.

KM 31 would thus seem at first sight to be a clear result of those twin colonialisms (the American and the Spanish) denounced by García Canclini; and perhaps a product of the globalizing triumph of commerce over film art. But the situation is more complex than that. Rejecting the local colour and national folklore that is so marketable abroad, *KM 31* was shot in the hardly exotic location of El Desierto de los Leones (which, disappointingly, is not a desert and harbours no lions). As a location, this gloomy pine forest (at least as it is depicted in the artfully faded blue and grey tones of the film) is more likely to recall Sweden or Switzerland rather than Mexico to a foreign audience. Indeed, the film did not do great business in the only non-Hispanic market where it received theatrical distribution, namely the UK.

Moreover, although *KM 31* is a horror movie that employs with some skill the filmic techniques typical of the genre, all too accessible to international viewers (such as the use of obscurely threatening off-screen space and sound), its plot relies on a key historical element directed exclusively to transborder Hispanic spectators. Collado's initially sympathetic character, known as Nuño, apparently the devoted boyfriend of a Mexican girl hospitalized in a coma, is in fact (or is he?) the reincarnation of a brutal colonial conquistador who seduced and abandoned the maiden who would be la Llorona (the native woman who weeps for her drowned children and is here identified with the twin sister of the modern girlfriend, Catalina).

It thus follows that some very specific historical traumas and debts are super-imposed on a generic transnational base, forming an 'assemblage' of multiple plateaux that affect each other mutually and are difficult to interpret, at once geographically and historically. Exemplary here is the climactic scene where, within a single shot boasting expertly realized digital effects, Castañeda moves from the foul underground sewer in which the modern lovers kiss to the sylvan stream where their colonial counterparts (played by the same actors in period dress) also embrace. The transnational casting, with its duelling Peninsular and Mexican accents, is thus essential to the film's backstory. As in the case of Chinese-language cinema, then, it may be that generalized versions of historical narratives function better than the concrete circumstances of everyday life as the foundation of an audiovisual culture potentially shared by all.

My second example is the third feature by Lucrecia Martel, *The Headless Woman*. Even though this last film received a hostile reception in Cannes (where Martel had in a previous year served on the jury), it seems fair to say that Martel is prized by critics and art audiences as one of the most promising of world auteurs (Bradshaw). Indeed, a poll of international film critics for *Sight & Sound* magazine rated *The Headless Woman* the best film of the year in 2008, in spite of the fact that it had not received even a festival screening in the UK, and had yet to gain theatrical distribution in any territory other than Argentina and Spain (James 2009: 17). One critic called it 'refined, mysterious, and troubling', while another praised its 'terrain of oblique unease' (2009: 23, 25).

Seeking to engage an autonomous aesthetic and a creative originality that many consider to be lost in contemporary film, Martel's features are often described as 'enigmatic'. Certainly their narratives wholly reject the transpar-ent motivation and causality of genre films. Thus *The Swamp* (*La ciénaga*, 2001), studied in detail by Falicov (2007: 122–6), opens with an accident, when drink-sodden Mecha stumbles into broken glass by the filthy pool at her decadent country estate; and it closes with another when the young son of Tali (the excellent Mercedes Morán) falls from a ladder and perhaps dies (we never find out). The audience, plunged into a tangled web of family relationships, remains as disorientated as the characters. In *The Holy Girl* (*La niña santa*, 2004), the 16-year-old daughter of a frustrated hotel-owner (Morán, once more) suffers a kind of mixed spiritual and erotic obsession with a middle-aged doctor, which remains largely unexplained, if clearly tragic in its effects.

The central premise of *The Headless Woman* is equally open-ended: a middle-aged woman in a provincial town once more, believing she has run over an animal or person in her car, experiences a kind of rupture with reality that takes the audience with her into a new and uncertain realm of existence. But if space is uncertain in Martel, then time is equally problematic. Opting for a daring anachronism, The Headless Woman makes repeated reference to the music and costumes of the 1970s, even as it clearly takes place in the present.

Martel's extraordinary cinematic vision, heightened by her eccentric off-centre framing, would appear to be as local as it is personal. In a dimension unlikely to be appreciated by her transnational admirers, her films, whose location remains stubbornly ambiguous, are shot in Salta, some 1600 km from Buenos Aires, which remains the unchallenged film capital of Argentina. While viewers from Salta may recognize some locations, Argentine audiences will also catch the tension between those settings and the actors or characters, such as Morán's, who originate in the distant capital. When Martel presented her film's UK premiere on 4 December 2008 at the Discovering Latin America festival at London's Tate Modern, she called attention precisely to this clashing of regional accents, inaudible to English speakers.

In spite of her tendency towards surrealism, then, Martel would seem to be firmly rooted in a specific place and time. Martel herself, often enigmatic in her commentaries on her own films, has claimed in an interview with Andrew O'Hehir (2008) that The Headless Woman has a precise political meaning, pointing obliquely as it does to class division in contemporary Argentina (the existence of two 'castes' who barely coincide) and to historical trauma (the linking of an obsession with the horrors of the past to a 'blindness' to the problems of the present). Martel's practice could thus perhaps be read as a subtle updating of that 'politicized aesthetic' promoted by Stam.

Two industrial factors militate against this localist reading of The Headless Woman's form, however. The first is that Argentine 'festival films' such as Martel's are not just regularly screened on the foreign circuit well before they make an often fleeting appearance in their so-called home market; they also receive significant foreign input into their development and production process. The screenplay for The Swamp won a Sundance award that enabled it to go forward; The Holy Girl was co-produced by the Spanish firm El Deseo, and its executives Pedro and Agustín Almodóvar were given a prominent name check on the film's US trailer. While such collaborations could be read as positive examples of the cultural affinities or creative clusters which Berry prizes in Chinese-language cinema, El Deseo is itself aware that sponsorship of young auteurs such as Martel, whose films may well lose money for them, remains a way of adding to the prestige or symbolic capital of Almodóvar himself (Pajuelo Almodóvar 2005). Where horror films like KM 31 rely on Hollywood genre templates, art movies like The Headless Woman thus depend on contacts with US indies and European art film, which actively determine to a large extent the kind of films made in Latin America.

Beyond these industrial questions of production and distribution (but inextricable from them) is the artistic question of the family resemblance between many such 'festival films', which (less distinctive than Martel's) can become as formulaic and anonymous as the genre movies from which they work so hard to differentiate themselves. It is easy to define such features in cinematic, narrative and performative terms. They employ little camera movement and extended takes without edits; they tell casual or oblique stories, often elliptical and inconclusive; and they often cast non-professionals whose limited range restricts their performance to a consistently blank or affectless acting style. 'Festival films' may well be shot in black and white, and will certainly lack a conventional musical score. As Tamara L. Falicov has noted (2007: 155), domestic critics have attacked a surfeit of 'silent, dark and indecipherable debut films' that failed to connect with local audiences.

One recent and significant transnational trend, going back at least to Carlos Reygadas' *Japón* (2002), is the use of a random toponym as a title. The Argentine Lisandro Alonso and the Mexican Fernando Eimbcke both employed this technique in films shown at the London Film Festival in October 2008: *Liverpool* (2008) and *Lake Tahoe* (2008), respectively. The place names, justified only in the final shots of each feature, remain conspicuously inappropriate for films shot and set in Ushuaia and Yucatán. For Bourdieu (1996: 137), the 'obscure and disconcerting title' serves in such cases to engage the attention and collaboration of the critic whose professional help, or perhaps collusion, is required to ensure that the full social meaning of the film is achieved.

I have argued, then, that genre movies (apparently international) may exploit transnational subtexts that remain more or less hidden to foreign audiences; 'festival films' on the other hand (normally known as art, auteur or specialist features), which are held to be personal and local, may well be yet more transnational than genre movies in both production and aesthetics. Certainly, popular comedies in Latin America could hardly be more specific in their reference, and are rarely seen abroad. One unremarkable Mexican example, contemporary with the films I treat here, is *Divine Confusion* (*Divina confusión*, Salvador Garcini, 2008), in which the ancient Greek gods descend on modern Mexico City, with predictably humorous results. Clearly such comedy of incongruity will remain inaccessible to foreign audiences and even critics, who are likely to be as unfamiliar with the Distrito Federal as they are with Mount Olympus.

One new genre, which mediates between the two extremes of genre movies and 'festival films', is the overtly transnational blockbuster, often spoken in English, which I have dubbed here the 'prestige picture'. Most clearly exemplified by González Iñárritu's *21 Grams* (2003) and *Babel*, this newly prominent genre illustrates at least two features of Berry's 'transborder cinema'. It signals a dispersion of production outside Spanish- and Portuguese-speaking home territories that calls into question the 'national presumption', based on financial or geographical criteria. And it employs a flexible post-Fordist mode of production, contracting contributors from around the globe for unique event movies.

One question to be explored, however, is whether such discrete projects, for all their good intentions (*Babel* laments the lack of communication between the peoples of the world), question the ideology of globalization in which culture (like capitalism) is seen as a quasi-natural 'flow' impeded only by commercial (or political) barriers. Beyond the Spanish-speaking countries, the question is also posed by Brazil. And as nomadic as his Mexican opposite numbers, Fernando Meirelles is, with Walter Salles, Brazil's most frequent traveller.

If *City of God* (*Cidade de Deus*, 2002) was the Brazilian *Amores perros* (a hugely stylish and inventive action drama) and *The Constant Gardner* (2005) was *21 Grams* (an English-language psychological piece), then *Blindness* is like *Babel*: a polyglot parable (in variously accented English and Japanese) on the human condition. Adapted from Saramago's well-known novel, this is the dystopian tale of an epidemic of 'white sickness' which, beginning as the first victim is struck down while driving his car in heavy traffic, leaves only Julianne Moore as 'the doctor's wife' sighted. Plucked from the chaos of an unnamed metropolis, an international cast (from the USA, Brazil, Mexico and Japan) is soon corralled into a hospital-cum-prison, where social order breaks down irrevocably. Although the premise evokes some specific political contexts (such as governmental responses to HIV), the anonymity of the characters (identified only by their professions) and the refusal to establish a precise location suggest much broader ethical ambitions: of community, conflict and cooperation *in extremis*.

The premise of *Blindness* is thus highly visual, based as it is on vision and perspective. Yet, as I wrote in my *Sight & Sound* review (Smith 2008), in spite of some effective action sequences, the film falls flat. The allegorical setting that seems acceptable on the page feels fake on screen, when well-known actors (who, like Moore and Gael García Bernal, are highly familiar from elsewhere) spout clichéd dialogue in a Babel of accents.

Yet even here, in a film identified as a co-production between Canada, Brazil, Japan, the UK and Italy, there is an argument for a localist reading. Although Saramago may be cited in the film's press-kit as a Nobel prizewinner, he clearly shares a key cultural referent with director Meirelles in their common Portuguese language. Moreover, although the hospital scenes were shot in an abandoned institution in Canada, the city sequences were filmed in Montevideo and São Paulo. The latter city marks something of a homecoming for the *paulistano* Meirelles, whose earlier *City of God* was so rooted in the rival metropolis of Rio, with which he was less familiar. It seems likely that closer analysis of other transnational prestige pictures would reveal a similar persistence of localism: certainly González Iñárritu took with him to distant Memphis, Tennessee, the creative crew that had served him so well on the chilango *Amores perros*.

More overtly than a genre film like *KM 31*, then, these more ambitious projects risk losing their cultural specificity as they aim for universal relevance; but they also serve, if we look more closely, as perilous plateaux whose diverse levels mutually affect and even undercut one another. And it is striking also that national territories still retain particularities that are due perhaps to comparative advantages which are at once artistic and financial. Thus, at least in terms of international distribution, Brazil has not produced the large corpus of low-budget 'festival films' of which Martel is only the best-known Argentine director; while Argentina has, in turn, not evolved a celebrated transnational auteur like González Iñárritu or Meirelles. Only Mexico, the disappearance of whose cinema García Canclini once predicted, has significant examples in all three categories: genre movies, 'festival films' and 'prestige pictures'. The practice of transborder filmmaking that I have identified here has thus by no means erased differences between cultural fields in the varied Latin American nations.

To conclude, I would like to return to the three models of the transnational that I sketched in the first half of my article, suggesting some new priorities for research. First of all, if it is indeed the case, as Stam suggests, that resistance, broadly defined, has taken the place of revolution (in film as in life), then we need new forms of theorizing this resistance and recognizing it in cinema, based perhaps on forms of agency that are not simply oppositional. In the second place, we need, as scholars, to expand the object of study (and the object of cultural value) beyond the fiction feature film championed by García Canclini to include (as in festivals such as Morelia, Mexico) shorts and documentaries, not to mention TV drama, which through its popularity and ubiquity stakes a claim to be the true mirror of the Latin American public.

Finally, we should with Berry go beyond economic and geographic criteria when we define transnational cinema, in order to construct a transborder model which values cultural affinities and creative nuclei, and properly accounts for all kinds of creative participation, a model which can do justice to the fragile but flexible productions of today's nomadic cinema. If many Latin American directors (both consecrated and new) seem no longer to believe that political commitment or aesthetic autonomy inevitably win out over entertainment and commerce, this need not mean that new forms of power do not exist and cannot be examined in their works – new forms which are called into being by the very transborder flow that has globalized creativity as much as it has finance.

References

Berry, Chris (2008) 'Transnational Chinese Cinema as Transborder Cinema'. Plenary paper read at 'Transnational Cinema in Globalizing Societies – Asia and Latin America' (University of Nottingham Ningbo, China, and Universidad Iberoamericana, Puebla), 31 August 2008.

Bourdieu, Pierre (1996) *The Rules of Art* (Cambridge, Polity).

Bradshaw, Peter (2008) 'How I Lost My Head for *The Headless Woman*', *The Guardian*, 24 November. Online at: http://www.guardian.co.uk/film/filmblog/2008/nov/24/latin-america-festival. Accessed 7 December 2008.

Castañeda, Rigoberto (2006) '*KM 31*: Notas del director'. Online at: http://www.lahiguera.net/cinemania/pelicula/3179/comentario.php. Accessed 6 December 2008.

Falicov, Tamara L. (2007) *The Cinematic Tango: Contemporary Argentine Film* (London, Wallflower).

García Canclini, Néstor (1994) *Los nuevos espectadores: cine, televisión, y vídeo en México* (Ciudad de México, IMCINE/CONACULTA).

García Canclini, Néstor (1997) 'Will There be a Latin American Cinema in the Year 2000? Visual Culture in a Postnational Era', in Ann Marie Stock (ed.) *Framing Latin American Cinema: Contemporary Critical Perspectives* (Minneapolis, University of Minneapolis), pp.246–58.

García Canclini, Néstor (2008) 'Latin American Cinema as Industry and Culture: Its Transnational Relocation'. Plenary paper read at 'Transnational Cinema in Globalizing Societies – Asia and Latin America' (University of Nottingham, Ningbo, China, and Universidad Iberoamericana, Puebla), 30 August 2008.

James, Nick (2009) 'Films of 2008', *Sight & Sound*, January, pp.16–28.

Noble, Andrea (2005) *Mexican National Cinema* (London/New York, Routledge).

O'Hehir, Andrew (2008) 'Why the Cannes Boo-Birds are Wrong', in *Salon.com: Beyond the Multiplex*, 25 May. Online at: http://208.17.81.143/ent/movies/btm/feature/2008/05/25/martel/index.html. Accessed 8 December 2008.

Pajuelo Almodóvar, Diego (2005) Presentation on El Deseo's financial strategy given at Universidad Complutense, Madrid, 1 December 2005.

Senado de la República (2008) 'Senadores buscan apoyar al cine mexicano', 18 September. Online at: http://comunicacion.senado.gob.mx/index2.php?option=com_content&do_pdf=1&id=4823. Accessed 8 December 2008.

Smith, Paul Julian. (2005) *Amores perros* (Barcelona, Gedisa).

Smith, Paul Julian (2007) '*KM 31*' (review), *Sight & Sound*, December, p.69.

Smith, Paul Julian (2008) '*Blindness*' (review), *Sight & Sound*, December, p.53.

Stam, Robert (2008) 'From Revolution to Resistance: Alternative Aesthetics in Transnational Media – The Cases of Brazil, Chile, and Mexico'. Plenary paper read at 'Transnational Cinema in Globalizing Societies – Asia and Latin America' (University of Nottingham, Ningbo, China, and Universidad Iberoamericana, Puebla), 29 August 2008.

Triana-Toribio, Nuria (2003) *Spanish National Cinema* (London and New York, Routledge).

Note

1 A Spanish version of some of the material in this article was read at 'Nación, imagen, lectura: coloquio internacional sobre cine en México' (coinciding with the Festival Internacional de Cine de Morelia), on 5 October 2008; and, in its current English form, as an inaugural lecture at the British Academy, on 18 November 2008. My thanks to the organizers of both events.

Chapter Five

Eduardo Noriega's Transnational Projections

Chris Perriam

This chapter addresses aspects of two of the questions posited in our Introduction: it examines some routes and patterns in the distribution of the cinematic image in the world, as mediated by the niche DVD market and the internet; and it explores a small but representative range of polycentric constructs of feeling and identity in relation to the work of, and responses to, a single actor caught up in a multilocational network of representations. It is an exploratory case study of the Spanish actor Eduardo Noriega, now in his late 30s and at the start of an international career, as an actor in transit between languages and audiences. By looking at his first bilingual and modestly transnational role, and by tracing some of the history of his internet presence through his official website, it will bring together two established conceptualizations of the idea of motion: movement away as a paradoxical consolidator of cultural expression (in an anthropological sense of deterritorialization); and the 'transport' of desire. The movement away is looked at in simple terms of location – where Noriega goes to make his images, and how his career is travelling. Desire is considered from the point of view of audiences, lone viewers, and web-connected fans and enthusiasts following not only 'the logic of all new media – selection from a menu of choices' (Manovich 2001: 126), but also on a more or less libidinized quest for virtual contact with this attractive actor. So the chapter is concerned with the ways in which actors' performances move their audiences, the links they activate between motion and emotion, and the identities which are lost and formed in the transit of their image. It will alight on some key moments in what is a typical modern screen actor's trajectory – from a career based in domestic television and film productions on to a move into European and American films, from the representation of more or less local issues on to wider ones such as terrorism, labour under global capitalism, revolution and regime change. Secondly, it will be discussing the ways in which images of Noriega are mobilized on the web, transnationalizing themselves and his professional personality, but also creating virtual and haptic intimacies on the mobile or domestic screen.

A constant in what is certainly a serious enough career as an actor has been the way that both domestic and transnational productions want to emphasize Noriega's sexual charisma, packaging his body in alluring ways while also exploring the fascination of the perverse: either in the punishments meted out to the characters he plays – as, notably, in *Open Your Eyes* (*Abre los ojos*, Alejandro Amenabar, 1997) and *Wolf* (*El lobo*, Miguel Courtois, 2004); or in the misogynistic or pseudo-psychotic behaviour of his characters – as in *The Devil's Backbone* (*El espinazo del Diablo*, Guillermo del Toro, 2001) or *Love Songs in Lolita's Club* (*Canciones de amor en Lolita's Club*, Vicente Aranda, 2007). On the web, that embodiment and charm is set at a considerable remove, of course, despite the saturating presence of images of the star's body, eyes and smile; however, arguably it is here that we see most clearly how motion and emotion come to structure response and performance in relation to the actor on a world stage, as will be seen in the third part of the chapter.

Central to theorizations of the screen in the proto- and post-cinematic senses is this issue of motion – or, rather, the lack of it for the viewer in front of the framing space of the peephole, picture border, large and smaller screen. The body is famously trapped in perspectival systems of representation (Manovich 2001: 103–6). Walter Benjamin, in 1936, might have been able to speak in relation to cinema, despite is shock tactics, of the viewer 'calmly and adventurously ... travelling' (Benjamin 1992: 229) because of the way film fakes entry into new spaces, and Anne Friedburg (1993: 2) could later still talk of 'a mobilized virtual gaze'. However, as Manovich points out (developing an image from Baudry), post-primitive cinema always represented 'a new, institutionalized immobility of the spectator [in which] the prisoners could neither talk to one another nor move from seat to seat' (2001: 107). So, while just over 212,000 original cinema-goers[1] saw one of the films to be discussed here, *Novo* (Jean-Pierre Limosin, 2002), in just such confined and focused circumstances, those subsequently seeing it on DVD (distributed for the English-language market, for example, by MGM/United Artists) could and can swap remarks on the action and the actors, change locations for viewing, and mix and match, speed through or freeze scenes as desired (indeed, some of the film's sex scenes are already self-referentially marked up for such a treatment by being filmed on security camera by a voyeuristic guard).

In both situations – in one through plot and career choice, in the other through mediatic and technological framing – the actor-image Noriega can be seen to be placed to one degree or other in positions where his image may be manipulated and articulated through its projection into other geographical, fictional and coded spaces, in a context of a more or less strong emotional pull being exerted on the user-viewer. He is therefore placed in a long history of professional journeys by actors crossing over, or back and forth, between countries and industries, stages and different screens (Phillips and Vincendeau, 2006). He also becomes aligned, despite his more consistent attachment (so far, at least), to the domestic markets in which he first trained and thrived, with the Spanish-born Antonio Banderas, Penélope Cruz and Javier Bardem, who more recently have invented for themselves something akin to 'hyphenated cultural lives' (Phillips and Vincendeau 2006: 4) through their work with North American directors, and their comings and goings, to different degrees, across the Atlantic (Perriam 2005, 2010). Above all, such actors in this transnational frame are of interest for the ways in which they carry in the image of their bodies – voice, gesture, allure, look, craft, kinesis – a volatile conflation of culturally distinctive desires and affective responses of a far less localized (because pre-personal) kind. This intensifying conflation, as actors' images travel or get under the skin of the viewer, leads to new formations of fantasy; new because of their doubly deterritorialized and deterritorializing effect on the economies of desire into which the travelling actor is inserted when performing abroad and on the foreign screen.

One of the purposes of this chapter, then, is to re-attach to the idea of the actor in motion on screen and across borders – Banderas in Argentina, California and Mexico; Cruz in California, Bahia and New York; Bardem in Cuba, in an ersatz Peru and in Texas[2] – to their role as provocateurs of emotion, emotion underpinned by affective response to the embodiment of pseudo-primal experiences (the flush of attraction, the sense of others out there, the sense of movement, the rush of fear or exhilaration), but also freighted with the territorial meanings the actors carry across from their socialized personal and professional experiences at home. The actor's transnational projections will not only be moving, touching, exciting or emotionally educational in effect, but will also bring resonances of the territory they have just worked in, trained in or gained fame in. A frisson of otherness, an accented-ness, and a stimulus to the recalibration of social and cultural assumptions, as well as of feelings, is part of the pattern in this polycentric dynamic of transmission. Deterritorialized in a straightforward way when they depart from their cultural and professional ground (drama school, local contacts, domestic networks), they become agents of deterritorialization in a more widely signifying and abstract sense, adapted in part from Deleuze and Guatarri by Néstor García Canclini to refer to 'territorial relocalizations of old and new symbolic productions' (1995: 229). García Canclini's suggestion is that the hybridizations involved in such symbolic and social delocations, and relocations across and between cultures, mean that:

all cultures are border cultures ... movies, videos, songs that recount events of one people are interchanged with others. Thus cultures lose the exclusive relation with their territory, but they gain in [communicative power] and knowledge. (1995: 261)

The specific movements of actors across industries and between audiences are part of this interchanging. Their work is situated in the always already decentred, disseminated, densely intercultural practice (these are García Canclini's terms: 1995: 258–9) of filmmaking in and for different global locations. They detach from but bear, at times, the traces of an original cultural space, which is, on occasion, relocalized or even restored. Pulling against this, of course, is the reterritorializing and homogenizing double effect of the marketing machine and the audiences it creates, which exoticize actors (especially in the cases of Banderas and Cruz), reduce them to generic or ethnic types, departicularize, and lessen the range and intensity of the effect of the performance and the image of the actor's body.

How Filmic Emotions 'Take Hold'

At this stage it will be useful to return to the concept of the 'transport' of desire, introduced earlier. Giulana Bruno's *Atlas of Emotion* (2002) is designed as a series of 'Journeys through art, architecture and film' (the book's sub-title), and sets out to 'relocate the moving image within a cultural history that engages with intimate geographies' (2002: 3). The emphasis here is on spatiality, and Bruno is exploring the implications of 'the haptic affect of "transport" that underwrites the formation of cultural travel' (2002: 6–7) – how we feel when we are given the illusion of moving through a culturally and emotionally charged space. However, as well as the images and the travelling viewer-subject, actors are key agents in bringing about transportedness and in conveying effect. This is especially true of the actors' images in progress through websites – which at times look like the galleries of framed pictures, or the 'haptic routes' of laid out panoramas and viewing devices which are part of Bruno's interest (2002: 171–203) – which, as much as the standard, seductive scenes of film fiction, make the viewer-user wish to reach out and touch, dance, or become one with the actor's body. For the picture-goer's and web-user's passion truly to be passion, she needs to identify not just with her own motion and with her temporarily expanded subjectivity at the place arrived at, but also to identify with – to meet in some sense or other – some actors there. If as part of her haptic and fantasy journeying she recognizes that these heavenly bodies are also new to the place and sometimes to the language (as is the case with Noriega and French in *Novo*), then one of the things that might move her is the sudden adjustment of the cultural meanings of where the actors have come from and where they have arrived at. Encountering the free-travelling actor on webpages focused on their person, deeds, views and looks is especially entrancing. Although, as Bruno argues, 'experiencing film involves being passionately transported through a geography', and proto-filmic exhibits of the early nineteenth century already had broken the 'equation of body with home and home with body' (Bruno 2002: 186), the actor's translated presence in the semi- or pseudo-interactive performance space which is the web on screen paradoxically repairs that somatic-domestic rift.

At one stage Bruno draws out early film theorist Hugo Münsterberg's understanding of cinema as, in her words, 'a vehicle of physiological activity', and she emphasizes how 'The realm of filmic emotion is mobilized as the very transformation of sensations'; thus she sees this as a 'partial view [of cinema]' which 'nonetheless enables us to grasp how filmic emotions "take hold" of our bodies in the space of the movie house' (2002: 261). Those identifications which I have been hypothesizing for the traveller-viewer and the travelling actor surely add to this effect.

Novo

Noriega's early career, and especially his embodiment of certain key representations of masculinity in, and conformed by, an era of specifically Spanish postmodernity, rapidly made him nationally iconic (Perriam 2001: 173–200). Subsequently, both the Argentine-Spanish *Burnt Money* (*Plata quemada*, Marcelo Piñeyro, 2000) and Mexican-Spanish *The Devil's Backbone* marked the beginnings of an intense involvement with international co-stars, and of a development of screen identities based on materials which are more or less Spanish in a new context of professional deterritorialization. That material is made up of the associations of earlier roles, the product of working with other young Spanish actors, the emergence of a specific, problematic new Spanish masculinity, a look. The new space of professional deterritorialization is one where there is necessarily an exploration of new modes of provoking the desire, admiration and interest of audiences, and the elaboration of new languages.

Let us focus for a while on the most obvious sense in which a new language needs elaboration in such a context. The sporadically nomadic or serial returnee actors mentioned above, when working in a language other than Spanish, are culturally repositioned in a sudden and discontinuous manner, as with Jean Gabin and others of the more decidedly émigré actors discussed by Vincendeau (2006). The translation of their accumulated screen persona into new linguistic contexts provokes a tacit intercultural dialogue, as well as culture shock in their old fans and new audiences.

With *Novo*, and a role mixing French with Spanish, Noriega properly began his career as a transnationally mobile actor, with English-language roles starting in Josh Evans' *Che Guevara*, shot in 2005 and out in 2008, the same year as *Transsiberian* (Brad Anderson) and *Vantage Point* (Pete Travis). In a low-key way, the film helps us to think about the connectedness of motion and emotion, about transfer into new territories and about the production of new formations of desire in relation to the mobile actor-image. Although Noriega is still Spanish-based, and in no sense émigré, it is useful to link him with those actors of other generations, for whom 'acting in a different language, their own relation to [national] identity changes' (Vincendeau 2006: 115). Similarly, 'the ways in which stereotypes work for and against the émigré actor', as discussed by Radnor (2006: 126), can readily be seen at work in Noriega's career.

The film is self-consciously about desirability, flux, origins and non-belonging. Its story is itself highly emotive in a well-tried way: an amnesiac Spaniard, Pablo, is living a life of attempted rehabilitation as 'Graham' in Paris, while his wife and son wait for him to recover. The eroticization and display of Noriega's body, and the enjoyment of Graham's body (by a girlfriend, Irène, whose name he has to inscribe on his chest to remember her, and by his female boss), is tightly related to the film's exploration of the habitual philosophical conundrums and the dilemmas associated with this type of plot (Figure 1).

However, it also brings across for French-language audiences what for young Spanish and Latin American audiences had already accrued to Noriega's image – a cool, intelligent, sexiness underscored with sad or sinister plot lines, disturbed masculinities, and a tangential relation to fragile national identities and

Figure 1   Noriega with Anna Mouglalis in Novo

histories. Added to this set of border and crossover effects is the film's post-modern dislocation of its Frenchness through transnationalizing reference sustained at a number of levels.

At the start of the film, after the display of its production credentials (Switzerland, France, Spain), attention is drawn in a woozy, Japanese comic strip manner to a non-specifically semi-tropical mountain scene on a lurid piece of graphic advertisement. The drinks vending machine, the facia of which we see, as the camera pulls back, itself has international aspirations or even prove-nance. It also serves as an establishing clue to the main plot line of *Novo*: acute short-term memory deficit. Graham cannot remember that you need to put a coin in the slot to get your drink; and he cannot remember it twice in the short five-part sequence we shall see here. His memory keeps crashing. He is watched from the point of view of a man who tails him across the urban landscape of Paris, and as the camera travels, a collage of multicultural and polycentric Paris is constructed. Skateboarding youths signify the diasporic presence of South East Asia and North Africa, their brilliant moves – as the camera moves through – a playful metaphor for the speed and difficult beauty of transcultural identity formation (in one briefly held medium close-up young, non-white and different France is represented in static portrait). The camera, Graham and the watcher move on through mean streets with visuals (cracked walls, a flurry of fly-posted text, bins, a skip) which deftly signal gritty French films of earlier decades, and then emerge into an even more unambiguously Parisian scene – the rue du Faubourg Saint Martin – dominated left uppe-centre screen by the red signage for a Franco-Lebanese restaurant. A pan upwards fixes upon the inscription-ded-ication of the building 'To the Working Classes', repositioning France as part of the constellation of the global socialism of yesteryear. The mobile visual context is clearly decentring in its overall effects.

Further to this – a constant in the rest of the film – language and code-switching are used as clear markers of otherness and deterritorialization. When Graham takes the new temp, Irène, on her induction tour of the building where he works, his recital of the distinguishing contents of the rooms is a mnemonic, out-loud labelling exercise which obliquely draws attention to Noriega's own heavily accented, mainly rote-learned French. It recalls the repetitions and for-gettings of the routines of early second-language learning. Later, in a key scene, the associations between failed recuperation of identity, a crisis of subjectivity and emotional dislocation are made linguistically by a fall back into Spanish. Graham's (once Pablo's) wife Isabelle (Paz Vega) is having an affair with the watcher in the sequence described above – Pablo's best friend in the past; Graham, in a moment of half-remission, both remembers her and senses her betrayal; exonerating her in Spanish, he explains that he cannot be betrayed because 'I am not here'. He slips out of the frame of stable identity, of ethical behaviour and of their construction through language.

What disintegrates Graham/Pablo in this way is his dependence on a code, but without a programme. Each move he makes in everyday life – with self-penned memos pinned around everywhere – is semi-random, a branching selection, as far as he is concerned, a kind of surfing. Acting in a French that he does not yet really know, Noriega himself is cast into a similar rootlessness, where he is charmingly but rashly dependent on just being there in the new, deterritorializing space of performance abroad. The once local Spanish star is set in contexts of transience and interchangeability. The diegetic focus on loss of subjective integrity spills over into the actor's career in a risk which, as it turned out, was worth taking.

The Noriega Website

One way in which Noriega has been cannily safeguarding, whilst also transforming, a sense of origin and identity ('Spanishness', that is) has been through the construction of a web presence, which makes the most of how websites may stabilize as well as disperse. They are as much archive as points of departure on branching adventures of selection or quests for the dispersal of identity and blocks of knowledge, for the abandonment of physical space, and for the destruction of the fixity of verbal language.

Like other Spanish actors with whom he has starred – Silvia Abascal, José Coronado, Carmelo Gómez and Najwa Nimri – Noriega has an official website, coordinated and structured in his case by Meltin SA.[3] Conventionally enough, it combines generalized publicity, an image gallery and biography-filmography which constructs a space for the actor as personality or star, telecommunication with a fan base and (better than some other sites) a source of documentation of scholarly and popular interest.

The site, then, offers useful documentation on the actor and his recent history, opening an easy route into international press and popular critical reception of him. The documentation is mainly traditional, old-media, static, textual information; but it points to several new trajectories and permits the generation of a rapidly branching set of performance-based meanings around Noriega. The 'Hemeroteca' (document archive) quickly reveals the recent transnational projection of Noriega's career in the form of increased (selected) coverage from beyond Spain: *Wolf* prompting articles in Argentina, Britain and France; *The Grönholm Method* (*El método*, Marcelo Piñeyro, 2006) prompting responses in Argentina (because of the link back to *Burnt Money* by the same director); his first North American venture in *Vantage Point* is shown to have been marked by the carefully archived, glamorous full feature 'Noriega da el gran salto' (Noriega makes the big leap) in the colour supplement of the prestigious daily *El País*.[4]

The site makes several significant connections, in a number of directions, between the development of acting skills and travel. For example, on his return from Buenos Aires and Montevideo at the end of 1999, Noriega attributed a growth in his maturity as an actor specifically to Piñeyro's skills as a director (implicitly, of actors), as well as to the fact that the actors had had the luxury of a full month of preparation and rehearsal.[5] In the 'Making Of' to The Grönholm Method, he (and the rest of the high-profile cast) also pays tribute to Piñeyro's skill as a director of actors. One of his web page's Hemeroteca items, from the Buenos Aires magazine Para ti, takes up the same theme, then leads into a passage showing Noriega's awareness of the Argentine cultural and professional diaspora in Spain, as well as of the new openness of audiences to the intermingling of Spanish and Latin American actors in films, and of the rise of market importance of co-productions (Salamanco, 2006). In what constitutes a telling response to the anxieties of dispersal and the challenges of making new screen identities, Noriega finds himself here making the somewhat sweeping claim that Spaniards and Latin Americans (his term: latinoamericanos) are conjoined by raíces, idioma and historia (roots, language and history).

Noriega's travels through this commercial and artistic space of the co-productions, and through his career, have indeed meant professional connections with actors from several cultures, his work with them allowing him to pull away from precarious dependency on that apparently lucky triad of rootedness, language and history, as well as on embodying Spanishness itself. Replying to Elisa (from Úbeda) in the website chat session in August 2006, Noriega refers to director Agustín Díaz Yanes' suggestion that he imitate Jeremy Irons' comportment in order to create a distinctive personality for the Conde de Guadalmediana in Alatriste (Agustín Díaz Yanes, 2006), then filming. Vigo Mortensen, in the eponymous fictional role, is acknowledged by Noriega in chat with 'Malagueña salerosa' ('Witty Chick from Malaga') as generous and attentive, suggesting another possible role model (Noriega does not exclude the grand heroic and the adventure movie role from his repertoire). On screen, Vantage Point sets Noriega's role as a policeman at the scene of the assassination of a high-ranking US delegate at a top-level security conference in Salamanca alongside Dennis Quaid, Matthew Fox, Saïd Taghmaoui, William Hurt, Forrest Whitaker, Ayelet Zurer and Sigourney Weaver, as well as on location in Mexico DF, Puebla and Cuernavaca. In Transsiberian he worked with Emily Mortimer, Woody Harrelson and Ben Kingsley in a film shot mainly in Vilnius, and on locations in Lithuania and China, whose setting is mainly – as the title suggests – one of the epitomes of transnational travel, and which is financed through a range of European sources.

With these fellow actors and multiple, shifting locations, then, comes a certain deterritorialization of the original Spanish Noriega. The website makes a point of the international cast into which Noriega is inserted; and in the

Hemeroteca we find a photo of him with Zurer, conventionally captioned with the phrase 'muy bien acompañadito' (in very good company) in the Mexican *Reforma* (*Gente*).[6] As *L'Officiel*'s guest of the month (June 2006), he is flagged as a name to watch, not as well known as Banderas, Bardem and Sergi López, but worth naming alongside them (Chéze 2006: 138). Festival and preview appearances align him with various names from other cultures and acting traditions – as well as positioning him internationally. In fairly straightforward ways, the site's tracking of such events makes Noriega an immediately present figure for the fan despite (and because of) his transit around the globe, and it connects the emotion of response to his look, style, performance and movement as a travelling player writ large.

Noriega's mediatic presence had already been transnationalized through the emphatically globalizing phenomenon of the videogame. On the website for *Open Your Eyes* (now no longer on open-server access), this took the form of a web-mediated quest game. In his discussion of the site, Jean-Paul Aubert (2002) draws attention to its unconventional structuring in relation to sites such as those hosted by Infocine or closely connected to the distribution companies. Instead of the usual tabs designed to lead the user at the computer into becoming the consumer in the box office and DVD store, the site in its day had no clear hierarchy of pathways, deployed multiple itineraries and circularities, and strove to create a cognate atmosphere to that of the film (2002: 133, 138). Modelled on videogame practices and gesturing towards the *film-concert* as theorized by Laurent Jullier (especially in that it combines specific technical requirements to see and hear it, combined with an emphasis on the presence of spectacle and dominance of sound [Jullier 1997: 140]), it emphasized the imaginative participation of the user (136). In such a structure, it might also be added, the actors, and notably Noriega, are encountered by the wandering web-user as visual clues in a mystery, or as sound-associations, as data almost; they are lifted out of the film world (despite the undeniable creation of a cognate atmosphere) into the mediascapes of the videogame and semi-interactive fan-site with the at once more cerebral and more spontaneous or affect-driven effects of reception and usage which these arenas promote. 'Flying through spatialized data', as Lev Manovich characterizes the classic videogame player and web flâneur/explorer (2001: 277), or, rather, stepping and selecting through it, the fan of the film and of Noriega finds him again in cyberspace.

Earlier in Noriega's career, *Nobody Knows Anybody* (*Nadie conoce a nadie*, Mateo Gil, 1999) aligned him at the level of plot with the videogame and technological/remote intervention in the events and experiences of the everyday world. There, Noriega's character, Simón, was denied the ability tactically to negotiate trajectories through the space of Seville and identity-based reality, and faces the disintegration of his subjectivity at the hands of technologically inspired and executed manipulations by Sapo (Jordi Mollà). In Paris, in *Novo*,

Noriega plays a man with no steer through time; in Seville, he had played a man with suddenly no direction through the cityscape of his life.

The publicity links of the website position the actor in a flexitime zone, which, depending on the physical location and cultural mobility of the user, mingles the already seen and the unseen; what is wrapped with what has not yet happened. So the 'Primeras imágenes' (Preview) section, when viewed towards the end of 2006, was of the much-delayed (and, in fact, never-to-be released) Madagascan-located version of *Othello*, *Souli* (Alexander Abela), *Che Guevara*, which went into commercial distribution two years later, and *Vantage Point*. In 2009 the French premier of *Little Indi* (*Petit Indi*, Marc Recha) as *C'Est içi que je vis* is announced, in advance of its October opening in Spain, drawing attention to a further linguistic twist to Noriega's career as he plays the character Sergi in Catalan.

The user can of course herself make interesting kinks in the timeline of selection when exploring the site by following an impulse to go off-screen, chase up pointers and invitations to reselect. The *Che Guevara* official site – now down – interspersed quotations from Che, with Noriega as Che in all of eight images, of which five are solo portraits (a tight-frame CU pensive/heroic shot from below; one from behind, Che looking out to sea; one in action; one of the executed hero; lastly, another close-up of him looking defiant but defeated). The arresting, if boldly standard, image of the hero gazing off to sea in epic absorption connects Noriega, for the length of time of sustaining of the cybernaut's minor thrill, with documentary history, with war – as also *Warriors* (*Guerreros*, Daniel Calparsoro, 2002), which translates Noriega to Kosovo – or, indeed, epic (as notoriously did *Alatriste*).

The site rapidly opens the way up to the revelation and seeking out of many distinct personas, many differently resonant cultural sites, juxtaposing, and overlaying genres, histories and associations centring on the actor. A slideshow of photo-portraits runs in the window top-left of this FlashPlayer site, mixing its biographical and iconographic impressions with the browsing of other areas. Not insignificantly, an expansive Tónica Schweppes advert (by Vinizius Young and Rubicam agency), filmed in March 2007, featured Noriega (and a stunt double) cliff-top and adventurous in Antofagasta, surveying the vast ocean, prior to a shirtless dive into its fizzing, risky and refreshing depths. It is this location (I suspect) that provides the portrait photo which is the right-hand block of the biography pages: of a dark-jerseyed, blue-jeaned Noriega perched bottom right on a high ledge, surveying a scene down left, and with most of the frame filled with geological splendour, as the screen grab shows (Figure 2).

Similarly, *Gente* (Buenos Aires), covering Noriega's visit to the Mar del Plata Festival in 2006, also has him posed close against a cliff-face. *Conde Nast Traveler* magazine's photo-shoot and coverage of Noriega in the Atlas Mountains, in 2009, also makes this geological gesture of inscription of the

Figure 2   Screen grab of Noriega's official website page, December 2006

nomadic acting subject (while also simply making Noriega glamorous in the world of leisure).[7]

But Noriega outdoors has more low-key and melancholy connotations, and the user-viewer might browse her shelves or download a clip or still in that direction too: in *My Angel* (*Mon Ange*, Serge Frydman, 2005), an inlet on the Belgian shores of the North Sea is the sparkling but bleak, bright backdrop to poignant performances of emotional and sexual commitment by Noriega and Vanessa Paradis, revealing as noted by *L'Officiel* his charismatic presence ('sa présence fascinante de charisme') (Chéze 2006: 139), also picked up on by Marc Recha in directing *Where Is Madame Catherine?* (*Les mains vides*, 2003, the same year as *Novo*) (Figure 3). Here a semi-bucolic outsiderdom, in a French-Spanish frontier setting, constructs strong emotional bonds between actor and viewer built around the ways that 'l'histoire... la lumière, le son et les paysages se placent sur le même plan' within a context of 'volonté de cinéma global' ('history ... light, sound and landscape occupy the same plane, within a context of aspiring to be world cinema', Breton 2004).

Moving to another part of the site, this charismatic presence is strenuously though beautifully built up by the gallery of photographers' images of him, which includes four by Bruce Weber, aligning him with a well-known iconography of highly posed, athletic-cum-languid male sexuality, and a set by Pedro Usabiaga, well-known in the Spanish-speaking and the gay world for his stylish male erotica. This, like the hyper-sexualization of his body in a number of the films, might risk turning the tables on the actor, who might be hoping to deploy the website to make his presence polysemic, protean even, as part of an

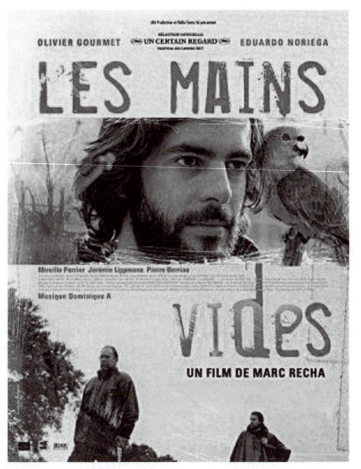

Figure 3   The DVD cover of Les mains vides *(dir. Marc Recha)*

aspiration (*volonté*) to a global identity, not a static and objectified *latino* beauty or bad guy. The multi-directionality of the site, though, counters this risk strongly.

In one direction it points the audience back to the star's necessary confected ordinariness and availability – or even the possibility of a genuine closeness to his public in Noriega's case – in a paradoxically delocalizing gesture. The Chat Room in a previous textual version took the web-traveller into the imaginations of interlocutors from Monterrey, Mexico DF, São Paulo, Montelimar, Charleroi, Lille, Lima, New York, Athens, Newcastle-upon-Tyne and Stara Zagora. Of the only four men (out of some 60 participants) who had participated at the time of my last log on to this version of the room (5 February 2007), two were clearly queer admirers: one, Miguel Ángel from Seville, was pretending to be interested in fencing techniques (on the back, no doubt, of the publicity for *Alatriste*), and Jose from Paterna, more directly, wanted to be in a photograph with Eduardo. Many of the heterosexual women taking part felt bonds of *simpatía*, approachability and warmth (sometimes, but not always, generated erotically). The Chat Room is now in video format.

The Visitors' Book, which continued the textual communication after 2007, draws the web traveller into small spaces of intimacy, as well as charting the many directions in which Noriega is being projected across the cinephile world. Ángela's message of 15 November 2006 announces its writer as 'la chica que te "abordo" dos veces en Vallecas y después que el hecho de verte ese día y que fueses tan amable conmigo me ayudó no sabes cuanto, pues estoy pasando un momento muy malo' ('the girl who "accosted" you twice in Vallecas and then the fact I'd seen you that day and that you were so nice to me you'll never know how much it's helped me because I'm going through a difficult patch'). To the heroics and high dilemmas of some of the actor's onscreen personas is added this highly localized and personalized dimension. For María, in Chile, the Schweppes tonic advert and Noriega's handsome presence at Antofagasta are, on 27 April 2010, 'una hermosa manera de ver mi País' ('a lovely way of seeing my country'); on the same day, Eleane writes informing him that 'tienes un grupo de fans en san luís potosí que te aman y te siguen desde que te descubrimos en tesis' ('you've got a group of fans here in san luís potosí who love you and have been following your career since *Thesis* [*Tesis*, Alejandro Amenábar, 1996). Sabahat writes, on 12 October 2009: 'This is Sabahat from Pakistan, dont worry I am not a TERRORIST, I am a simple woman. I am a fan of yours. You are really doing a great job regarding acting. You are superb. I like you most because of your role as CHE and I am a follower of CHE so this is why I like you most'. Everywhere on the site, motion and emotion, unique, punctual presence and flash-facilitated, protean unattainability come together as projections of Noriega's image, as it is transacted and reinscribed across various sites and boundaries. As one French magazine, again accessible via the page's Hemeroteca, puts it: '*Depuis* [having done the two French-language roles, and now *Wolf*], *il est reparti se métamorphoser aux quatre coins du globe*' ('he has gone off to the four corners of the globe to transform himself again').

The pleasure of surprise, the charms and mysteries involved in the routes, and combinations chosen when browsing the site, are several: that encounter in Vallecas, which briefly grounds and humanizes the star, returns him to Spain and its capital and its problems; the constant repositioning of the once Spanish actor at the 'four corners of the globe' – Antofagasta, San Luis Potosí, Tyne and Wear, and Pakistan; visual reminders of Graham/Pablo's daily astonishment in *Novo*, as he pieces together an identity, his dysfunction matching the cybernaut's own cultish bricolage using fragments of an actor's identity. All these signs and routes activate screen-projected, framed desires which are the product of motion and emotion contained, yet set loose. '[F]ilmic emotions "take hold" of our bodies in the space of the movie house', Bruno suggested (2002: 261), and Noriega in French, or Noriega pieced together and exhibited on the website, also mobilizes emotions that grip and transform, making new routes and patterns in the transit of images, and of those involved in making them on screen.

References

Aubert, Jean-Paul (2002) 'Quand le cinéma espagnol assure sa promotion. Étude de la web page d'*Abre los ojos*', in Groupe de Recherche sur l'Image dans le Monde Ibérique-américain/Groupe de Recherche sur l'Image dans le Monde Hispanique (eds) *Penser le cinéma espagnol 1975–2000* (Lyon, Université Lumière-Lyon 2), pp.131–41.

Benjamin, Walter (1992) 'The Work of Art in the Age of Mechanical Reproduction', in Hannah Arendt (ed.) *Illuminations*, trans. Harry Zorn (London, Fontana), pp.211–44.

Breton, Émile (2004) 'Entre Catalogne et Rousillon', *L'Humanité*, 11 February: no page reference. Bibliotèque du film, Paris, digital archive.

Bruno, Giulana (2002) *Atlas of Emotion: Journeys in Art, Architecture, and Film* (London and New York, Verso).

Chéze, Thierry (2006) 'Eduardo Noriega', *L'Officiel* (June), pp.138–9. Online at: http://www.eduardonoriega.com/hemeroteca/2006/officiel_06/officiel_06.pdf. Accessed 6 March 2010.

Friedburg, Anne (1993) *Window Shopping: Cinema and the Postmodern* (Berkeley, University of California Press).

García Canclini, Néstor (1995) *Hybrid Cultures: Strategies for Entering and Leaving Modernity*, trans. Christopher L. Chiappari and Silvia L. López (Minneapolis and London, University of Minnesota Press).

Jullier, Lauren (1997) *L'écran post-moderne: un cinéma de l'allusion et du feu d'artifice* (Paris, L'Harmatan).

Manovich, Lev (2001) *The Language of the New Media* (Boston, MIT Press).

Perriam, Chris (2001) *Stars and Masculinities: From Banderas to Bardem* (Oxford, Oxford University Press).

Perriam, Chris (2005) 'Two transnational Spanish stars: Antonio Banderas and Penélope Cruz', *Studies in Hispanic Cinemas* 2:1, pp.29–45.

Perriam, Chris (2010) 'Javier Bardem: Costume, Crime, and Commitment', in Ann Davies (ed.) *Spain on Screen* (London, Palgrave Macmillan), pp.114–28.

Phillips, Alastair and Ginette Vincendeau (eds) (2006) *Journeys of Desire: European Actors in Hollywood, A Critical Companion* (London, BFI).

Radnor, Hilary (2006) 'Louis Jourdan – the "hyper-sexual" Frenchman', in Phillips and Vincendeau (eds) (2006), pp.125–32.

S.B. (2006) 'Eduardo Noriega', *Studio* (May). Online at: http://www.eduardonoriega.com/hemeroteca/2006/studio_mayo_06/pdf/studio_mayo_06.pdf. Accessed 15 January 2010.

Salamanco, Veronica (2006) 'Eduardo Noriega', *Para ti* (Actualidad) (17 March), pp.414–18. Online at: http://www.eduardonoriega.com/ hemeroteca/2006/paraTi_arg_marzo/pdf/paraTi_arg_marzo.pdf. Accessed 15 January 2010.

Vincendeau, Ginette (2006) '"Not for Export": Jean Gabin in Hollywood' in *Journeys of Desire: European Actors in Hollywood*, in Phillips and Vincendeau (eds) (2006), pp.115–24.

Notes

1 Lumière database of admissions of films released in Europe: http://lumiere.obs.coe.int. Accessed 19 March 2007.

2 Banderas in *Evita* (Alan Parker, 1996), *The Mask of Zorro* and *The Legend of Zorro* (Martin Campbell, 1998 and 2005), *Frida* (Julie Taymor, 2002), and *Once Upon a Time in Mexico* (Robert Rodríguez, 2003); Cruz in *Captain Correlli's Mandolin* (John Madden, 2001), *Woman on Top* (Fina Torres, 2002) and *Vanilla Sky* (Cameron Crowe, 2001); Bardem in *Before Night Falls* (Julian Schnabel, 2001), *The Dancer Upstairs* (John Malkovich, 2002) and *No Country for Old Men* (Ethan and Joel Coen, 2007).

3 The website is at http://www.eduardonoriega.com/web1024.html. Last accessed 8 May 2010.

4 The link takes the viewer to http://www.eduardonoriega.com/hemeroteca/2007/paisSemanal07/paisSemanal07.pdf. Last accessed 15 January 2010. The bare-chested action shots, moody over-the-shoulder looks, and gritty prison-cell setting accompanying the text, are useful examples of the seductive projection of the actor as both meaningful and desirably accessible.

5 *Sur* (Málaga, Spain), 26 December 1999, p.62. Link from the Noriega website Hemeroteca broken as at 15 January 2010.

6 Linked at http://www.eduardonoriega.com/hemeroteca/2006/gente_10_7_6/gente_10_7_6.pdf. Accessed 6 March 2010.

7 Online at http://www.eduardonoriega.com/hemeroteca/2009/travelerJun2009/travelerJun2009.pdf. Accessed 15 January 2010.

Chapter Six

From world cinema to World Cinema: Wong Kar-wai's *Ashes of Time* and *Ashes of Time Redux*[1]

Felicia Chan

When Wong Kar-wai began shooting *Ashes of Time* (*Dongxie Xidu*, 1994), he was not yet known as the filmmaker who was to give the world the hyper-kinetic *Chungking Express* (*Chongqing Senlin*, 1994), a film widely acknowl-edged to have launched his international career. By the time *Ashes of Time Redux* was released in 2008, Wong had acquired a global reputation for being an 'auteur of time' (Teo 2005a), cemented in particular by the wide critical success of *In the Mood for Love* (*Huayang Nianhua*, 2000). Re-combined from various scattered prints, *Ashes of Time Redux* (hereafter referred to as *Redux*) is a 'refreshed' rather than re-made version of the original film (hereafter referred to as *Ashes*). Re-edited with digitally remastered visuals and a re-recorded soundtrack, *Redux* in many ways feels like the spruced-up sibling of the earlier film. However, I contend in this chapter that each film is a product of its time, and so needs to be read in relation to the circumstances from which it emerged, as well as (now) against one another. I argue that the newer version, while looking and sounding better – and certainly being more 'slick' – than its grainy predecessor, exists *alongside* the older one as an alternate film, rather than replacing it. In addition, the duplication of these films plays out on another level: Wong's obsession with repeating the past and with time. In 1994, *Ashes*, as a quirky innovative film, stood as an example of world cinema in a descrip-tive sense: it was part of a large corpus of non-English language films that were not necessarily available to English-language markets, for various political, social and commercial reasons. In 2008, *Redux*, as a film that was released after the filmmaker had gained his international reputation, thereby (re-)entered his *oeuvre* and by association the 'canon' of World Cinema (in the qualitative sense); or, as a reviewer for *Screen International* writes, Wong's 'most poetic, experimental film belongs not in the curiosity cabinet but on the big screen' (Marshall 2008).

I make my case in two parts: the first addresses the place of *Ashes* at the end of the cycle of the *wuxia* genre in 1994, and *Redux* at the rebirth of that same genre in 2008 following the global success of *Crouching Tiger, Hidden Dragon* (*Wohu Canglong*, Ang Lee, 2000); and the second addresses the role that the star-studded cast plays in both films with regard to the changing fortunes of the Hong Kong film industry in the intervening years.

Wuxia Fortunes

Although *Ashes* did not secure a US theatrical release in 1994, and thus had a limited international release (only Southeast Asia and France), it was nonetheless still widely referred to in scholarly writings on Wong's work. One of the more notable analyses of *Ashes* is Ackbar Abbas' (1997) reading of the film as a symptom of what he called Hong Kong's culture of 'disappearance'. The narrative of *Ashes* is loosely based on a well-known martial arts novel series from the 1940s by Louis Cha (whose Chinese pseudonym is Jin Yong), called *The Eagle-Shooting Heroes* (*Shediao Yingxiong Zhuan*, sometimes also known as *The Condor-Shooting Heroes*), which runs into four volumes. Rather than adapt the novels, Wong's film speculates on the lives of the main characters – Huang Yaoshi, nicknamed 'Dongxie' (Evil East, played by Tony Leung Ka-fai), and Ouyang Feng, nicknamed 'Xidu' (Malicious West, played by Leslie Cheung) – before they had become the characters in Cha's novels. If not in great detail, the series is known among Chinese audiences because of the widespread popularity of its written form, as well as the proliferation of film and television adaptations, mostly shot 'in conventional genre terms' (Teo 1997: 197). As such, the characters are relatively familiar to East and Southeast Asian audiences, which traditionally make up the bulk of the market for Hong Kong cinema, in much the same way as archetypal characters like Robin Hood and King Arthur may be familiar to Western audiences, who may never have read the original medieval ballads from which the characters emerged. Although presented as a martial arts film, *Ashes* eschews almost all of its conventions, or is 'in defiance of the genre', in Abbas' words (1997: 59): instead of displaying the agility and prowess of martial combat, the simple moralities of good versus evil and the characters' polarized differences, the film stresses the similarities between them. The key similarity that binds them all is not just their lack of fulfilment and action, but the interminable waiting in between events – features that have come to characterize nearly all of Wong's films, and with which Lu and Yeh go as far as to associate Deleuze's theory of movement- and time-images embedded in the cinematic form itself (Lu and Yeh 2005: 16). All we know of their heroic deeds, if any, is narrated in voice-over or titles, and never enacted; what little fighting is conducted on screen is rendered so blurred as to be unwatchable. As Abbas describes:

> The ambiguities of heroic space can be suggested by how action is represented ... It is no longer a choreography of action that we see ... but a composition of light and color where all action has dissolved – a kind of abstract expressionism or action painting. (1997: 59)

While these ambiguities may be read as allegories for the anxieties concerning Britain's handover of Hong Kong to Chinese jurisdiction in 1997 – Lo writes that '[the characters'] angst bespeaks the social atmosphere of Hong Kong near the end of time and its ambivalence to Chineseness' (2005: 100) – they may equally be read as signalling the decline of a once-popular genre, and an industry in profound crisis.

When *Ashes* emerged in the mid-1990s, the *wuxia* genre in Hong Kong cinema had all but disappeared from the big screen, having migrated to television in the 1980s. The genre may be distinguished from the *kung fu* genre in the history of Hong Kong cinemas, and in the 1960s and 1970s their distinctive styles were clearly delineated (Teo 1997: 98). The *wuxia* films, which peaked in the 1960s, were Mandarin-speaking and focused on fantasy period stories, with elaborate costumes and elegant swordplay. The genre declined in the 1970s with the rise of the *kung fu* films. These emphasized fist-fighting (rather than sword-fighting) and the athleticism of the body (as opposed to the wire-work favoured in *wuxia* films). This distinction between the two styles of cinema also corresponded with the historical and political distinctions between the Mandarin-language and Cantonese-language cinemas that characterize much of Hong Kong's output during this period. The twin histories are too intricate to enter into detail here; however, suffice it to say that the Mandarin-language cinema has its roots in northern and mainland China, whose continued political turbulence in the past century (especially during the Japanese occupation of the Second World War, the civil war in 1949 and the Cultural Revolution in 1966) drove many who worked in the film industries there to what was at the time the British Crown Colony of Hong Kong (Fu 2003). The Cantonese-language cinema rose in the 1970s as part of a growing movement to reclaim Hong Kong's cultural space for the southern Cantonese-speaking residents: Mandarin and *wuxia* were seen as being closely associated with northern China, while Cantonese (the language of the southernmost province, Canton, or Guangdong) and the *kung fu*, fist-fighting martial arts styles were generally considered of southern origin (Teo 1997: 98). The two styles eventually merged, and the demarcations between them became less and less distinct – indeed, *Ashes* itself is a Cantonese-language film, though for some territories like Singapore, with strict state policies on language in public culture, it would have been dubbed into Mandarin. Nevertheless, the nostalgia for the period fantasies of the late 1960s and early 1970s continues to hold sway for filmmakers of a particular generation – Ang Lee spoke of just such a nostalgia when he made *Crouching Tiger, Hidden Dragon*, his own tribute to the lost genre (see Lee 2000), though one which ultimately revived it in a different form (Chan 2008).

Read in this context, it is not too far-fetched to perceive the blurred opening fight sequence in *Ashes*, choreographed by Sammo Hung (a contemporary of Jackie Chan, and renowned actor and action director in his own right), as a modernist take on an old, familiar genre. What Abbas describes as a kind of abstract expressionism does not seem to parody or ironize the genre inasmuch as 'the implications of the genre are followed to their catastrophic conclusions, giving us in the end the complex continuum of a blind space and a dead time' (Abbas 1997: 58–9). When we do 'catch a glimpse of a human figure', Abbas notes 'it is always at the moment of dealing out death or in the throes of dying' (1997: 59). Indeed, the characters in *Ashes* are all, metaphorically, at a stage of death, a kind of stasis in which life slips by while they sit and wait and yearn for what might or might never have been. The long, lingering close-ups of faces, every star image rendered beautifully melancholic by the rich play of light and shadow, show off Christopher Doyle's cinematography to its full effect. In the world of the film, heroism becomes not about what one *does*, but how one waits. And, yet, does waiting arrest time or prolong it? Does waiting offer hope or despair? Indeed, if Clint Eastwood's elegy to the western was to cast himself as an ageing gunslinger in *Unforgiven* (1992), Wong's answer to the death of the *wuxia* film seemed to be to cast two of Hong Kong's biggest stars as the younger selves of older heroes, only to have them behave as if they were already at the end of their lives, their youth spent and their idealism withered away. When we watch and wait and mourn with the characters, we are also invited to watch and wait and mourn for a time when films were simpler to understand, romance more promising and life more forgiving. The titles towards the end of the film tell us that the characters move on to bigger and better things (even eventual death), but the linearity of film history draws us towards the conclusion that even those times have passed – these characters have lived those better lives in other, earlier, films.

For, by 1994, the frenetic heights of production the Hong Kong film industry had experienced in the 1970s and 1980s, when over 100 films were produced annually, had also passed (Leung 2008: 71). In addition, during this period, almost all of the best-selling films at the box office were domestic productions:

Eleven of the top twenty films of the 1970s were Hong Kong movies, and the top four far ahead of the first Hollywood import to make the list (*The Towering Inferno*). In some years, no foreign film even ranked in the top ten. European bureaucrats railed against Hollywood imports, but it was European audiences who made global hits of *The Lion King*, *Forrest Gump*, *Batman*, *Home Alone*, *Ghostbusters*, *Aladdin*, *Mrs. Doubtfire*, *Beverly Hills Cop* and *Back to the Future*. All failed in Hong Kong. (Bordwell 2000: 34)

By the mid-1990s, the tide had turned. In 2004, domestic production hit a low of 63; and in 2005, it had slipped further to 55 (Leung 2008: 74). The reasons were many, including the 1997–99 Asian financial crisis (which meant the regional markets for Hong Kong films also collapsed); the SARS epidemic in southern China in 2003; piracy and the rise of the VCD format (see Davis 2003); the costly transition to multiplex theatres; and changing audience tastes and preferences (Hendrix 2003; Leung 2008).

The closing montage in *Ashes* pays double homage to the genre, by establishing Ouyang Feng, Leslie Cheung's character, as Lord of the West, intercut with the occasional image of Hong Qi (Jacky Cheung) and Huang Yaoshi (Tony Leung Ka-fai), who go on to become fighters in *The Eagle-Shooting Heroes* saga. However, by far the most airtime in the final montage is given to Murong Yin/Yang, the sister-brother pair played by the iconic Brigitte Lin Ching-hsia. By the time of the film's initial release, the Taiwanese Hong Kong actress and star – described by one fan as Julia Roberts, Audrey Hepburn, Grace Kelly, Marlene Dietrich and Elizabeth Taylor combined (Tetsuya 2005: viii) – had retired from show business, following her marriage to a business tycoon. The flashback images in the final sequence are performed almost as a salute to the actress, and especially to the role that defined the latter part of her career – that of a cross-dressing transgender martial arts exponent in Tsui Hark's *Swordsman* series (Chan 2006). The styling of Murong Yin/Yang in *Ashes* is almost exactly like that of Lin's character, 'Asia the Invincible', in the *Swordsman* series, and at one point in the *Ashes* montage, Lin's character even looks directly into the camera, confronting the spectator with the same steely-eyed gaze she is known for as Asia the Invincible.

In 2008, *Redux* entered a substantially different market environment, notably following the unprecedented success of Ang Lee's *Crouching Tiger, Hidden Dragon* in both Asia and the West (Chan 2004, Chan 2008; Lu 2005). It is a film that has been noted as sparking the revival of the *wuxia* genre in Chinese-language cinemas, spurred on by renewed interest in the West (Teo 2005b). The success of *Crouching Tiger* spawned big-budget, transnational productions designed for an international audience, such as Zhang Yimou's *Hero* (*Yingxiong*, 2002) and *House of Flying Daggers* (*Shimian maifu*, 2004), as well as historical epics for a predominantly Asian audience (albeit with an eye on the West), such as the monumental two-part *Red Cliff* (*Chibi*, John Woo, 2008) and *Mulan* (Jingle Ma, 2009); it also revived – intermittently – the self-belief of a failing industry, through the relative successes of the *Infernal Affairs* (*Wujiandao*) trilogy (Andrew Lau and Alan Mak, 2002–03) and *Kung Fu Hustle* (Stephen Chow, 2004) (see Leung 2008).

By 2008, Hong Kong was a Special Administrative Region of the People's Republic of China, and any anxieties over the handover experienced prior to 1997 had met with a certain 'anti-climax'. As a Hong Kong resident remarks:

> On the day China reclaimed Hong Kong, the international media expected doomsday news stories but ended up having none. The sovereignty transfer was smooth; stock and property prices soared; dissidents were still protesting on the streets and no one was arrested. The handover ceremony seemed to be an anti-climax and international interest in Hong Kong quickly died down. (Ma 2000: 173)

The waiting in *Ashes* that signified the waiting for Hong Kong's change of political masters in 1997 is potentially transmuted in *Redux* to the waiting for the expiration of Hong Kong's special status – the 'one country, two systems' promise of the PRC that Hong Kong would remain 'unchanged' for 50 years from the handover – a theme Wong explores in his film *2046* (2004) (Rayns 2005; Taubin 2005).

If he was relatively unknown in 1994, by 2008, Wong's reputation as international auteur was firmly established: while taking a break from *Ashes*, he had made *Chungking Express*, which became a 'cult hit' (Wright 2002) internationally (Quentin Tarantino 'presents' the film on US DVD produced by Miramax); in 1997, he won the Best Director award at Cannes for *Happy Together* (*Chunguang zhaxie*, 1997); and in 2000, *In the Mood for Love* took the award at Cannes for Best Actor (Tony Leung Chiu-wai), as well as the Technical Grand Prize (Christopher Doyle et al.). It is in this context that *Redux* was received, especially since many mainstream newspaper reviewers did not have the chance to see the 1994 version. It is interesting to note that what puzzled critics experiencing the film for the first time in 1994 continued to puzzle critics experiencing it for the first time a decade and a half later, with slight variation. The *Guardian*'s critic wrote:

> It is an intriguing film in some ways, with lovely swirling images, and Wong's distinctive emphasis on close-ups and faces, suggesting an interiority of mood and feeling. With its ironic duplications and symmetries of unrequited passion – a woman caresses a man while both are thinking of another – it's a forerunner of the very much superior *In the Mood*

for Love. But I must frankly say I found its flashbacks and general structure muddled and opaque, and I am unsure how rewarding the film's
intricacies and indulgences look now. (Bradshaw 2008)

Redux is here read as a precursor to *In the Mood for Love*, although it bears
significant differences to the 1994 version. In 1994, *Ashes* developed Wong's
preoccupations with time and waiting at the mid-point between his early films
(*As Tears Goes By* and *Days of Being Wild*) and his later hits (*Happy Together*
and *In the Mood for Love*); in 2008 the film is read against the critic's own
pivotal encounter with – and seduction by – *In the Mood for Love*. While *Ashes*
signalled the ultimate destruction of the time in the waiting room, *In the Mood
for Love* and *2046* elevated the art of waiting into such studied glamour and
elegance that *Redux* seemed unable to match up.

Nevertheless, it is the polish of *Redux* – the colours are richer, the images
sharper, the music clearer – compared with the early experimentation of *Ashes*
that takes it into the domain of what is today described (however con-
tentiously) as 'transnational' cinema, as cinema that circulates around 'the
world'. By virtue of its higher visibility, *Redux*, more than *Ashes*, may be said to
inhabit the two main realms of 'World Cinema' addressed in the debates on the
subject: the first is the realm of world cinema as 'the cinema of the world ... a
global process', the cinema that 'is not the other, but ... is us' (Nagib 2006: 35);
and the second, of World Cinema as the body of work that emerges out of the
discourses of economic globalization, thereby making a distinction between 'a
theory of world cinema and a world theory of cinema' (Leary 2008: 58). There
is, in a sense, the world cinema that exists because the films exist, and then
there is the 'World Cinema' that is made, through a process of canonization
that includes awards ceremonies, reviews and international distribution deals.
Redux, in its new, improved state, acquires what I can only describe as a certain
global style that has come to characterize transnational Chinese cinema after
Crouching Tiger – a style that embodies a conscious look and feel of sumptuousness, of high production values, yet one that also seems to eschew commercialism and aspire towards 'art'. For instance, the saturated colours of the newly
digitized photography in *Redux* recall the rich hues in Zhang Yimou's *Hero*
(whose cinematographer was also Christopher Doyle), while the deep yellows
of the desert landscape recall the desert sequence in *Crouching Tiger*, even
though the original film predates them both. Additionally, the mellifluous
strains of Yo-Yo Ma's cello solos on the re-recorded soundtrack are strikingly
similar to Tan Dun's scoring of *Crouching Tiger*, the musical theme of which is
also performed by Ma. In other words, if *Ashes* looked back on what Hong Kong
cinema was and might have been after the 1980s, *Redux* seems to promise what
(transnational) Hong Kong or Chinese cinema could be and may have been
after 2000.

Starring: Leslie et al.

A key difference between these two films, and any other arthouse film with a slow pace and bewildering narrative, is the fact that they employ some of the biggest names in Hong Kong show business. A poster for *Ashes* in 1994 lines up each star in equal measure horizontally across its length – Leslie Cheung, Brigitte Lin Ching-hsia, Tony Leung Ka-fai, Jacky Cheung, Carina Lau, Charlie Young and Tony Leung Chiu-wai – singling out none (Figure 1). The only star missing from the line-up is Maggie Cheung; however, she is credited with a 'special appearance' in the film. Apart from Young, who debuted with this film – and she was cast only after Joey Wong, who co-starred with Leslie Cheung in *A Chinese Ghost Story* (*Qiannü Youhun*, Ching Siu-tung, 1987), withdrew from the film – these faces are so recognizable and visible in Hong Kong popular culture that it is sufficient for their names to be etched in small print in a corner of the poster. The close integration between the popular culture industries in Hong Kong is exemplified by the fact that many of the territory's film stars are also TV stars and pop singers, with appreciably large fan bases and, hence, significant 'trans-border' influences (see Chua 2004).

There are certain differences between the Hong Kong and Hollywood star systems which have received little scholarly attention to date. Susan Dominus points out several of these in her interview feature with Maggie Cheung for *The New York Times*, two of which I address here for how they might impact on the reception of *Ashes* and *Redux*. The first is the lack of exclusivity or special treatment, in comparison to the vast entourages that accompany Hollywood stars; the second a sense of kinship among filmmakers, and between them and their fans, as I shall explain in later pages. Dominus recounts the cross-cultural observations of Olivier Assayas, Cheung's ex-husband:

> Assayas said ... he was surprised to find in Cheung a performer whose charisma was completely uncoupled from the Western notion of celebrity, which holds that great performances demand indulgence and coddling. To the contrary, *there's a diligence – almost a dutifulness –* common to Cheung's circle of Hong Kong performers, most of whom put up with the industry's grueling production schedules. Cheung has raced her way through some 75 films, making as many as 11 in one year during the height of the Hong Kong film industry in the late 80's. 'You sleep in cars, you sleep on the set, anywhere you can', she said. Working on one of the Police Story films with Jackie Chan, she had to run through a stack of bed frames, several of which collapsed on her head, sending her to the hospital for 17 stitches. (Dominus 2004, emphasis mine)

Read in this context, the perception of *Ashes* as an arthouse film – Frederic Dannen writes that it 'must rank with the most self-indulgent pictures ever made' (1997: 51) – ought to be considered alongside a madcap B-movie parody called *Eagle-Shooting Heroes* (*Shediao yinxiong zhi dongcheng xijiu*, Jeff Lau, 1993). The relationship between the two films reveals much about the production culture that enables Wong to make his arthouse films. Jeff Lau, the director of *Eagle-Shooting Heroes*, is one of the producers of *Ashes*, and when Wong showed no sign of finishing his film by the Chinese New Year of 1993, Lau decided to make his own Chinese New Year special (Tetsuya 2005: 86).[2] *Eagle-Shooting Heroes* places the entire cast of *Ashes* in a brutal parody of itself, complete with an over-the-top musical declaration of love performed to Rossini's 'William Tell Overture'. Played with broad humour and loud gesticulation, along with cheap *papier-mâché* sets and tin-foil weapons, the actors gamely lampoon their roles in *Ashes* in a vein very similar to the British *Carry On* films. Far from being a criticism of Wong's style, *Eagle-Shooting Heroes* is in fact produced by Wong himself, and his Jet Tone company. During another brief hiatus in the filming of *Ashes*, Wong produced and directed his first hit, *Chungking Express*, starring Brigitte Lin and Tony Leung Chiu-wai, which was made in two months (Dannen 1997: 51). In other words, the voracity of the production industry in Hong Kong and the interconnectedness of its popular-culture industries create an air of relative familiarity among cast and crew, to the extent that projects are brought into fruition as much from contracts and legalities as they are with personal favours and goodwill. In an interview for the *Redux* DVD released in the UK by Artificial Eye, cinematographer Christopher Doyle – an Australian who established his career in Taiwan and Hong Kong, but who has also worked with Gus Van Sant, Jim Jarmusch, James Ivory, M. Night Shyamalan, Philip Noyce and Neil Jordan – remarks on the differences in working cultures between Hong Kong filmmaking and that in the West; in Hong Kong, he says 'we are friends first'. Likewise, the interpellation between the high- and low-brow, the arthouse and commercial, has led David Overby to

Figure 1   *Poster of* Ashes of Time *(1994)*

note: 'It reminds me a lot of Hollywood ... before the great split between commerce and art' (quoted in Bordwell 2000: 91).

The decline in the industry in the late 1990s has significantly reduced the number of these cheaply made-on-the-fly productions, for which much of Hong Kong cinema in the 1980s was known. The desire to emulate the success of *Crouching Tiger* with better scripting and higher production values, and thus a turn towards more foreign co-productions, is already changing the production culture and aesthetics of the films (see Hansen and Seno 2001; Leung 2008). The release of *Redux* during this period of reinvention allows Wong to reposition himself within the current global arena of 'World Cinema'. One blogger notes that:

> 'Wong Kar-wai the challenging auteur' is himself being reinvented as 'Wong Kar-wai the prescient epic-maker' ... Both *Redux* and these other releases point to his arrival at a jumping-off point similar to that reached by Ang Lee circa *Crouching Tiger, Hidden Dragon*. Having mastered and reshaped expectations within the international festival and 'art house' distribution circuits, Wong is now going global at the level of more popular genres – a level which now includes, as it did not in 1994, the *wuxia* epic. (Johnson 2008)

Fourteen years after *Ashes*, the stars' careers have also evolved: some have retired (Brigitte Lin); others have retired and returned (Charlie Young); some remain active and popular in Hong Kong (Jacky Cheung, Carina Lau); others attempted a European crossover but never quite made it (Tony Leung Ka-fai starred in Jean-Jacques Annaud's *The Lover/L'Amant*, 1992; he remains active in Hong Kong); still others have crossed with reasonable success (Maggie Cheung and Tony Leung Chiu-wai) (see, for example, Dominus 2004; Rose 2004); and one, most notably and tragically, has committed suicide (Leslie Cheung), and his death resonates heavily in the revised film. Several years after he leapt to his death off the Mandarin Oriental hotel in Hong Kong at the age of 46, his demise is still mourned by fans, and in 2009, one of the events on the day of commemoration was the screening of a special trailer of *Redux* cut from his scenes (China Hush 2009). Indeed, the closing sequence in *Redux* is re-edited to eliminate the presence of the other stars, leaving the last actions, and images, for Cheung, who paradoxically ages in the final sequence in a way he now never will.

The shifts in Hong Kong's political circumstances and film cultures have now rendered the nostalgia in *Redux* less for the loss of a beloved genre than for the passing of a certain golden age to which beloved stars belonged. New and younger stars have emerged in Hong Kong, but like the passing of Hollywood's Golden Age when the studios broke up, the glamour of old appears to be gone, replaced with a lingering sense that this particular group of stars will never be seen in the same film again. Cheung, in particular, holds a special place in Hong Kong stardom in that his career could be mapped across the rising trajectory of the industry during the 1980s, not just as an actor, but also as one of the 'kings' of 'Cantopop' (Cantonese pop music). Richard Corliss, *Time* magazine's veteran film critic, paid this tribute to him:

> Here was a new kind of star: beautiful, tender, toxic. James Dean with a mean streak, or a deeper Johnny Depp. ... Beyond this attitude, this star was an actor. Leslie didn't simply mesmerize or bully the camera; he worked subtle wonders before it. (Corliss 2003)

Despite the SARS crisis in 2003, thousands turned up for Leslie Cheung's funeral on the streets of Hong Kong, many from abroad, and thousands more watched the procession on television. In the industry and to his fans, the star was frequently referred to as 'Gor Gor', which is Cantonese for 'elder brother'.

This sense of familial kinship is the second characteristic that Dominus identifies in her feature on Maggie Cheung. The smallness of the industry and the sheer proliferation of projects encourage familiarity and intimacy not just among the cast and crew, but also with the fans. Dominus cites Assayas' experience as the ex-husband of a superstar once again:

> Even Assayas, from whom she's been separated for years, can't cross a hotel lobby in Shanghai without being swarmed, because of his former association with Cheung. 'In China, they care even more about their stars than in America', Assayas said, 'and they're also less shy about approaching them. I don't know what it is. It's less of an individualist society, maybe – *it's like they feel their stars belong to them, are part of the family – they're someone in the family who made good, and they feel they belong to them*.' (Dominus 2004, emphasis mine)

Yiman Wang writes that the internet has contributed to Leslie Cheung's posthumous fandom, and that its virtual space 'is particularly important in preserving and reviving Leslie fandom and extending to it a "dead celebrity" culture. It does so by producing the illusion that the idol does not cease to exist upon his death, but rather becomes omnipresent' (Wang 2007: 330). Thus, if the poster of *Ashes* celebrated the collective stardom of a group of actors, the poster of *Redux* features only Cheung, captured in mid-spin, his arm outstretched and sword thrust forward, frozen forever in eternal youth (Figure 2). In this sense, *Redux* not just participates in, but *adds to*, this shared memory and collective nostalgia (Wang 2007: 333), turning what was a relatively obscure film into a requiem for a talent prematurely lost.

Figure 2   Poster of Ashes of Time Redux *(2008)*

Ashes to Ashes (Redux)

The mythology behind the journey from *Ashes* to *Redux* serves as a fitting meta-text for much of the films' concerns. *Ashes* was simply not widely released. The few non-pirated DVD versions were difficult to procure: diehard fans lucky enough to track them down would have found two versions released by Hong Kong companies, one by World Video and the other by Mei Ah Entertainment. Of the two, it is usually acknowledged that the former is the more dismal; a fan reviewer complains:

World Video has released a domestic English market version of *Ashes* but it is such a travesty, it does not even deserve a full review. The company simply took their poor quality Chinese market version and matted off the bottom third of the picture, to cover up the original Chinese and English subtitles, and put new video generated English subs on top. The result is a compositional disaster and a far from appropriate presentation for any film, let alone one as beautifully composed as this; Wong and Doyle should sue. (Charles 2003)

Mei Ah Entertainment's prolific output of VCDs and DVDs (and laser discs, at one time) fares only marginally better. The company's rendition of *Ashes*, among a list of other faults, is said to possess 'instances of gatefloat and graininess that cause noticeable compression flaws ... There is no menu and the chapter stops are simply placed at five minute intervals throughout' (Charles 2003).[3] Wong notes in the *Redux* press kit: 'Over the years, I've come to realize that there are several different versions of *Ashes of Time* in circulation, some approved by me, some not' (Wong 2008: 3).

The decision to rework *Ashes* was not initially motivated by artistic concerns, but practical ones. The director relates:

As we launched into the work, we discovered that the original negatives and sound materials were in danger: the laboratory in Hong Kong where they were stored was suddenly shut down, without warning. We retrieved as much as we could, but the negatives were in pieces. As if we were searching for a long-lost family, we began looking for duplicate materials from various distributors and even the storage vaults of overseas Chinatown cinemas. As this went on, we came to realize that there are hundreds of prints locked up in Chinatown warehouses in those cities which used to show Hong Kong movies. *Looking through all this material felt like uncovering the saga of the ups and downs of Hong Kong cinema in the last few decades. And this history, of course, included* Ashes of Time. (Wong 2008: 3, emphasis mine).

Ashes was very much a victim of the times: the laboratory storing the negatives had succumbed to the 1997 Asian financial crisis, and prior to its move to its current premises in 2001, the Hong Kong Film Archive lacked the resources to adequately preserve Hong Kong's film history, though the archive today boasts facilities dedicated to dehumidification and storage, as well as to screening and public exhibition (see *Hong Kong Film Archive*). This quixotic journey to retrieve lost prints also highlights the fact that cinema may circulate transnationally outside of established and well-recorded routes. In contrast, *Redux* is distributed theatrically by Fortissimo Films in Europe, and on DVD by Sony

Pictures Classics in the United States, and by Artificial Eye in the UK, complete with a 'making of' documentary, theatrical trailer, and cast and crew interviews.

In looking back at 'the saga of the ups and downs of Hong Kong cinema in the last few decades', the journey from *Ashes* to *Redux*, from obscure example of world cinema to boutique gem in World Cinema, may have inadvertently, but fittingly, enacted a temporal and textual *tête-bêche* now seen to be characteristic of Wong's films (see Yue 2008) – one in which the films, because of their current relation to each other, must now unendingly fold back on themselves. The worldliness of cinema is usually read in spatial terms (see Andrew 2006; Leary 2008). However, the journey from *Ashes* to *Redux* reminds us of the medium's temporal dimension, especially of the ways in which the resurrection from 'death' – of a film, a genre and a star via new technologies (see Mulvey 2006) – can enable, and also be enabled by, the global – 'world' – circulation of cinema.

References

Abbas, Ackbar (1997) *Hong Kong: Culture and the Politics of Disappearance* (Hong Kong, Hong Kong University Press).

Andrew, Dudley (2006) 'An atlas of world cinema', in Stephanie Dennison and Song Hwee Lim (eds) *Remapping World Cinema: Identity, Culture and Politics in Film* (London, Wallflower Press), pp.19–29.

Bordwell, David (2000) *Planet Hong Kong: Popular Cinema and the Art of Entertainment* (Cambridge, Harvard University Press).

Bradshaw, Peter (2008) 'Ashes of Time Redux', *The Guardian*, 12 September. Online at: http://www.guardian.co.uk/film/2008/sep/12/actionandadventure. Accessed 17 June 2010.

Chan, Felicia (2006) '*Wuxia* cross-dressing and transgender identity: the roles of Brigitte Lin Ching-hsia from *Swordsman II* to *Ashes of Time*', *EnterText* 6:1. Online at: http://arts.brunel.ac.uk/gate/entertext/issue_6_1.htm. Accessed 17 June 2010.

Chan, Felicia (2008) '*Crouching Tiger, Hidden Dragon*: cultural migrancy and translatability', in Chris Berry (ed.) *Chinese Films in Focus II* (London, Palgrave Macmillan), pp.73–81.

Chan, Kenneth (2004) 'The global return of the *Wu Xia Pian* (Chinese sword-fighting movie): Ang Lee's *Crouching Tiger, Hidden Dragon*', *Cinema Journal* 43:4, pp.3–17.

Charles, John (2003) *Ashes of Time. Hong Kong Digital 154*. Online at: http://www.dighkmovies.com/v3/154/154.html. Accessed 18 June 2010.

China Hush (2009) 'Fans pay tribute to Leslie Cheung on Sixth Death Anniversary', *China Hush*, 1 April. Online at: http://www.chinahush.com/

2009/04/01/fans-pay-tribute-to-leslie-cheung-on-sixth-death-anniversary/. Accessed 17 June 2010.

Chua, Beng Huat (2004) 'Conceptualizing an East Asian popular culture', *Inter-Asia Cultural Studies* 5:2, pp.200–21.

Corliss, Richard (2003) 'That old feeling: days of being Leslie', *Time Asia*. Online at: http://www.time.com/time/arts/article/0,8599,440214,00.html. Accessed 2 September 2005.

Dannen, Frederic (1997) 'Hong Kong Babylon: A reporter looks at the Hollywood of the East', in Frederic Dannen and Barry Long (eds) *Hong Kong Babylon: An Insider's Guide to the Hollywood of the East* (New York, Hyperion), pp.1–56.

Davis, Darrell William (2003) 'Compact generation: VCD markets in Asia', *Historical Journal of Film, Radio and Television*, 23:2, pp.165–76.

Dominus, Susan (2004) 'Why isn't Maggie Cheung a Hollywood star?', *The New York Times*, 14 November. Online at: http://www.nytimes.com/2004/11/14/movies/14CHEUNG.html. Accessed 17 June 2010.

Fu, Poshek (2003) *Between Shanghai and Hong Kong: The Politics of Chinese Cinemas* (Stanford, Stanford University Press).

Hansen, Jeremy and Alexandra A. Seno (2001) 'A touch of realism', *Asiaweek*, 20 July.

Hendrix, Grady (2003) 'Hong Kong horror: the 90s and beyond', *Senses of Cinema* 29. Online at: http://archive.sensesofcinema.com/contents/03/29/hong_kong_horror.html. Accessed 17 June 2010.

Hong Kong Film Archive. Online at: http://www.lcsd.gov.hk/CE/CulturalService/HKFA/en/1–1.php. Accessed 17 June 2010.

Johnson, Matthew David (2008) 'Ashes of Time Redux', *The China Beat*, 11 July. Online at: http://thechinabeat.blogspot.com/2008/11/ashes-of-time-redux.html. Accessed 17 June 2010.

Leary, Charles (2008) 'Electric shadow of an airplane: Hong Kong Cinema, World Cinema', in Leon Hunt and Leung Wing-Fai (eds) *East Asian Cinemas: Exploring Transnational Connections on Film* (London, I.B.Tauris), pp.57–68.

Lee, Ang (2000) 'Foreword', in Linda Sunshine (ed.) *Crouching Tiger, Hidden Dragon: A Portrait of the Ang Lee Film* (New York, Newmarket Press), p.7.

Leung, Wing-Fai (2008) '*Infernal Affairs* and *Kung Fu Hustle*: panacea, placebo and Hong Kong cinema', in Leon Hunt and Wing-Fai Leung (eds) *East Asian Cinemas: Exploring Transnational Connections on Film* (London, I.B.Tauris), pp.71–87.

Lo, Kwai-cheung (2005) *Chinese Face/Off: The Transnational Popular Culture of Hong Kong* (Urbana and Chicago, University of Illinois Press).

Lu, Sheldon H. (2005) 'Crouching tiger, hidden dragon, bouncing angels: Hollywood, Taiwan, Hong Kong, and transnational cinema', in Sheldon H.

Lu and Emilie Yueh-yu Yeh (eds) *Chinese-Language Film: Historiography, Poetics, Politics* (Honolulu, University of Hawai'i Press), pp.220–33.

Lu, Sheldon H. and Emilie Yueh-yu Yeh (2005) 'Introduction: mapping the field of Chinese-language cinema', in Sheldon H. Lu and Emilie Yueh-yu Yeh (eds) *Chinese-Language Film: Historiography, Poetics, Politics* (Honolulu, University of Hawai'i Press), pp.1–24.

Ma, Eric Kit-wai (2000) 'Re-nationalization and me: my Hong Kong story after 1997', *Inter-Asia Cultural Studies* 1:1, pp.173–9.

Marshall, Lee (2008) 'Ashes of Time Redux', *Screen International*, 20 May. Online at: http://www.screendaily.com/ashes-of-time-redux/4039049. article?sm=4039049. Accessed 17 June 2010.

Mulvey, Laura (2006) *Death 24x a Second: Stillness and the Moving Image* (London, Reaktion Books).

Nagib, Lúcia (2006) 'Towards a positive definition of world cinema', in Stephanie Dennison and Song Hwee Lim (eds) *Remapping World Cinema: Identity, Culture and Politics in Film* (London, Wallflower Press), pp.30–7.

Pang, Laikwan (2002) 'The global-national position of Hong Kong Cinema in China', in Stephanie Hemelryk Donald, Michael Keane and Yin Hong (eds) *Media in China: Consumption, Content and Crisis* (London, Routledge Curzon), pp.55–66.

Rayns, Tony (2005) 'The Long Goodbye', *Sight and Sound* 15:1, pp.22–5.

Rose, Steve (2004) '"It never gets any easier": interview with Tony Leung', *The Guardian*, 23 February. Online at: http://www.guardian.co.uk/film/2004/feb/23/1. Accessed 17 June 2010.

Taubin, Amy (2005) 'The Long Goodbye', *Film Comment* 41:4, pp.26–9.

Teo, Stephen (1997) *Hong Kong Cinema: The Extra Dimensions* (London, British Film Institute).

Teo, Stephen (2005a) *Wong Kar-Wai: Auteur of Time* (London, British Film Institute).

Teo, Stephen (2005b) 'Wuxia Redux: *Crouching Tiger, Hidden Dragon* as a Model of Late Transnational Production', in Meaghan Morris, Siu Leung Li and Stephen Chan Ching-kiu (eds) *Hong Kong Connections: Transnational Imagination in Action Cinema* (Durham, Duke University Press), pp.191–204.

Tetsuya, Akiko (2005) *The Last Star of the East: Brigitte Lin Ching Hsia and Her Films* (Los Angeles, Akiko Tetsuya).

Wang, Yiman (2007) 'A star is dead, a legend is born: practicing Leslie', in Sean Redmond and Su Holmes (eds), *Stardom and Celebrity: A Reader* (London, Sage), pp.326–40.

Wong, Kar-wai (2008) Director's Notes. *Ashes of Time Redux* press kit, 3. Online at: http://www.sonyclassics.com/ashesoftimeredux/. Accessed 17 June 2010.

Wright, Elizabeth (2002) 'Wong Kar-wai', *Senses of Cinema*, Great Directors. Online at: http://archive.sensesofcinema.com/contents/directors/02/wong. html. Accessed 17 June 2010.

Yue, Audrey (2008) '*In the Mood for Love*: intersections of Hong Kong modernity', in Chris Berry (ed.) *Chinese Films in Focus II* (London, Palgrave Macmillan), pp.144–52.

Notes

1 The author thanks Angelina Karpovich for her thoughts on and assistance with East Asian film fandom.
2 The Chinese New Year season is traditionally a lucrative time for filmmakers in Hong Kong. The films released during this period tend to be commercially driven, and, in the spirit of the celebrations, either light-hearted comedies or blockbuster crowd-pleasers (see Pang 2002: 61–2).
3 'Gatefloat' refers to the slight wobble produced when the film strip is not aligned properly in the projector.

PART III

THE DIASPORIC
PROJECT

Chapter Seven

Beyond World Cinema? The Dialectics of Black British Diasporic Cinema

Rajinder Dudrah

How might we theorize and analyse Black British diasporic cinema in its relationship to world cinema? Is it better considered part of, or beyond, the discourses that have thus far attempted to map out world cinema? This chapter will offer an analysis of the diegetic possibilities that select post-1980s Black British diasporic cinema (of combined British, African, Caribbean and South Asian heritages) might engender as a way of understanding the relationship(s) between world and diasporic cinema. In order to do this I want to offer a reading of key segments of three selected films (*Southall, A Town Under Siege*, Colin Prescod, 1982; *Bhaji on the Beach*, Gurinder Chadha, 1993; and *Babymother*, Julian Henriques, 1998), through a theoretical exchange between the work of Lúcia Nagib (2006), Stephanie Dennison and Song Hwee Lim (2006), and Kobena Mercer (1994: 53–66, 69–96). This exchange will help set up both the relationship of world and diasporic cinema, and provide a useful framework to understand the contribution of Black British diasporic cinema to debates about race and nation – one of the central concerns of this cinema.[1]

Thinking World and Diasporic Cinemas Together

Let us begin with a definition of world cinema by Lúcia Nagib as a first step towards further discussion (Nagib 2006). Drawing on Ella Shohat and Robert Stam's original contribution to debates about and critique of multiculturalism in and through dominant global media and its images, Nagib, anticipating many of the concerns of the current volume, extended their idea of 'polycentric multiculturalism' (Shohat and Stam 1994: 48–9) to polycentric cinema. Nagib is keen to move away from thinking about world cinema in a binary relation to Hollywood cinema exclusively. For her, polycentric cinema is the 'inclusive method of a world made of interconnected cinemas' (Nagib 2006: 34), and she goes on in that 2006 essay persuasively to argue that:

> World cinema is simply the cinema of the world. It has no centre. It is not the other but it is us. It has no beginning and no end, but is a global process. World cinema, as the world itself, is circulation.
>
> World cinema is not a discipline, but a method, a way of cutting across film history according to waves of relevant films and movements, thus creating flexible geographies.
>
> As a positive, inclusive, democratic concept, world cinema allows all sorts of theoretical approaches, provided they are not based on the binary perspective. (Nagib 2006: 35)

Dennison and Lim (2006), developing debates on world cinema, in a related frame of inquiry to that of Nagib, make a case for making sense of diasporic cinema in a reciprocal relationship to world cinema. Arguing against one popular understanding of world cinema 'as the sum total of all of the national cinemas in the world', they argue that this perspective limits a take on world cinema by presupposing and privileging a notion of the nation or nation-state as fixed and bounded, which 'risks overlooking modes of film practices that include, among others, Third Cinema, women's or feminist cinema, queer cinema, and many regional, sub-state, transnational, diasporic and nomadic cinemas' (2006: 6–7). These cinemas pose a challenge to thinking in terms of exclusive claims on nation, race and ethnicity. This is an important standpoint in locating and interpreting diasporic cinema, and one that arises from an understanding of debates within Black British cinema.

Elaborating these discussions in relation to diasporic cinema, the work of Black British cultural critic Kobena Mercer (Mercer 1994: 53–66, 69–96) is fitting in this regard, not least his useful account of Black British diasporic cinema's trajectory postwar and especially since the 1980s. Mercer's work can be usefully situated in relation to a wider dialogue between other scholars, critics and activists interested in this period through the intellectual practice of Black British cultural studies (see, for instance, Hall 1981; Bhabha 1983; Gilroy 1983, 1987; Parmar 1990; West 1990; Baker, Diawara and Lindeborg 1996; Owusu 1999).

In a seminal essay, Mercer (1994: 53–66) argues persuasively about the interventionist and creative role of postwar Black British filmmakers, while also charting their history as emergent voices in British art and cultural production, since at least the 1960s, when filmmakers Lloyd Reckford, Lionel Ngakane and

Horace Ove, amongst other artists, were producing work. More interested in the period broadly across the years of the 1980s, Mercer documents the emergence of a generation of cinematic activists through production companies such as Ceddo, Sankofa, Retake and the Black Audio Film Collective; all working in and focusing on issues in British cities, not least to do with race and nation. Their work is described as part of a 'cultural struggle in the domain of image-making' over Black and white representations and their historical relations, and also where the complexities rather than homogeneity of Black experiences in Britain begin to emerge (Mercer 1994: 55).

One film of the time which has received particular critical acclaim since its release is *Handsworth Songs* (Black Audio Collective, 1986). It deals with the fallout from the riots that occurred in Lozzells Road, Birmingham in 1985. Not all of its reviews were positive, however. Mercer traces how it received a negative response from Salman Rushdie and stirred a brief debate amongst Black British critics in the pages of *The Guardian* newspaper – Rushdie was supported, in part, by Darcus Howe, though critically taken to task by Stuart Hall. At the heart of this exchange was a tussle over claims to the validity of political realism in representations about Black people, which Rushdie in his review was claiming to know more about – to this end his article was aptly titled 'Songs doesn't know the score'. Hall and others, as well as the commentary of Mercer (1994), felt differently and in fact argued that what is missing is a viable tradition of critical appreciation that can make sense of the emergence of Black British film, especially during the course of the 1980s, as in dialogue with and drawing on a dual inheritance from both Third World and First World filmmaking cultures (Mercer 1994: 54–5). Mercer goes on to argue, using films by these 1980s Black British filmmakers as examples, that to think usefully about black film criticism is to recognize that such a tradition does not yet fully exist. He argues for using the films themselves as a way to interrogate both Eurocentric discourses about aesthetics vis-à-vis film language, and at the same time using the films as ways of intervening in white modernist representations of the emergence of the Black subject (see also Mercer 1994).

Mercer posits a useful critique, informed by the cutting edge of Black British cultural studies, that seeks to uncover and dismantle white-black binaries and suggest alternative ways of framing and considering representation. Using Mercer, then, as a way of adding actual texture to and elaborating on the arguments of Nagib (2006), and Dennison and Lim (2006), builds a useful tripartite framework to dismantle a hierarchical or binary-based notion of world cinema, and simultaneously to demonstrate through cultural critique and analysis the issues at play in making sense of Black British diasporic cinema. My three films have been chosen for the following reasons. Firstly, that each of them, in related yet different ways, helps us to see, after Nagib, that world cinema is not the other, but it is us. It has no beginning and no end, but is a global process and, like the world itself, is in circulation. This is especially the case for *Southall, A Town Under Siege* (Colin Prescod, 1982), as I will argue in relation to its screening at a Black arts and cultural centre in Birmingham, UK. Secondly, they remind us through their sounds and images of the fallacy in privileging a notion of the nation or nation-state as fixed and bounded in racial terms, in and through media representation. And thirdly, they are different examples of the eclecticism in Black British diasporic filmmaking, that through their film form and audiovisual representations allow us to decipher statements about modern Black Britons as subjects in diaspora.

Southall, A Town Under Siege at The Drum, Birmingham

Southall, A Town Under Siege is one of four films by Prescod, collectively titled *Struggles for Black Community*. Commissioned by Channel 4 in its early radical television heyday, these films mark the presence of Black British communities in pre- and postwar, Britain and explicitly acknowledge their contribution in the social uprisings and remaking of modern-day urban life. This particular historical film focuses on how Southall organized resisting racist and fascist attacks between 1976 and 1981. Southall's militancy had been initiated by community organizations of the 1950s, created to help Black workers combat racism in the workplace, as well as to deal with discrimination in the community; and as state racism increased, the community fashioned new weapons of struggle (see also Campaign Against Racism 1981 on this history).

In October 2009 the film was shown at the Drum, a multipurpose centre for Black British arts and culture in the inner-city area of Aston, Birmingham. The screening was followed by an audience discussion with the film director (Figure 1).[2] It was a weekday evening, and about 25 people, Asian, black, white, mixed race, late-teens and adults, both men and women, had gathered to see the film, and meet and discuss with Prescod afterwards. Prescod was introduced by Pervaiz Khan, Artistic Director of the performing arts company Duende, who has long been involved in community politics and Black arts in Birmingham. There was a noticeable camaraderie between the two, already colleagues and friends, and Khan was pleased to have been able to invite the director to the Drum. Prescod spoke briefly, introducing the film, but also the importance of the place and space where it was being shown. Prescod was involved with others in the setting up of the Drum in the late 1990s, and referenced it as an important and unique venue, 'one of its only kind left in Britain' that was still operating in an inclusive and progressive sense of the term of Black in the creative fields, attempting to bring together different members of Birmingham's diverse populace to think about key and pressing issues, not least to do with race and nation, through arts and culture.

Figure 1   Advert for the screening of Colin Prescod's film, as displayed on the Drum's website

Prescod also addressed the issue of Black History Month in the UK, within which his film was being shown. He echoed an argument (one that has been made in the USA, the originating home of Black History Month) that Black History is not just about celebrating the lives and exploits of a few key individuals, or taking stock of Black heritage for one month in the year. For cultural commentators like Prescod, Black History does not, and should not, exist as a separate thing. When Black History is disconnected from other history and held up for display for a limited time, it runs the risk of speaking only to a narrow nationalism and can distort the nature of the very contribution it claims to celebrate. Following these poignant words, and others, the film's DVD was screened onto a large canvas.

I am guessing from my observations of the audience's body language and responses that most present were familiar, or at the very least aware, in general terms, of the history that Prescod was referring to, and on which his film was based. There was a sense too that the audience comprised of community workers, intellectuals, students, teachers and local people from Birmingham, who had come to watch and partake in a retelling and re-showing of this slice of postwar history. Documentary footage taken by the filmmaker was edited and juxtaposed against white media documentary clips of far-right political parties, such as the British National Party, to more mainstream parties such as Labour and the Conservatives, all concerning the impact of perceived ills of non-white immigration on economic resources and the culture of British society. This was countered by Black figureheads (including an early Prescod himself), who argued and demonstrated the facts of Black immigration to Britain as helping rather than hindering the postwar economy. Such a hostile climate of dominant discourse and rhetoric, as weighted against mass non-white settlers, led, in part, to violent clashes in the street as racism was widespread in terms of access to housing, employment and other facets of public life (see Solomos and Back 1996; Solomos 2003). The strategy of the film is clear: it serves as a counter-discourse to conservative and inaccurate white ideologies, both in the use of alternative sounds and images, and in accounts of histories as recounted through the experiences of Black people themselves and facts about their lives. Mercer, observing the importance of Prescod's four films and the use of informed talking figureheads, surmises:

> This oral testimony combines with political analysis advanced by activists and intellectuals featured in the film to present an alternative definition of the situation. As *Struggles for Black Community* shows, the historicizing emphasis in such critical counter-discourse is an over determined necessity in order to counteract the de-historicizing logic of racist ideologies. (Mercer 1994: 57)

Prescod's *Southall* film, then, gives voice to those silenced and excluded by media racism, and in doing so recasts them as active agents in the making of postwar London. This was also a point that was saliently observed and appreciated by the film's audience in the post-screening discussion. In fact, the film prompted a healthy interchange of questions and answers between the filmmaker and those present, as well as exchanges, albeit brief, amongst the audiences themselves. Some of the subjects raised included the contemporary relevance of the term 'Black' as a political signifier, to the role of intellectuals and activists in community formation, to how best to disseminate these stories of struggle to wider sections of the British populace.

Having been part of this event, one had the impression that this was a small yet nonetheless important space where modern British history and representations of it, especially through the contributions of Black Britons, was recalled and reinstated through audiovisual exhibition and discussion. Placing Prescod's film alongside the critical commentary by Mercer (1994: 53–66) that supplements it, one begins to appreciate its impact and freshness even today. The film documents a recent and turbulent time in British culture and society, and – anticipating Mercer's commentary – offers a counter-hegemonic reading of the dominant white ideological story of race and immigration espoused by the far right, and even the state of the time. Watched in the light of the commentary, it bears out Mercer's assertion of the importance of tracking such films individually and collectively as part of an emergence of Black British film production since the postwar period, which crystallized in a debate about film form and critical readings about representation in the depiction of Black people. Granted, Mercer was interested in the political viability of a culture of independent Black filmmaking, while also concerned with the commercial success that such films ought to attain, or at the very least the existence of a media culture where they can be seen en masse. Whether or not this culture has been achieved, Mercer leaves us with a set of pressing points for consideration about Black British film form and its attendant representation that I take up further in relation to the other two films.

Bhaji on the Beach: **Blackness and Asianness**

Bhaji on the Beach was well received critically and went on to do well at the box office, securing the success and lasting popularity of its director, Gurinder Chadha, and its writer, Meera Syal. Critical commentary on the film has largely explored it in terms of postcolonial or diasporic cinema (Ciecko 1999), or more specifically in terms of a cultural studies reading of the emergence of British-Asian cultural identity (Bhattacharyya and Gabriel 1994). It has also largely been discussed in terms of narrative and theme as follows: a group of inter-generational South Asian women make a day trip from Birmingham to Blackpool, on their journey discovering each other, as well as coming to terms with their personal issues of British-Asian community, identity and belonging (Desai 2004: ch. 5). However, little attention has been paid to one of the key plots in the film, that of the interracial romance between the young South Asian woman Hashida (Sarita Khajuria) and her British Caribbean boyfriend Olly/Oliver (Mo Sesay); and it is this aspect of the story that I wish to take up.

Hashida and Oliver's love story is spread throughout the film over 11 key scenes or episodes, interspersed and edited alongside stories of the other female characters, blending into a coherent narrative film. The scenes can be broken down and briefly described thus. Scene 1: Hashida takes a pregnancy test and we discover the father of her child-to-be as Oliver. Scene 2: The couple meet at Olly's student flat and argue about their relationship, and whether to keep the child or have an abortion. Scene 3: Olly discusses the issue with his British Caribbean friend Joe (Fraser James), who advises Olly to leave Hashida. Scene 4: Hashida calls Olly from a pay-phone en-route to Blackpool, and they argue again due to a breakdown in communication. Scene 5: Olly discusses the matter with his father (Rudolph Walker), who strongly advises him to be a man and take responsibility for the situation, standing alongside Hashida. Scene 6: Olly goes to Hashida's parental home to find Hashida and then leaves for Blackpool on his motorbike. Scene 7: Hashida's pregnancy becomes public knowledge amongst the wider female group at Blackpool, and she receives mixed and even prejudicial responses from the women. Hashida retorts back. Scene 8: Hashida attends a family-planning clinic in Blackpool for advice about her pregnancy options. Scene 9: Olly finds and begins to reconcile with Hashida at an art gallery, where Hashida has paused for thought and comfort. Scene 10: Hashida and Olly reconcile as they kiss and make up near Blackpool pier. Scene 11: Hashida and Olly stay behind in Blackpool on Olly's motorbike, and wave goodbye to the women's group as they leave on their minibus.

Hashida and Oliver's romance is depicted from the outset through conventional strategies of narrative cinema, interlaced with inter-generic elements of social drama and comedy too. This humanizes their story as everyday, and as part of a set of socio-cultural issues that seek to explore the opening-up of Black identity as complex and non-homogenous by the early 1990s, especially in terms of black African, Caribbean and brown South Asian relationships. From the outset in scene 1, their relationship is depicted as socially fraught and secretive, due to Hashida's being unable to communicate freely and openly with Olly over the telephone – she has to quickly and nervously replace the handset as soon as she hears her mother calling off screen. In fact, the lack of communication between these two characters, throughout scenes 1, 2, 4 and 6, stands in as a wider preamble for difficulties between black and South Asian individuals, and sections of their communities as dealing with one another through mutual respect and understanding.

Scene 3 is also telling of this disconnection in social relations in the conversation between Olly and Joe, where Joe alludes to the dissolution of the notion of Black political subjectivity, when he claims that 'Black don't mean notwhite anymore', and laments the loss of respect between Asian and black groups in general terms. Stuart Hall usefully articulates this position for us in terms of Black British representation as 'the end of the innocent notion of the essential Black subject' and goes on to say:

> the end of the essential black subject is something which people are increasingly debating, but they may not have fully reckoned with its political consequences. What is at issue here is the extraordinary diversity of subjective positions, social experiences, and cultural identities which compose the category 'black'; that is, the recognition that 'black' is essentially a politically and culturally *constructed* category, which cannot be grounded in a set of fixed trans-cultural or transcendental racial categories and which therefore has no guarantees in Nature. What this brings into play is the recognition of the immense diversity and differentiation of the historical and cultural experience of black subjects. (Hall 1988: 28)

Chadha and her creative team are part of a movement in Black British film- and media-making, who have taken up and articulated such issues that Hall remarks upon. Rather than offer simple and easy representations that profess good Black subjects versus bad white ones, they look both between and beyond black and brown identities, as well as their political alliances, problems and heterogeneities, and seek to criss-cross between them.

Whereas in scene 3, Joe, another young black male contemporary of Olly's, tries to persuade him to forget the girl and move on, as the relationship has been difficult from the outset, scene 5 juxtaposes this with another viewpoint, that from Olly's father, who chastises Olly for so easily thinking of letting go of Hashida and leaving her to her own devices. His advice to his son is to deal with the issue head-on in terms of trying to understand that to marry an Asian girl is also to marry into family, even whilst acknowledging that Olly has been having a less than public relationship due to social prejudices. The film in this scene, and others, deals explicitly with how sections of both the black and South Asian communities might view each other, and, at times, can hold opposed but nevertheless similarly ultra-conservative positions. Hashida and Olly's romance presents this as drama and as dramatic possibility that might have the strength to overcome such obstacles. Scenes 8–11 attempt to audio-visualize just that.

While Hashida is taking advice from a health professional about her preg-nancy options, including possible abortion, Olly is seen searching for her along the seafront and riding the side streets of Blackpool on his motorbike in scene 8. This montage contains no dialogue and instead follows the characters in action, as they are at a sensitive crossroads in their partnership. What accom-panies this scene as its non-diegetic signifier is the song 'Mera Laung Gawacha' (My Lost Jewellery). This is a British Bhangra track, based on the lyrics of a very popular Punjabi folk song remixed by the British Asian artist Bally Sagoo, with female vocals sung by Jayshree and male vocals by artist Cheshire Cat.[3] The song is about a woman who has lost an item of jewellery (her nose piece), possibly through intimate action with her lover, and she sings to him to retrace their steps in order to try and retrieve the item before anybody else finds it. Not only is this song a fitting eulogy for the two protagonists in the film who are conducting their relationship in private, but also the genre of the music is a fit-ting companion to some of the themes the film raises. British Bhangra is an intermix of lyrics in Punjabi with snatches of English and Patois Dub catch-phrases, alongside musical sounds that fuse together the beats of the Indian drums – the *dhol*, *dholak* and *tablas* – with pop, reggae, RnB, rock and other musical sounds from around the world (Dudrah 2002, 2007). This song is an urban British-Punjabi-Ragga-Dub-based inflection, which professes multiple musical heritages and associated cultural identities simultaneously; and, further still, the male vocalist, Cheshire Cat, is a white-British singer who raps in a predominantly black-identified lyrical form, thereby complicating further and disrupting issues of fixed and bounded identities. The track is a deliberate placement therefore, meant to extend the film's advocacy of mixed-race rela-tionships, and their new possibilities through the black and brown male and female characters.

Scenes 9 to 11 also extend this cultural diplomacy, and use the genre of romance as it articulates with modern Black British sensibilities and South Asian filmic conventions associated with the romantic couple. Scene 9 pres-ents Hashida taking refuge for pause and contemplation in an art gallery, where an exhibition of the British portrait artist Mervyn Peake is on display. Hashida, in fact, inspired by Peake, is seen earlier as having drawn pictures of Olly and herself which adorn his student flat, and art is clearly one of her passions. Olly

Figure 2   Hashida and Olly are united amidst the colourful backdrop
of Blackpool illuminations

also turns to the gallery to search for Hashida after seeing a poster advertising the exhibition. Two kindred spirits, then, are seen to slowly regain each other: Olly gets down on his knees and makes a gentle gesture of reconciliation, while caressing her fingers as tears slowly roll down her cheeks. The medium shot and gentle capturing of this scene, in the predominantly white gallery space, creates a contemporary and subtle mood of genuine affection, while also placing our protagonists as very British *and* Black subjects, who are inflected both by popular art forms such as hybrid Bhangra music (scene 8) as well as modern art. Scenes 10 and 11 use the Blackpool illuminations to offer a colourful backdrop to the dark evening setting, which is heightened as an aesthetic cause for celebration with the couple reaffirming their commitment to each other. Upbeat contemporary British music, mixing light jazz with minor orchestral compositions, and subtle tabla and Bhangra basslines, carry these three scenes, ending on a high by scenes 10 and 11. The music here, as well as elsewhere in the film, has been crafted by composers John Altman and Craig Pruess, with additional music from Kuljit Bhamra who has also composed for British Bhangra artistes. Here, vibrant colours and music, suggesting merriment and togetherness, draw on a tradition in popular South Asian filmmaking where the same signs and codes are often used; not least in, say, Bollywood cinema (see Gopal and Moorti 2008) (Figure 2).

Babymother

This film is one that has not been widely written about, certainly less so than *Bhaji on the Beach* (see Moseley-Wood 2004). *Babymother* was co-funded by Channel 4 Films, with Lottery money from the Arts Council of England and Formation Films, which was headed by the film's director Julian Henriques and producer Parminder Vir. It was made with a budget of £2 million, which it was unable to recuperate from either box office-returns or video-rental sales. The film was given financial backing to produce it, but next to no budget was set aside for its publicity, nationally or internationally. Nonetheless, it is a vibrant film about black popular music, inner-city life and the struggles of its central black female character. Anita (Anjela Lauren-Smith) is the baby-mother, a young woman in her early 20s with two young children. She lives on a run-down housing estate in north-west London, and dreams of becoming a successful ragga and dancehall artist, together with her two friends Sharon (Caroline Chikezie) and Yvette (Jocelyn Esien). However, a number of obstacles stand in her way (Figure 3).

Anita not only has to struggle as a single unemployed mother, but also has to negotiate the social expectations placed on her by her partner Byron (Wil Johnson). Byron is an established ragga performer, and while he recognizes Anita's talent and potential, he wants her to be his babymother, not a dance-hall artiste. The rapport between the two characters is lively and, at times, feisty. They sing to and dance with each other alongside their narrative dialogues. In one scene, where Byron tries to make up with Anita after diss-ing her at a dancehall performance, having earlier promised her she could sing along-side him, Byron sings to Anita softly and romantically, aiming to appease her through a serenade. Anita is with her friends, Sharon and Yvette, and they dismiss Byron, replying in a tart ragga comeback in which Anita hits out lyrically and musically against Byron's earlier deception and chauvinism for not being able to accept her as a female artiste.

The film also draws attention to its setting in north-west London, a place that is important as an urban conduit for ideas of diaspora to flow through and be nuanced within a British setting. Harlesden and its surrounding areas are figured from the opening credits, and through the sights and sounds and the different characters that we encounter throughout the filmic diegesis. Caribbean dialects are mixed and spoken with a north London vernacular slang: 'safe, whagwaan, innit'. The audience is witness to a changing social landscape of urban Britain and London in particular, albeit one still largely entrenched in issues of race and class. This is further heightened and coupled with the film's recourse to a double strategy of filmic discourse, combining both a British social realist tradition of media-making with Black British forms of expression. The credits open to a refrain of ragga music and lyrics, celebrating the female form

Figure 3   *DVD cover of* Babymother, *with its three central female
friends in ragga and dancehall dress*

and Black feminist sensibilities, as Anita promenades proudly and playfully in
loud dancehall regalia through the high street with her children in hand. Her
friends and passers-by join in and cheer her on, as they celebrate in and become
the everyday of the street. As the credits start to draw to a close, a trumpet
plays thoughtful and mindful mid-to-long notes over the ragga music, interlac-
ing a reference to the mundanity of everyday working- and lower-class life in
Britain. The two references are drawn together to form an aesthetic which
incorporates a postwar British social-class perspective that is framed by and will

be dealt with, during the course of the film, through Black British popular cultural forms.

The dancehall (as dance floor/music genre) also features as a central space throughout the film, not least as where Anita wants to make her name. She has a dancing stand-off with her female rival Dionne (Tameka Empson), struggles with her partner and promoters to perform on stage, and by the film's climax the dancehall is the extended space where for several minutes Anita and her partners, Sharon and Yvette ('Neeta, Sweeta and Nastie'), take on Byron in front of a live audience in a dancehall singing-off competition. The dancehall, then, is an outlet for the performance of the social self, for women to put on a show alongside and in relation to men, for Caribbean diaspora-infused fashion styles to be worn large, and celebratory costumes to be shown off and seen in, and where issues in heterosexual gender and sexual politics can be figured in dance and explicitly sung out loud.[4] The camera is highly mobile here, working in between and amongst the crowd, capturing their active participation in the event as they too dance, hoot and holler, along with and against the performers. Fast-edit cuts switch the scene from the MC on stage to the crowd, from the standpoint of the camera as the live audience, to the artistes on stage, and back again. The call and response, and the showdown lyrics and dance moves between Neeta and Byron, are juxtaposed with the crowd on the dance floor and the promoters at the side of the stage, culminating in a tense moment of performance and anticipation, until Neeta emerges victorious.

A simple and conventional narrative tale, then, broadly located within the genre of British social realism, is also aestheticized and audiovisually conveyed through the strategies and styles of Black British vernacular cultures.

Beyond World Cinema?

At the outset of this chapter, in its title and its opening remarks, related questions were posed about the relationship between world and Black British diasporic cinema. The dialectic of Black British diasporic cinema helps us to consider both 'Black/-ness' *and* 'British/-ness' as not mutually exclusive, in racial or cultural terms, but as articulated together to produce versions of themselves anew in and through audio and visual representation. The versions we get to see and hear in Black British diasporic cinema are partly to do with issues of history (colonialism, race, racism, power), and, at times, its ideological misuses positing Black and white groups in dominant and subordinate relationships, which are then re-cast and re-presented (*Southall, A Town Under Siege*); partly to do with definitions about Blackness itself, and, at times, the fraught social relationships between black and brown social groups that have historically comprised a postwar political term of resistance (*Bhaji on the Beach*); and partly to do with contemporary issues of social identities expressed through popular culture as evidence of diasporic British identities (*Babymother*). Black British cinema is also always an engagement with the modern Black and British complex subject, in and through aesthetic, socio-cultural and political enunciation using the repertoire of cinematic aural and visual signs and signifiers, deployed strategically and simultaneously.

If a concept of polycentric world cinema is a democratic one which enables us to see, hear and experience the world and its cinemas as interconnected and interrelated (Nagib 2006: 34–5), then Black British diasporic cinema is very much part of this, while also striving to extend the intellectual and conceptual configurations of this term, and to move it beyond its current parameters.

References

Alexander, Claire (2002) 'Beyond black: re-thinking the colour/culture divide', *Ethnic and Racial Studies* 25:4, pp.552–71.

Baker, Houston, Manthia Diawara and Ruth Lindeborg (eds) (1996) *Black British Cultural Studies: A Reader* (Chicago, University of Chicago Press).

Bhabha, Homi (1983) 'The other question: the stereotype and colonial discourse', *Screen* 24, pp.18–36.

Bhattacharyya, Gargi and John Gabriel (1994) 'Gurinder Chadha and the Apna Generation', *Third Text* (Summer), pp.55–63.

Campaign Against Racism and Fascism/Southall Rights (1981) *Southall: The Birth of a Black Community* (London, Institute of Race Relations).

Ciecko, Anne (1999) 'Representing the spaces of diaspora in contemporary British Films by women directors', *Cinema Journal* 38:3, pp.67–90.

Cooper, Carolyn and Alison Donnell (eds) (2004) *Interventions. International Journal of Postcolonial Studies*, Special Topic: Jamaican Popular Culture, vol. 6, n.1.

Dennison, Stephanie and Song Hwee Lim (eds) (2006) *Remapping World Cinema. Identity, culture and politics in film* (London, Wallflower Press).

Desai, Jigna (2004) *Beyond Bollywood: The Cultural Politics of Diasporic South Asian Film* (New York, Routledge).

Dudrah, Rajinder (2002) 'Drum N Dhol: British bhangra music and diasporic South Asian identity formation', *European Journal of Cultural Studies* 5:3, pp.363–83.

Dudrah, Rajinder (2007) *Bhangra: Birmingham and Beyond* (Birmingham, Punch Records and Birmingham City Council).

Gilroy, Paul (1983) 'Channel 4: Bridgehead or Bantustan', *Screen* 24, pp.130–6.

Gilroy, Paul (1987) *There Ain't No Black in The Union Jack* (London, Unwin Hyman).

Gutzmore, Cecil (2004) 'Casting the first stone! Policing of homo/sexuality in Jamaican popular culture', *Interventions. International Journal of Postcolonial Studies* 6:1, pp.118–34.

Hall, Stuart (1981) 'The whites of their eyes: racist ideologies and the media', in George Bridges and Rosalind Brunt (eds) *Silver Linings* (London, Lawrence & Wishart).

Hall, Stuart (1988) 'New ethnicities', in Kobena Mercer (ed.) *Black Film, British Cinema*, ICA Documents 7 (London, Institute of Contemporary Arts), pp.27–31.

Hippolyte, Idara (2004) 'Collapsing the oral-literary continuum: Jamaican dancehall and anglophone Caribbean literary culture', *Interventions. International Journal of Postcolonial Studies* 6:1, pp.82–100.

Hope, Donna P. (2004) 'The British link-up crew: consumption masquerading as masculinity in the dancehall', *Interventions. International Journal of Postcolonial Studies* 6:1, pp.101–17.

Mercer, Kobena (1994) *Welcome to the Jungle. New Positions in Black Cultural Studies* (London/New York, Routledge).

Moorti, Sujata and Sangita Gopal (eds) (2008) *Global Bollywood. Travels of Hindi Song and Dance* (Minneapolis, University of Minnesota Press).

Moseley-Wood, Rachel (2004) '"Colonizin Englan in Reverse" – Julian Henriques' *Babymother*', *Visual Culture in Britain* 5:1, pp.91–104.

Nagib, Lúcia (2006) 'Towards a positive definition of world cinema', in Dennison and Song (2006), pp.30–7.

Owusu, Kwesi (ed.) (1999) *Black British Culture and Society: A Text Reader* (London, Routledge).

Parmar, Pratibha (1990) 'Black feminism: the politics of articulation', in Jonathan Rutherford (ed.) *Identity, Community, Difference* (London, Lawrence & Wishart).

Shohat, Ella and Robert Stam (1994) *Unthinking Eurocentrism: Multiculturalism and the Media* (London/New York, Routledge).

Solomos, John (2003) *Race and Racism in Britain* (London, Palgrave Macmillan).

Solomos, John and Les Back (1996) *Racism and Society* (Basingstoke/New York, Palgrave Macmillan).

West, Cornel (1990) 'The new cultural politics of difference', in Russel Ferguson, Martha Gever, Trinh T. Minh-ha and Cornel West (eds) *Out There: Marginalization and Contemporary Cultures* (New York, The New Museum of Contemporary Art), pp.19–38.

Notes

1 The term 'Black British' is used in its postwar British usage as a collective term referring to a political identity of resistance and renewal. Here a notion of Black British political identity is formulated through the similar experiences of racial discrimination and strategies of anti-racism amongst African, Caribbean and South Asian social groups. It is in this context that I use the term 'Black' throughout this chapter (with a capital B to refer to political identity), but where necessary I distinguish some of the social and cultural particularities between the different groups concerned as black African and Caribbean (with a lowercase b), Asian/South Asian in terms of ethnic origin, region and cultural practices. This is also how the term has been used and engaged with by Black British cultural critics and filmmakers, as I will demonstrate in the chapter. For an account of the history of Black British political identity, see Alexander (2002).

2 The Drum and Duende presents *Struggles for Black Community: Southall, A Town under Siege* (1982), Thursday 29 October 2009, 7pm. For details of the event as it was advertised on the Drum's website, see: www.the-drum.org.uk/event/struggles-for-black-community-southall-a-town-under-siege; last accessed 20 June 2010. See also www.the-drum.org.uk/about-us.

3 The song is taken from Bally Sagoo's 1992 album *Essential Ragga*, produced and distributed by Oriental Star Agencies in Birmingham.

4 On the styles and conventions of the dancehall as genre and performance, see, for instance, the special journal issue of *Interventions* edited by Carolyn Cooper and Alison Donnell (2004), and in particular the essays by Hippolyte (2004) on oral and literary cultures in the music, Hope (2004) on the performance of masculinity in the genre, and Gutzmore (2004), who addresses the performance of homophobia in dancehall while also suggesting other implicit queer possibilities.

Chapter Eight

Speaking in Tongues: Ang Lee, Accented Cinema, Hollywood[1]

Song Hwee Lim

Recent scholarship in film studies has increasingly acknowledged the limitations of the 'national cinema' paradigm to the extent that, if it is not entirely jettisoned, it must at least be problematized, rather than taken as a self-evidential category of analysis (Higson 2000). Several other conceptual categories have been mooted in its place, including transnational cinema, world cinema and accented cinema (encompassing exilic and diasporic cinemas), all of which highlight the various forms of filmmaking practice that cross national borders, and unsettle the notion of the national from both within and without. In an age of globalization that has witnessed massive migration of peoples, capital, cultures and ideologies, the national (and national cinema) can no longer sustain its myth of unity, coherence and purity. Rather, the disjunctive order of the global cultural economy (Appadurai 1990) must be brought to bear on the specificities of each case study of national and cross-border filmmaking activity.

All the above categories, implicitly or explicitly, are engaged in a 'dialogue' with Hollywood (Cooke 2007), a cinema which remains a dominant force in the production, distribution and exhibition of mainstream, commercial films in many parts of the world. Whether we like it or not, Hollywood, as a 'shorthand for a massively industrial, ideologically reactionary, and stylistically conservative form of "dominant" cinema' (Shohat and Stam 1994: 7), is often embedded in the discursive construction of these new categories of analysis, at times as the undesired Other to be distinguished against, or otherwise as an unmentionable shadow lurking in the dark. My intention to bring Hollywood into play in this chapter is both borne out of theoretical and conceptual imperatives as much as a strategic one, because my focus here is the Taiwanese director Ang

Lee, whose career has been based in the United States from the very beginning. While Lee can variously be claimed as a national (Taiwanese) director, a transnational Chinese director, a world cinema director and an accented (diasporic) director, I believe all these categories cannot be fully accounted for unless we also consider his career in the United States, where he has directed films (including a blockbuster) in a globally dominant mode of production. Speaking in multiple tongues, Ang Lee epitomizes a director who can not only move between different cinemas, but is also simultaneously located in all of them, thus exposing these categories of analysis as neither mutually exclusive nor all-encompassing.

More importantly, via the example of Ang Lee's career, I want to rethink the notion of accented cinema which, in Hamid Naficy's construction at least (2001), only concerns itself with filmmaking activities situated in an exilic or diasporic condition emerging from migratory routes from Third World and postcolonial societies to Western cosmopolitan centres. I propose to reconfigure Naficy's restrictive definition and narrow specificity, which 'preclude full realization of its critical potential' (Suner 2006: 377), in three ways. First, that the route of migration for accented directors should not be limited to a hierarchical one from the Third World to the First World, and this will be illustrated through the specificity of modern Chinese and Taiwanese history; second, what happens to the notion of accented cinema when a filmmaker from the Third World begins making films in the mode of 'dominant cinema ... without accent' (Naficy 2001: 4) such as Hollywood? Finally, instead of being assumed as having no accent, Hollywood must be reconceptualized as bearing an accent that has been, for historical reasons, dominant to an extent that it passes as universal (read unaccented) in many parts of the world, including Taiwan where Lee grew up, when it is just as culturally specific and accented as any other cinema. As a result of this interrogation, the very notion of 'accent', and the discourses and mechanisms that sustain the distinction between accented and non-accented cinemas, will also be challenged.

Accented Cinema: Ang Lee as Diasporic Director

At the time of writing, Ang Lee has made 11 feature films, five of which are in Chinese languages (including Mandarin, Shanghainese and Cantonese) and the other six in English languages (including British English and American English). It is noteworthy that Lee started his career very much in the mode of a national cinema director. His first three films, *Pushing Hands* (*Tuishou*, 1992), *The Wedding Banquet* (*Xiyan*, 1993) and *Eat Drink Man Woman* (*Yinshi nannü*, 1994), popularly known as the 'father knows best' trilogy, were made under the aegis of Taiwan's Central Motion Picture Corporation (CMPC) and benefited from national schemes of sponsorship.[2] While Lee's career dovetails with those of first-generation Taiwan New Cinema directors such as Hou Hsiao-hsien and Edward Yang, who made their mark in the 1980s, Lee's first two films do not share their obsession with Taiwan's history, modernity and society, but are diegetically located outside Taiwan and attempt to give voice to a diasporic experience.

Indeed, *Pushing Hands* and *The Wedding Banquet* fit comfortably in Naficy's notion of an accented cinema, with 'amphibolic, doubled, crossed, and lost characters; subject matter and themes that involve journeying, historicity, identity, and displacement; dysphoric, euphoric, nostalgic, synaesthetic, liminal, and politicized structures of feeling; interstitial and collective modes of production; and inscription of the biographical, social, and cinematic (dis)location of the filmmakers' (Naficy 2001: 4), being the hallmarks of these films. *Pushing Hands* traces an elderly father's journey from mainland China to the United States to live with his son, his American daughter-in-law and their son, only for him to end up moving into a dingy flat in Chinatown to live by himself owing to the difficulties he faces in communicating with his daughter-in-law and in adapting to a new environment. *The Wedding Banquet* opens with the disembodied voice of a mother from Taiwan addressing her son in New York, in the form of a letter recorded in an audiotape, exemplifying the epistolary narrative form highlighted by Naficy (2001: 5), while the message in the voiceover sets the stage for a conflict between the parents' wish for their son to get married and have children to carry on the family name, and the son's homosexuality. Set in the United States, these two films can thus be categorized as diasporic cinema for their thematic concern with the negotiation of cross-cultural and intergenerational conflicts arising from a condition of diaspora. They also conflate categories and cross-national boundaries insofar as they simultaneously belong to a national cinema and a diasporic cinema, raising questions about the relation between the national and the diasporic, from filmmaking practices and historical trajectories to individual and collective subjectivities.

The example of Lee's first two films is symptomatic of a larger question about the position of Taiwan cinema in relation to questions of the national and the diasporic because of Taiwan's jagged modern history.[3] Taiwan came under Japanese occupation in 1895 as a result of China's Qing regime's defeat in its war with the Japanese. Following Japan's surrender in 1945 at the end of the Second World War, Taiwan was 'returned' to a China then under Nationalist (Kuomintang, or KMT) rule. When the Nationalist Party lost its civil war with the Chinese Communist Party (CCP) in 1949, it retreated and established the Republic of China (ROC) on Taiwan, bringing with it a displaced population of about 1.3 million people who became known in Taiwan as *waishengren*, literally people from outer provinces. The native Taiwanese, including Han Chinese, who have settled on the island since the seventeenth century and are known as *benshengren* (literally people from this province), and the indigenous aboriginal population, were effectively doubly colonized, first by the Japanese, then by a mainland-Chinese regime technically still at war with the People's Republic of China (PRC) which occupies the mainland.

In light of this history, films produced under the ruling Nationalist Party in Taiwan, with CMPC as its cinematic apparatus, can be regarded as a diasporic or exilic cinema, though this is a potentially controversial claim that has, as far as I am aware, yet to be made by film scholars or historians. Nevertheless, the Nationalist regime has been a *de facto* government-in-exile which imposed martial law in Taiwan from 1949 to 1987, and the Party remains open to talks of reunification with the CCP, in contradistinction to the nativist, pro-independence Democratic Progressive Party (DPP) which took over political power from the Nationalists between 2000 and 2008. With regard to film production, CMPC's mandate was 'to make films that promoted a nationhood authorized and governed by the Nationalist party' (Yeh and Davis 2005: 18, 25). In particular, films produced by the CMPC in the 1960s and 1970s tended to idealize an imagined homeland located not on the island that the KMT regime then occupied, but on the much larger piece of land that it wished to return to.

While Lee was born in Taiwan in 1954, his status as a second-generation *waishengren* arguably places him within this diasporic cinema in terms of its linguistic and cultural orientation. It is no surprise that Lee's 'father knows best' trilogy is mainly spoken in Mandarin, the language imposed by the KMT regime on Taiwan. Unlike films by Hou Hsiao-hsien, Wang Tung, Wu Nien-jen and Chang Cho-chi, which engage with a native Taiwan culture deeply influenced by 50 years of Japanese colonization, and often spoken in Holo and Hakka (regional languages spoken by the *benshengren* communities),[4] Lee's trilogy largely represents a *waishengren* experience of diaspora and displacement (in the case of the first two films, a double displacement, first from mainland China to Taiwan, then from Taiwan to the USA). *Pushing Hands* and *The Wedding Banquet* adhere to Naficy's concept of accented cinema, tracing the journey of a Third World film-maker to the Western cosmopolitan centre of New York. However, the cinema produced by an exilic state apparatus such as CMPC, and by directors who continue its legacy, must surely be a diasporic/exilic cinema in essence if not yet in name. The representation of the *waishengren* community in Lee's trilogy (particularly his only film set in Taiwan, *Eat Drink Man Woman*), while categorically different from the propagandist and nationalistic films churned out by CMPC in the heyday of the Cold War era, can nonetheless be situated within this expanded sense of accented cinema whose historical consciousness and structure of feeling originate from a (main)land that has become increasingly mystified as the possibility of the mission to return diminishes with time,[5] and whose spoken tongue clearly carries accents located in provinces outside of Taiwan.

Therefore, via the examples of the KMT regime and Ang Lee's trilogy, I want to extend Naficy's narrow definition of accented cinema to include different kinds of migratory routes that are not hierarchically structured between the so-called First and Third Worlds. This extension is necessary, I would argue, because it not only undermines the (post)colonial logic inherent in Naficy's construction, but also highlights other relations of power, other 'scattered hegemonies' (Grewel and Kaplan 1994) that have hitherto been neglected in scholarship in film studies precisely because they do not fit neatly into existing theoretical models; their historical realities are too messy; or they are located in places that simply fall outside the radar of producers of knowledge based in Anglo-American and Eurocentric institutions. The intriguingly intra-national route such as that taken by the KMT regime, which left behind a nation-state only to establish another across the Taiwan Strait, has produced a hegemonic cinema that is at once national and diasporic, indeed a national cinema in diasporic/exilic form. Lee's 'father knows best' trilogy, while representing experiences of the Chinese and Taiwanese diasporas in the United States and Taiwan, is also an exilic cinema that is spoken in a decidedly different accent in the context of Taiwan's lived reality, where the majority of the population speaks a different tongue (Holo).

The examples of the KMT regime and Ang Lee's trilogy demonstrate that, far from operating in an interstitial and artisanal mode of production (Naficy 2001: 40–62), an accented cinema that travels within the Third World (indeed, within a 'nation'), rather than from the Third World to the First World, can occupy an official, hegemonic position that benefits from state sponsorship while exercising its own powers of censorship and control. Moreover, this broadened definition of diasporic/accented cinema could take into account an intra-Asian journey, such as that of the Malaysian-born Tsai Ming-liang who has based his entire career in Taiwan, highlighting issues about the status of the Chinese population and its languages in Malaysia, and about Chineseness as a transnational imaginary. It could also include directors whose careers are based in their homelands but whose films exhibit diasporic and/or exilic thematic concerns and styles, such as Bahman Ghobadi, Wong Kar-wai and Nuri Bilge Ceylan (Suner 2006), exploring different configurations of relations between the homes and the diasporic spaces. This extended notion of accented cinema can more fully consider all kinds of migratory routes, irrespective of their origins and destinations, debunking the hierarchical (post)colonial logic whilst being always attentive to the power dynamics embedded in these cross-border activities.

Speaking in Tongues: Ang Lee as Hollywood Director

Ang Lee made his first foray into English-language filmmaking with *Sense and Sensibility* in 1995. Indeed, Lee's career post-'father knows best' trilogy has been mainly in a different tongue, as he followed *Sense and Sensibility* with five more

English-language films (*The Ice Storm*, 1997; *Ride with the Devil*, 1999; *Hulk*, 2003; *Brokeback Mountain*, 2005; *Taking Woodstock*, 2009), and he has made only two more Chinese-language films since (*Crouching Tiger, Hidden Dragon* (*Wohu canglong*, 2000); *Lust, Caution* (*Se, jie*, 2007)). In this sense, Lee's filmmaking trajectory is not that dissimilar from those of émigré directors past and present, who have forged a new career in Hollywood making films in a language different from their mother tongue. While Naficy notes the careers of those he calls 'great transplanted directors', such as Alfred Hitchcock, Douglas Sirk and F.W. Murnau (2001: 19), his exclusive focus on filmmaking practices that are marked by displacement, decentredness and deterritorialization fails to illuminate the trajectories of transplanted filmmakers whose careers in Hollywood negotiated a different set of dynamics, that of acculturation, integration and reterritorialization. In other words, Naficy is more concerned with filmmakers who bring their accents to, and who preserve their displaced selfhoods in, their host countries. This theoretical model, however, does not adequately address filmmakers such as Ang Lee, who have spoken in different tongues and accents in the process of being assimilated and becoming the other.

Given that Taiwan was shielded by the United States during the Cold War era, the process of acculturation may have begun even before one has travelled to the other shore. In the case of Ang Lee, Shu-mei Shih proposes that knowledge of American culture has become a given for educated Taiwanese, 'to the extent that a national subject from Taiwan can be readily transformed into a minority subject in the US' (Shih 2000: 91). Doubly displaced, Lee has emphasized in an interview his identity as a second-generation mainlander, and the alienation that this group feels in Taiwan and in the United States (Berry 2005: 331–2). Multiple displacements, however, can be both a consequence of and a condition for what Aihwa Ong terms 'flexible citizenship' (1999), and it is precisely this flexibility that has made possible Lee's versatile career.

What does it entail to be flexible, especially in relation to speaking in a different language and working in a different film industry? Lee has spoken candidly about how he struggled to command respect while directing *Sense and Sensibility*, this being his first English-language film and set in a time and place that were unfamiliar to him, and how Emma Thompson and the production designer gave him tutelage in the art and history of the Regency period (Berry 2005: 338). Lee's first attempt to speak in a different tongue reveals an unequal power relation, for to acquire a new language or to put on a different accent is to place oneself constantly in the inferior position of being judged, scrutinized, examined. Like passing a test, one has to also pass as native/authentic, in much the same way that actors and actresses have to sound convincing when playing roles set in a different context, or transgendered people trying to pass as the other gender in appearance and mannerism. This position, however, is a double-edged one, as one's acquisition of the accent/language could be judged to have passed (in both senses) and thus welcomed into the host family, or the remnants of one's original accent/language could be celebrated under the logic of multi-culturalism so that one's cultural difference is not perceived as a hindrance to integration, but, paradoxically, as hybridizing and rejuvenating the host culture.

I believe the latter dynamic underpins much of the reception of Lee's English-language films so that, despite Lee hailing from a neo-colonial Taiwan heavily influenced by popular culture of the United States and his film school training in New York, the reading of some of his films, notwithstanding their seemingly all-American themes, is invariably coloured by his cultural differ-ence, his otherness. For example, while Lee claims that he does not divide his work between Chinese film and American film (Berry 2005: 338), scholars, critics and journalists clearly enjoy finding links between them. One of the key tropes for discussing Lee's films has been Confucianism, especially in relation to patriarchal ideology. This may be understandable in the context of the 'father knows best' trilogy, but the trope of Confucianism persists nonetheless, ranging from analysis of Lee's subsequent films, such as Hulk (Marchetti 2009), to a work ethic ('sincerity and diligent craftsmanship') that Lee purportedly brings to Hollywood (Yeh and Davis 2005: 13). Elsewhere, Chris Berry (2007) has written on 'The Chinese Side of the [Brokeback] Mountain'. Such kinds of reading unwittingly imply that Lee could never attain full membership as an American director, his identity forever hyphenated, his Chineseness valorized, even though his film style may adhere more fully, to borrow the title of David Bordwell's book (2006), to 'the way Hollywood tells it' than to the accented style in Naficy's construction.

To more fully appreciate Lee's modus operandi in Hollywood, it is worth considering the different modes of production that Lee has engaged in since making Sense and Sensibility. The budget for Hulk, at a staggering $160 million (Berry 2005: 325), was more than 200 times the budget for The Wedding Banquet, made for a mere $750,000. A much bigger budget, however, could also mean less autonomy and control over both his source materials and the end products; for example, the studios decided not to grant Ride with the Devil and The Ice Storm full theatrical release or promotional support in the United States, resulting in these being the least well-known of his films (Berry 2005: 338). In addition, Lee has stopped making films based on his own scripts since the post-'father knows best' trilogy period, as he claims he wrote scripts in his early career only because nobody was giving them to him (2005: 339). Both of these factors – changing industrial condition and withdrawal from writing credits – have had the effect of undercutting Lee's personal imprint on his films.

To identify Lee's authorial signature would require, in the spirit of earlier studies of Hollywood directors, an examination of recurring themes and motifs, or of mise-en-scène, to ascertain if the genius of the individual has been able to transcend the genius of the system (Bazin 1968). On the level of themes and motifs, Lee is unique in having made two films on homosexuality that are groundbreaking in the context of their respective cinemas. *The Wedding Banquet* is widely regarded as the first Chinese-language film that problematizes homosexuality as a theme (Lim 2006: 41), and *Brokeback Mountain* (hereafter *Brokeback*) has been claimed as groundbreaking in the history of Hollywood because it 'brought a gay couple to the forefront of US genre cinema' (White 2007: 20). For me, however, *Brokeback* rather demonstrates the narrow limits to which Hollywood would allow such homosexual representation. In his excellent reading of *Brokeback*, D.A. Miller distinguishes between what he calls 'homocinema', a sampling of whose major works include Pasolini's *Theorem* (*Teorema*, 1968), Oshima's *Taboo* (*Gohatto*, 1999), Fassbinder's *Querelle* (1982) and Hollywood cinema:

> Hollywood cinema knows only two options: to make homosexual desire invisible, in a closet intended for general use, or to make the Homosexual super-visible, as a minoritized 'problem'. In homocinema, what is uncloseted is not the Homosexual, but the nexus of desire, pleasure, and fantasy that normal culture develops around him. In the open circulation of these elements – in their emigration from the person and category of the Homosexual – homocinema finds a radical potential for disrupting social and symbolic order. (2007: 60, n.8)

Taking a cue from Miller's argument, I want to suggest that Hollywood's inability to visualize homosexual desire in a radical manner may or may not be traceable to any institutionalized or individual homophobia, but is instead firmly located within its very mode of address – the exalted form of the classical narrative. That is to say, within the internal logic of a narrative form that demands an early establishment of a story's premise; the development of plot elements and the tying up of every loose end as closure, all governed by generic conventions; the compulsion of the narrative force that can only drive things relentlessly forward; and the overriding causal dynamic dictating that everything has to have an explanation; there is very little room left for any narrative possibilities, homosexual or otherwise.

On the level of *mise-en-scène*, the opening sequence of *Brokeback* epitomizes the classical narrative form. To establish the premise of the film, which begins with the encounter between two cowboys in Wyoming in 1963, the film employs six standard shots to show the arrival of Ennis del Mar (Heath Ledger) (Figures 1–2):

1   Night. Establishing static extreme long shot of landscape; title of film appears at the centre of screen; truck enters from bottom right of screen (shot length: 18 seconds).

Figure 1   Ennis (Heath Ledger) arrives at Wyoming in Brokeback Mountain

Figure 2   Ennis arrives at his destination

2   Night. Closer framing of shot 1. Tracking extreme long shot of truck travelling from right to left of screen; truck exits screen left (shot length: 8 seconds).

3   Night. Static long shot of truck approaching from background of the screen from the left to the foreground and exits screen right (shot length: 11 seconds).

4   Morning. Medium shot of truck slowly arriving then stopping at foreground of screen on the right, ending at medium close-up; Ennis jumps

off the truck; as he puts on his jacket and the truck exits screen right, the words '1963, Signal, Wyoming' appear on bottom centre of screen; Ennis exits screen left (shot length: 22 seconds).

5   Morning. Static extreme long shot of Ennis entering from screen left and walking towards building in background (shot length: 9 seconds).

6   Morning. Static medium long shot of Ennis standing outside building (shot length: 5 seconds).

Such is the economy of these shots that it takes just over one minute to show a journey that covers several hours from night till day, landing Ennis at his destination. While the evocative score by Gustavo Santaolalla accompanying this opening sequence is sparse and slow paced, with an average shot length of 12 seconds, the editing of the shots seems hurried precisely because of the compulsive force that pushes the narrative forward as if it has somewhere to go. Sure enough, the next sequence shows the passing of a train followed by the arrival of Jack Twist (Jake Gyllenhaal), and their love story is ready to unfold.

Compare this to the opening shot of the Turkish film *Distant* (*Uzak*, Nuri Bilge Ceylan, 2002), which also follows the journey of a protagonist (Figures 3–4). Here, a static long take allows more than one full minute for the protagonist to walk from the middle of the screen as a tiny figure in the background, until he arrives at the foreground of the screen in medium shot, where he pauses, then wanders off screen left. The camera, however, does not follow him immediately, nor is there a cut. Rather, it stays still for five seconds before panning slowly to the left to reveal an empty road dissecting snowy hills. The protagonist is gone, but we hear and then see a car arriving from the

Figure 3   The protagonist in Uzak begins his journey

Figure 4   The protagonist in Uzak *flags down a car*

background of the screen. The protagonist returns to the foreground of the frame from screen left to flag the car down. We do not see the protagonist board the car. Instead, the film cuts to the black-and-white opening credits before the car reaches the protagonist, and the rest of his journey is suggested through the diegetic soundtrack of the car engine slowing down then picking up again following the slamming of the car door.

This one-take opening scene lasts more than two-and-a-half minutes. Like the opening sequence of *Brokeback*, it serves to set the premise of the film in terms of a protagonist heading somewhere else to look for work. Unlike *Brokeback*, it is unhurried, and leaves time and space for the imagination. Rather than speed up the action through editing, it creates suspense through ellipsis during the brief disappearance of the protagonist, thus keeping the audience wondering. It does not rely heavily on extra-diegetic music to convey emotion, but instead allows the diegetic sounds of cocks, birds and dogs to evoke the tranquility of the landscape and the solitude of the protagonist. It also has somewhere to go, but it is not in a hurry to get there. That is to say, the journey does not merely function as a means to a narrative end, but is worth contemplating in itself and is just as important as the destination.

On the stylistic level, the contrast between these two opening sequences clearly marks Lee's Hollywood film as drastically different from *Distant*, discussed by Suner (2006) as an example of accented cinema. With *Brokeback* in 2006, Lee became the first Asian to win the Best Director award in the Academy's history, confirming him as a fully paid-up, albeit flexible, citizen of Hollywood. Lee's success at the Academy Awards signals his complete integration into Hollywood-style filmmaking, though he arguably maintains his accented filmmaking with Chinese-language films such as *Lust, Caution*. Lee's parallel career thus complicates Naficy's model of accented cinema and raises the following questions. Can a filmmaker be simultaneously making accented and unaccented films? Or must the very distinction between accented and unaccented cinema be challenged?

Unaccented Cinema? Provincializing Hollywood

Ang Lee's career clearly demonstrates the limitations of Naficy's model of accented cinema, whose remit is confined not just to films made in exile and diaspora, but also to filmmakers whose location remains liminal and interstitial (Naficy 2001: 20). As I have argued from the outset, this model fails to take into consideration filmmakers like Ang Lee whose careers begin as diasporic and liminal, but have, via strategies of flexibility, gained full citizenship in mainstream filmmaking. Moreover, by privileging only one route of migration, that from the Third World to the First World, Naficy's model neglects the other myriad forms of migration deserving equal attention, and risks valorizing the First World as the only desired destination. As Suner rightly points out in her critique of Naficy's model: 'As long as it takes emigration to the West as a prerequisite for the entitlement to speak universally, however, this approach would leave the hierarchical division between the West and the rest intact' (2006: 378).

More problematic, for me, is Naficy's distinction between accented and unaccented cinema that leaves the latter category completely unquestioned. On current theoretical paradigms for discussing films, Naficy argues, via Rick Altman, that classificatory approaches are not neutral structures, but 'ideological constructs' masquerading as neutral categories (2001: 19). However, his only mention of unaccented cinema in his book is one line in the introduction, in which he states: 'If the dominant cinema is considered universal and without accent, the films that diasporic and exilic subjects make are accented' (4), without qualifying what is dominant cinema, who considers it as without accent and why, or critiquing this distinction. Naficy, therefore, does not question the masquerading neutrality of what he calls a dominant cinema without accent. As a result, his theoretical model contributes to a widespread but erroneous distinction between Hollywood and the rest, which continues to plague discussions of national cinemas in general and of world cinema in particular. It also allows the dominant (Hollywood) cinema to pass as the norm against which all other cinemas must be measured, without questioning its unqualified hegemonic position, its discursive legitimacy and the violence it inflicts on other cinemas by the sheer force of its capitalist power, which is essentially a form of cultural imperialism.[6]

In this regard, the false dichotomy between accented and unaccented cinema is analogous to the linguistic one from which it draws its metaphor, that of received pronunciation (RP) as standard/unaccented, and regional pronunciation as bearing an accent, even though the idea that a standard English accent had some special claim to be a model has long been questioned (Honey 1989: 11). More disturbingly, given its reinforcement of the distinction between the West and the rest, with its privileging of the one route of migration that begins in the Third World and ends in the First World, the false dichotomy is also analogous to the construction of the white race as universal, neutral, unraced, and the other races as particular, different, 'coloured'. In his seminal book on whiteness, Richard Dyer notes the paradoxical situation in which there is an 'absence of reference to whiteness in the habitual speech and writing of white people in the West', despite the fact that whites, in Western representation, 'are overwhelmingly and disproportionately predominant, have the central and elaborated roles, and above all are placed as the norm, the ordinary, the standard' (1997: 2–3). He goes on to argue that 'there is something especially white in this non-located and disembodied position of knowledge, and thus it seems especially important to try to break the hold of whiteness by locating and embodying it in a particular experience of being white' (1997: 4). Following Dyer, I would propose that Hollywood, rather than being considered as dominant and unaccented, must be recast in film studies in light of its particularities, its cultural specificities, its situatedness, its difference. Similar to the historian Dipesh Chakrabarty's effort to provincialize Europe (2000), a dislodging of Hollywood from its presumed centrality and universality will illuminate the discourses, processes and mechanisms through which it has come to occupy this dominant position. In other words, we need to provincialize Hollywood.

Ang Lee's journey from Taiwan to the United States is not simply the process of losing one accent and acquiring a different, more exalted one, even though those in East Asia have been accustomed, after more than a century of experience of different forms of colonialism and cultural imperialism, to regard Lee's success in Hollywood as 'the pride of all Chinese people'. As the level of migration continues to intensify in the age of globalization, as more and more people – and cinemas – are able to speak in multiple tongues, we also need to dismantle the self/other distinction that continues to perpetuate the myth of the West versus the rest, Hollywood versus world cinema. While Lee's career could be split along linguistic lines, it is worth recalling that film was celebrated as a utopian universal language in its early years, albeit before the introduction of sound brought to it a Babelistic turn. As Miriam Hansen points out, the celebration of film as a universal language was accompanied by, on the one hand, the American film industry's efforts to ensure US films' dominance on both domestic and world markets, and, on the other hand, the emerging codes of classical narrative cinema (1991: 78–9). By projecting the career of Ang Lee through the lens of Naficy's notion of accented cinema, I hope to have demonstrated that the phenomenon of speaking in multiple tongues in cinema must challenge us not only to break down those aforementioned binaries, but ultimately to also rethink the very language of film itself, to question its presumed universality, and to treat all cinemas as particular, peculiar and provincial, while not discounting their abilities to communicate and connect beyond their cultural, linguistic and formal specificities.

References

Appadurai, Arjun (1990) 'Disjuncture and difference in the global cultural economy', *Theory, Culture & Society* 7:2–3, pp.295–310.

Bazin, André (1968) 'De la politique des auteurs', in Peter Graham (ed.) *The New Wave: Critical Landmarks* (London, Secker & Warburg), pp.137–55.

Berry, Chris (2007) 'The Chinese side of the mountain', *Film Quarterly* 60:3, pp.32–7.

Berry, Michael (2005) *Speaking in Images: Interviews with Contemporary Chinese Filmmakers* (New York, Columbia University Press).

Bordwell, David (2006) *The Way Hollywood Tells It: Story and Style in Modern Movies* (Berkeley and Los Angeles, University of California Press).

Chakrabarty, Dipesh (2000) *Provincializing Europe: Postcolonial Thought and Historical Difference* (Princeton, Princeton University Press).

Cooke, Paul (ed.) (2007) *World Cinema's 'Dialogues' with Hollywood* (Basingstoke, Palgrave Macmillan).

Dyer, Richard (1997) *White* (London and New York, Routledge).

Grewel, Inderpal and Caren Kaplan (eds) (1994) *Scattered Hegemonies: Postmodernity and Transnational Feminist Practice* (Minneapolis, University of Minnesota Press).

Hansen, Miriam (1991) *Babel and Babylon: Spectatorship in American Silent Film* (Cambridge and London, Harvard University Press).

Higson, Andrew (2000) 'The limiting imagination of national cinema', in Mette Hjort and Scott MacKenzie (eds) *Cinema and Nation* (London, Routledge), pp.63–74.

Honey, John (1989) *Does Accent Matter? The Pygmalion Factor* (London and Boston, Faber & Faber).

Lim, Song Hwee (2006) *Celluloid Comrades: Representations of Male Homosexuality in Contemporary Chinese Cinemas* (Honolulu, University of Hawaii Press).

Marchetti, Gina (2009) 'Hollywood and Taiwan: connections, countercurrents, and Ang Lee's *Hulk*', in Tan See-kam, Peter X. Feng and Gina

Marchetti (eds) *Chinese Connections: Critical Perspectives on Film, Identity, and Diaspora* (Philadelphia, Temple University Press), pp.95–108.

Miller, D.A. (2007) 'On the universality of *Brokeback Mountain*', *Film Quarterly* 60(3), pp.50–60.

Naficy, Hamid (2001) *An Accented Cinema: Exilic and Diasporic Filmmaking* (Princeton and Oxford, Princeton University Press).

Ong, Aihwa (1999) *Flexible Citizenship: The Cultural Logics of Transnationality* (Durham and London, Duke University Press).

Republic of China Yearbook (2008) Online on the Republic of China's Government Information Office website at: http://www.gio.gov.tw/taiwan-website/5-gp/yearbook/ch3.html. Accessed 30 April 2009.

Shih, Shu-mei (2000) 'Globalisation and minoritisation: Ang Lee and the politics of flexibility', *New Formations* 40, pp.86–101.

Shohat, Ella and Stam, Robert (1994) *Unthinking Eurocentrism: Multiculturalism and the Media* (London and New York, Routledge).

Suner, Asuman (2006) 'Outside in: "accented cinema" at large', *Inter-Asia Cultural Studies* 7:3, pp.363–82.

White, Rob (2007) 'Introduction' to special feature on *Brokeback Mountain*, *Film Quarterly* 60:3, pp.20–1.

Yeh, Emilie Yueh-yu and Darrell William Davis (2005) *Taiwan Film Directors: A Treasure Island* (New York, Columbia University Press).

Yoshimoto, Mitsuhiro (2006) 'National/international/transnational: the concept of trans-Asian cinema and the cultural politics of film criticism', in Valentina Vitali and Paul Willemen (eds) *Theorising National Cinema* (London, BFI Publishing), pp.254–61.

Notes

1 I would like to thank Kien Ket Lim for inviting me to a conference on Ang Lee in Taiwan in December 2006, where this chapter took its embryonic form, and Lúcia Nagib for inviting me to the Theorising World Cinema Workshop II in Leeds in November 2007, where the chapter then took a different incarnation. Thanks also to Chris Perriam for his insightful suggestions as discussant at Leeds and to participants at both workshops for their useful comments.

2 It should be noted that even these early films complicate the 'national cinema' model, as they were co-produced by CMPC and an American company, Good Machine.

3 Some of the following information on Taiwan's history is culled from the online version of *The Republic of China Yearbook 2008*, available on the webpage of the Government Information Office of the Republic of China.

4 It should be noted that Hou, born in 1947 in Guangdong province in China, is also a *waishengren*, though many of his early Taiwan New Cinema films deal with *benshengren* experience because of the source of the screenplay.

5 This mythical landscape finds its ultimate manifestation in the fictitious *jianghu* (rivers and lakes) of the *wuxia* (martial arts) world in Lee's *Crouching Tiger, Hidden Dragon* (*Wohu canglong*, 2000).

6 As Judith Mayne also argues: 'The classical Hollywood cinema has become the norm against which all other alternative practices are measured. Films which do not engage with the classical Hollywood cinema are by and large relegated to irrelevance. Frequently, the very notion of an "alternative" is posed in the narrow terms of an either-or: either one is within classical discourse and therefore complicit, or one is critical of and/or resistant to it and therefore outside of it' (in Yoshimoto 2006: 36).

PART IV

THE REALIST
PROJECT

Chapter Nine

From Realism to Neo-Realism

Geoffrey Nowell-Smith

Debates about realism and the cinema go back right to the origins of film and indeed further still, since they are a continuation of earlier debates about realism in literature, about realism in painting, about painting and photography, and so on.

These have been, and still are, particularly acute issues in relation to cinema because of the presumed privileged relationship of the film camera to the movement of the outside world that comes into its field of view. For the French critic André Bazin in the 1940s and 1950s, cinema was a means by which the intrinsic objectivity of the photograph could be extended into a temporal dimension (Bazin 1958).[1] For the German Siegfried Kracauer (1960), cinema represents the 'redemption of physical reality' by means of the cinematic apparatus. Even earlier, for the Hungarian Béla Balázs in 1924, it was through cinema that man becomes visible – what he called '*der sichtbare Mensch*' – without the mediation of language (Balázs 1924).

For writers of other schools, however, the cinema is not about reality so much as the imaginary. For another French writer, Edgar Morin, in 1956, the man cinema creates is not man made visible, but imaginary man – '*l'homme imaginaire*' – and man becomes imaginary, and an inhabitant of imaginary worlds, practically at the beginning of cinema: to be precise, at the moment when, from being a primitive photographic device, called the cinematograph, it begins to put shots together and posit a relationship between them (Morin 1956).

More recently we have seen the advancement of views like those of the philosopher Stanley Cavell (1979), for whom the cinema creates alternative worlds, which may be quite unlike the real world but are most interesting when they are lifelike and resemble it. Or the position espoused by another philosopher, Slavoj Žižek, who sees the cinema as a paradigm of psychic organization. The worlds the cinema creates, for Žižek, are interesting and valuable to the extent that they speak of desires beyond the gates of ordinary perception.

The apparent unreality of the worlds encountered in cinema – or even their apparent reality – touches us because they put the spectator in touch with what is normally invisible, which is the nature of our desire. Cinema looks real, and yet it is obviously unreal; but, to the extent that it finds desire for us, this unreal creation is real after all.[2]

These sets of ideas are clearly in conflict with one another, and which set one thinks appropriate to call into play will depend partly on the thinker and partly on the film being thought about. Different ideas can be held by the same person in relation to different films, or even sometimes in relation to the same one. A film can operate at different levels, and someone watching it can relate to it at different levels either at the same time or alternately. Take, for example, Vittorio De Sica and Cesare Zavattini's 1948 film *Bicycle Thieves* (*Ladri di Biciclette*). This film is generally seen as a more or less objective account of everyday life and the consequences of mass unemployment in Italy after the Second World War. But it can also be experienced as an evocation of anxiety in the manner of Hitchcock. On this reading, the stolen bicycle is what Hitchcock would call a McGuffin; what really sets the film going and holds the spectator's attention is the hero's inability to acknowledge his moral indebtedness to his wife. (Conversely, I suppose one could read Hitchcock's *North by Northwest* (1959) as not about the Cary Grant character's guilt at all, but as a documentary about North American transport systems. I would not go quite that far, though it is worth noting in parentheses that at one point the name of Cary Grant was touted as a possible lead for *Bicycle Thieves*.)

How one reads a film, however, is not a matter of more or less arbitrary personal choice. Also involved is the context in which the film was made and first seen, and that in which it is seen today. There have been periods in cinema history when films have been made to be viewed in a mainly realist key, as stories about the real world – in the sense of the physical and social world that we inhabit on this planet. This can be the case, even though the particular part of this real world that the film portrays might be remote from our immediate experience: the people in it might be too poor or too rich, or have different-coloured skin or sexual preferences, or some other attribute, and so not be us. But their real world existence remains unquestionable and what grounds the film. Meanwhile, at other times in history, films have been more about worlds clearly demarcated as imaginary, not related to anyone's daily reality, but possibly expressive of imaginary truths – which are not untruths just because they are imaginary.

In this respect, the Second World War is a massive watershed in the history of the cinema. In the years leading up to 1939, broadly speaking, realism was out, and the cinema appealed to imagination and desire. There are exceptions – for example, films of Jean Renoir such as *Toni* (1935), *Les Bas-fonds* (1936), adapted from Maxim Gorky's *The Lower Depths*, or most famously the prison-camp story *The Grand Illusion* (*La Grande Illusion*) from 1937. But more commonly, and not only in America, the cinema rejoiced in being seen as a dream factory to the world. It was the age of Astaire–Rogers musicals, of historical romance, of screwball comedy. Novels or plays, which in their original incarnation were works of broadly realist inspiration, became in the cinema pure romance or crazy comedy. Take Thackeray's *Vanity Fair*, a great work of social satire, brought to the screen by Rouben Mamoulian in 1935 as the melodrama *Becky Sharp*, with Miriam Hopkins in the title role. Or Ben Hecht and Charles McArthur's play *The Front Page* (1929), witty and satirical, which it remains in its first film version directed by Lewis Milestone in 1931, but which becomes a romantic comedy, and a hilariously funny one, when it is filmed again by Howard Hawks under the title *His Girl Friday* in 1939. And where Hollywood led, other film industries followed, though usually with less panache.

The Second World War changed the cinema fundamentally, though it did not do so overnight. In 1942, when the United States had entered the war but was not yet seriously embroiled in it except at sea, the Warner Bros. studio produced a film called *Casablanca*, an enduringly popular love story directed by Michael Curtiz, and set on the fringes of the war then being fought in Europe and North Africa. It is a magically evocative film, one which spectators can watch again and again, or which indeed one can switch on and not even watch, just listen to the soundtrack. One can listen to Max Steiner's lush musical score, to the rasp of Bogart's voice and the gentle modulations of Ingrid Bergman. One can savour the experiences of memory, of renunciation, of liberation and triumph. One can even, like Richard Klein, author of a book called *Cigarettes Are Sublime* (1993), use it as therapy to help one give up smoking, since no cigarette you smoke in real life will ever be as satisfying as those smoked by Bogart and other characters in the movie. But as a truthful representation of the Moroccan city of Casablanca, of the relations between the Nazi regime and its Vichy puppet, of European resistance to occupation, of the impending Holocaust, of anything to do with the war being waged across the world, you can forget it. There is perhaps one moment of political truth, and that is when the resistance leader Victor Laszlo, played by Paul Henreid, gives a little speech about how for every resister killed, a thousand will spring up in his place. This same speech is reused in 1944 by Howard Hawks in his film *To Have and Have Not*, and has become a cliché. But it is something that every occupying power needs to remember, even (or perhaps especially) if the occupying power is American. For the rest, the film is the purest hokum.

Cut now to Italy. Here the escapist war film has also not disappeared, as is shown by *The White Ship* (*La nave bianca*), a film shot by Roberto Rossellini in 1941, in which selfless nuns in naval uniform toil to care for the wounded from a stricken vessel. In what cause the vessel was stricken the audience is not told, but they are assured that the nuns are on their side, and presumably God is as well. Meanwhile, in 1942, far from the fighting, a young man called Luchino Visconti begins shooting a film about murder, greed, jealousy and betrayal, adapted from an American crime novel, James M. Cain's *The Postman Always Rings Twice* (1934). Visconti was in an odd position. This was his first film as director, and such limited filmmaking experience as he possessed had been acquired, not making escapist comedies or historical romances in Fascist Italy, but working with Renoir, one of the few realists in 1930s cinema – specifically on *Les Bas-fonds* and *Partie de campagne* (1936).

For the film version, entitled *Ossessione*, Visconti strips out bits of the plot action of Cain's novel, and replaces its casually evoked Californian background with the sight and sounds of the Po Valley in northern Italy. The story remains a bit melodramatic, but the location shooting and the naturalistic acting ensure that the film is firmly situated in its new setting. The film also showed more of the seamy side of Italian life than the censors thought decent. It was banned, briefly unbanned and then withdrawn after a very limited release. It did not properly surface again until 1949, since after the fall of Fascism it was injuncted by the victorious Allies on the grounds that the rights to Cain's story belonged to MGM.

The film opens with a lorry loaded with hay drawing up outside a country inn cum petrol station. A handsome but shabbily dressed man clambers out of the back, with hay on his clothes and in his hair. He stretches languorously, standings around for a while trying to get his bearings. After a while he enters the inn, where a woman is cooking and singing seductively as she cooks. Two things are instantly established. On the one hand a new spirit of realism in representation, and on the other a promise that this new spirit will not prevent there being romance and drama to come.

Five years after the film's abortive first release, one of the scriptwriters on the film, Antonio Pietrangeli, rhapsodized about the opening scene where the hero, Gino, is first discovered on the back of the lorry: 'How, then, shall we baptise Gino in *Ossessione*? We can call him, if you like, Italian neorealism' (Pietrangeli 1948).

Fair enough, up to a point. It is a scene that must have taken the audience by surprise, if only for its lack of respect for the actor, a well-known heart-throb. But the comment is also unduly rhapsodic, and decidedly after the event. *Ossessione* did not magically bring Italian neo-realism into existence. Neo-realism did not yet exist, and for it to exist, two further things had to happen.

The first thing that had to happen was historical and contingent. The war had to hit home. It was not only in Italy that the war acted as a stimulus to realism. A new respect for reality can be seen in British wartime films, like Humphrey Jennings' *Fires Were Started* (1943) or Anthony Asquith's *The*

Way to the Stars (1945), even in Noel Coward's *In Which We Serve*, in 1942. It can be seen in William Wellman's *The Story of GI Joe*, made in 1944 when the Americans knew what war was about and the limited place of heroics within it.

Neo-realism really began when filmmakers turned their cameras on war and even more on its aftermath. The war for Italians had two phases. During the first phase – up to 1942 or early 1943 – Italy was allied to the Germans, and had troops in the Balkans and North Africa. The cinematic legacy of this phase is slim. The second phase – 1943 to 1945 – lasted from the Allied invasion of Sicily, through the fall of Mussolini, the partisan struggle against the Germans, and the gradual advance of the Allies up the peninsula. This is what is commemorated in neo-realism, with inevitably a time lag but a very short one.

Whereas, on the whole, phase one of the war was something most people wanted to forget, phase two had a strong resonance and its commemoration was also a way of posing the question: what next? We have suffered, we have fought, what is to be our reward?

Neo-realism required this context in order to thrive, but it was by no means the only possible response to it. The war was, if you like, a necessary condition for the emergence of neo-realism, but not a sufficient one, and what emerged might have been something else. In France, for example, which was also occupied, resisted and changed sides not once but twice in the course of the war, nothing like neo-realism sprang up when the conflict came to an end.

This brings us to the second factor, which was in a way quite accidental and therefore even more contingent than the fact of war and reconstruction, but at the same time is more essential, since it is definitional of what neo-realism turned out to be. For neo-realism is precisely an aesthetic of the contingent, the accidental, the reality that is not foreseen by the artist before the work of art comes into being. And in this sense *Ossessione* is not yet neo-realist, though it gets quite close.

The concept of realism that underlies *Ossessione* is a conventional and literary one. It is that of verisimilitude and of the work of art as an imitation of life. Art as mimesis. There is reality and there is language, and realist art is the transfer of amorphous reality into the structured terms of language, the use of words to produce a lifelike resemblance of the things of which reality is supposed to consist. Visconti and his friends on the magazine *Cinema* were great admirers of the late nineteenth-century novelist Giovanni Verga, who aspired to a use of language which adhered to reality in such a way as to make it appear that when the novel spoke inside the reader's head it was not a wordsmith speaking, but the described reality communicating itself directly through the reader's skull. This is my gloss on Verga's celebrated letter to his friend

Salvatore Farina in 1880, prefaced to the short story 'Gramigna's lover' ('L'amante di "Gramigna"', 1880) – which incidentally Visconti had wanted to film before *Ossessione*, but hadn't been allowed to. Verga writes:

> This story is a human document. ... I shall tell it to you just as I picked it up in the country byways, just about with the same simple and picturesque words of popular storytelling ... without trying to find it in the lines of a book, through a writer's lens. ... The artist's hand will remain absolutely invisible and the work of art will seem to have made itself on its own, to have matured and emerged spontaneously, like a fact of nature, without retaining any point of contact with its author, or any mark of its original stain. (Verga 1880)

What crucially happened in 1945 was that a handful of fiction filmmakers went out into the street and started taking pictures, trying to fit the composed, scripted, fictional elements into the world that surrounded them. This was not an entirely new procedure. There was a lot of street shooting in the silent era, but the problems of recording sound had driven filmmakers into the studio in 1930 and they had hardly ventured outside since then. (Think of *Casablanca*: every single shot, including those purporting to be out of doors, was done indoors in the studio.)

There were practical questions involved here, like the fact that in 1945 there weren't many studios to shoot in anyway: companies had gone bust, premises had been bombed; the best studio of all, the renowned Cinecittà, had been requisitioned by the Allies for use as a transit camp for refugees. But the main reason for street shooting was aesthetic. Rather than translate your vision of reality into a set of instructions to give to the set designer so he can recreate it, you get reality to impress itself directly on film by means of the camera. The process of translation from three-dimensional real world to two-dimensional screen image is thus immensely simplified: indeed, it hardly seems a process of translation at all.

With *Ossessione* we are at a point where an answer seems to have been found to what we might call Verga's dilemma. That is to say, the problem of the realist writer who wishes to make himself invisible and make reality speak directly, with the least possible intervention of obvious literary construction. But of course there is construction. The filmmaker and the filmic apparatus are not a perfectly transparent vessel. They bend, they compress, they flatten, they impose themselves on reality, and necessarily this effort is visible. Moreover, if it is not visible, it is only as a result of an act of deception. In realist filmmaking the imposition is kept to a minimum, but there is still an idea to be enacted, there is a translation of the idea into the filmmaking process and a retranslation back into the impression of reality offered to the spectator.

However, in the process of making films in the new or partly new way, the Italian filmmakers came up against a phenomenon they did not expect to be there, which was the unexpected. How do you deal with the unexpected? There is nothing unplanned in *Ossessione*. Every shot is a shot of what the director intended to shoot. Maybe to shoot in a particular cramped location the cinematographer had to place the camera in a less than ideal position, or use a different lens than would have been ideal, but these adjustments were all made to fit a preconception and make sure it could still be translated into film.

But with some of the immediate postwar films, especially Roberto Rossellini's *Rome Open City* (*Roma città aperta*, 1945) and *Paisà*, (1946), or De Sica's *Shoeshine* (*Sciuscià*, also 1946), a new element enters. Reality is recalcitrant. It won't be bent. You want to film what is there, but what is there is not what you expected to be there, or at any rate not exactly what you had foreseen as being there when you put the script together – or even when you surveyed the proposed location ahead of shooting just two weeks ago. In the very shifting, uncertain and in many ways uninterpretable reality of postwar Italy, there was too much that was unpredictable and uncontrollable by the filmmaker.

Federico Fellini wrote, looking back over his time with Rossellini during the making of *Paisà* in 1946:

> Rossellini searched, he pursued his film through the streets, with the Allied armoured cars rumbling past a couple of feet behind his back, folk at the windows shouting and singing, hundreds of people trying to sell us something or steal something from us, in that incandescent hell, that teeming anthill that is Naples ... and again in Rome, and again in Florence, and in the Po Delta, i.e. in most of the episodes which compose that remarkable film. (Fellini 1980: 44)

What Rossellini realized, and De Sica too to a lesser extent, was that this immersion in a reality you could not control was a good thing. Instead of bending reality to your preconception of it, you should go with the flow. You should be the bending reed. You still have a script, you still have a story that must reach its end, you still have actors who know, or think they know, what character it is they are meant to impersonate. But out there on the street, life goes on, it is constantly in danger of invading the screen in unexpected or unanticipated ways. The filmmaker therefore has a choice. Does he hold this invading reality at bay so he can get on with making the film as scripted and planned? Or does he let it in, and reshape the film according to the dictates of what he has found?

The pragmatic choice hold it at bay or let it in, conceals a fundamental philosophical difference as to what realism in cinema was about. The first person to realize this, at a philosophical or theoretical level, was the French critic André Bazin.

In the early 1950s, Bazin found himself in dispute with Italian critics of a Marxist persuasion over the nature of neo-realism. Basically, the Marxists said: neo-realism is a movement which promotes realism and realism is about capturing social reality. Without a proper conception of social reality, the film-maker literally does not know which way to turn or in which direction to point the camera. Rossellini was widely criticized in Italy at the time for having lost his way, for no longer having the concept of reality which had animated *Rome Open City* and *Paisà*. He'd gone soft, partly because he was so besotted with Ingrid Bergman, with whom he had fallen in love when shooting his film *Stromboli* in 1949, and was now married to. He was making films which were all about spiritual longings incarnated in the person of his saintly wife. Where, they asked, was the realism in that?

The leading spokesman of the Marxists was Guido Aristarco, editor of the journal *Cinema Nuovo*. Aristarco was, in fact, a devotee of the Hungarian Marxist George Lukács, who had a very particular notion of realism in literature, which Aristarco thought could be applied to film. For Lukács and Aristarco, the ideal realist work, irrespective of medium, was one which perceived bourgeois society from inside, but with a critical perspective embedded in the narration. Essentially this was a theory of literature, whose adaptability to cinema remained to be tested.

Bazin, however, started with a phenomenological notion of reality, of the world as it presents itself to consciousness. And he also started with an idea of cinema according to which the camera, as a mechanical recording device, acts as a perfect mediator between consciousness and the world because of its neutrality, and because it can transcribe phenomena without translating – or without the need for the intervention of a translator.

The particular film which Aristarco had attacked (Aristarco 1952) was Rossellini's *Europe '51* (*Europa '51*), with Ingrid Bergman and Alexander Knox, made in 1952. (Even more virulent attacks had been made on Rossellini's first film with Bergman, *Stromboli*, on its release in 1950.) Bazin's counter-attack, entitled 'Défense de Rossellini' (Bazin 1962: 150–60),[3] concerns the next of Rossellini's films with Bergman, *Journey to Italy* (*Viaggio in Italia*), released in 1954 and treated with contempt by all the critics, except for Bazin and his friends on the magazine *Cahiers du cinéma*. These friends had names like François Truffaut, Jean-Luc Godard, Jacques Rivette, Eric Rohmer, whom no one had heard of at the time but who became very famous later.

Bazin tries to capture the originality of neo-realism compared with previous realisms by means of a metaphor. He starts by apologizing for not being a philosopher and having to fall back on metaphor, and then he writes:

I would assert of the forms of classic art and traditional realism that they construct works like one builds houses, with bricks or cut stone. It is not a question of arguing against the usefulness of houses, or their possible beauty, or the perfect adaptation of bricks to this use, but it can be agreed that the reality of the bricks lies less in its composition [by which he means material composition, the molecules it is made of] than in its shape and its resistance. It would not occur to one to define it as a piece of clay; its specificity as a mineral is of little importance: what matters is the convenience of its volume. A brick is an element of a house. So much is clear in appearance itself. One could say the same about the cut stones which form a bridge. They are perfectly shaped to form an arch. But the blocks of stone scattered in a river bed are and remain rocks; their reality as stone is not affected if, jumping from one to the next, I take advantage of them to cross the river. If they have provisionally made that use possible for me it is because I have been able to contribute to the accident of their layout my own touch of invention, adding the movement which, without changing their nature or appearance, has given them a provisional meaning and use.

In the same way, the neo-realist film has a meaning, but *a posteriori*, to the extent that it allows our consciousness to pass from one fact to another, from one fragment of reality to the next, whereas meaning is given *a priori* in classical artistic composition: the house is already there in the brick. (Bazin 1962: 157)[4]

Journey to Italy is a film in which a wealthy, middle-aged childless couple go to Italy on holiday. Being forced together in a strange city provokes a crisis in their marriage, which at the end of the film is dubiously resolved.

So far so good. And so conventional. But they don't just go to any city, they go to Naples. They are not just any couple, but Ingrid Bergman and George Sanders. The actress was the director's wife and the Rossellini-Bergman marriage, like that of the characters played by Bergman and Sanders, was under strain.

Rossellini of course has a script. But the way he films it involves letting his location intrude on the experience of his characters and allowing free rein to the personality of the actor impersonating the character.

In the film there are various scenes with the couple together, but more interesting from our point of view are those when the Bergman character, Katherine, takes the car (a Bentley coupé) and visits the city on her own. Probably the most celebrated of these is the one in which she visits the Archaeology Museum, where she has what can best be described as an erotic-mystical experience of startling ambiguity. On the one hand, the Greco-Roman statues in the Museum overpower her with their intense beauty and physicality; on the other hand, the vulgar patter of the old man guiding her through the galleries fills her with a deep sexual revulsion. More interesting still than this highly choreographed event are the shots of her driving the Bentley through the streets. Her irritation with her husband, spilling over into an irritation with her surroundings, is expressed through a voiceover commentary. But these surroundings infiltrate her mind without her apparently being aware of it. On this and later visits, she sees babies, pregnant women, funerals, bones in catacombs and many sights to which she reacts, sometimes with disgust and at best with profound ambivalence. What she sees – crosscut with shots of her face as she manoeuvres the car through the crowded streets, muttering as she goes – seems like almost random footage of the world pressing in on her in its everyday, disordered materiality. But in its very randomness it speaks to her about the sterility of her own existence, paving the way for a second quasi-mystical experience towards the end of the film, when she and her husband witness the uncovering of the interlaced bodies of two lovers buried under volcanic ash.

These are Bazin's stepping stones, which are not designed to be a bridge, but which get you across the river nonetheless. They are what for him made neorealism unique, and not only for him, but for the New Wave filmmakers who followed Rossellini in exploring the path along which events seemed to lead them.

It might be objected here that the 'stepping stones' in Journey to Italy are pretty artfully laid out – and indeed have to be, if they are to deliver the richness of intellectual content that writers on the film, such as Laura Mulvey (2000), have rightly discerned in it. It could also be objected that the montage in the scenes when Katherine is driving around Naples is in defiance of all the precepts for which Bazin is famous. Was he not a great enemy of montage effects, and the promoter of the uninterrupted long take that preserves the integrity of space and time?

Neither objection seems to me well-founded. The stepping stones are an extended metaphor, not to be taken too literally or in a rigorously binary fashion. It is not as if films are either like stepping stones or like bridges, with no possibility of anything in between. It is rather that the metaphor suggests a possibility of there being films which are less preconceived than most and to which the stepping-stone image would be more appropriate, and that is certainly the case with Journey to Italy. As to the question of montage, it is again a misreading of Bazin to think that he was against montage under all circumstances, or that films split rigorously into those which were montage films and those in which the long take, depth of field and spatio-temporal continuity were consistently dominant. If that were the case, what about Citizen Kane? The fact is that Bazin's commitment to the long take, etc. was always qualified. Particular techniques were to be recommended to the extent that they made more of reality visible, and the long take, etc. usually did this.[5] (Conversely, montage techniques tended to distort or hide this same reality.) But it was the purpose that counted, not the means of achieving it.

But what was this reality that Bazin thought, that the cinema, properly used, was uniquely suited to revealing? First of all, it was phenomenal; that is to say, a world of phenomena as they manifested themselves to human consciousness. (This was the unspoken *differend* between him and Aristarco, for whom the 'phenomenal form' in which reality presented itself to consciousness was not identical with reality itself.) Secondly, this phenomenal world was by nature contingent, and one in which the encounter between the human subject and surrounding contingency was marked by freedom of the will (whatever difficulties individual subjects might have in exercising it).

What Bazin saw in neo-realism was the possibility of cinema encountering the world of contingency with open eyes, and thereby transcending the traditional notion of artistic realism as a structured mimesis or imitation of the world. Underlying the belief in this possibility was a philosophical position which modern sophisticates would regard as naive, invoking as it does notions of transparency, whether of the world to consciousness or consciousness to itself. But it is precisely the function of art to open windows that have been closed by the operations of ideology – including those that have been closed by those who claim that all visions of the world are ideological in essence, and that what Bazin asserts that Rossellini is doing in *Journey to Italy* is a priori an impossibility. Art is also a 'what if?', and the basic 'what if?' of *Journey to Italy* is: 'What if one were to position oneself to encounter the world as Rossellini shows Bergman encountering it – a world of real objects, real people, embedded in a real situation?' Quibble with this premise, and you foreclose the possibility of seeing something you otherwise would not have seen. This something is not just a dose of phenomenal reality, but a sense of what Žižek, following the French psychoanalyst Jacques Lacan, calls the Real, the bedrock not amenable to symbolization.[6] In opening up this possibility, neo-realism, as a form of film-making which uses the cinema apparatus to remind us in a material way how reality makes us, rather than us commanding reality through our ability to make fictions about it, still has a lesson to impart.

References

Aristarco, Guido (1952) 'Europa '51', *Cinema Nuovo* 1 (15 December).

Balázs, Béla (1924) *Der sichtbare Mensch oder die Kultur des Films* (Vienna and Leipzig, Deutsch-Österreichischer Verlag); trans. E. Carter and R. Livingstone, in Balázs, Béla, *Early Film Theory: 'Visible Man' and 'The Spirit of Film'* (London, Berghahn, 2010).

Bazin, André (1958) *Qu'est-ce que le cinéma?* vol. I (Paris, Editions du Cerf).

Bazin, André (1962) *Qu'est-ce que le cinéma?* vol. IV (Paris, Editions du Cerf).

Bazin, André (2009) *What Is Cinema?*, trans. and ed. Timothy Barnard (Montreal, Caboose).

Cain, James M. (1934) *The Postman Always Rings Twice* (New York, Knopf).

Cavell, Stanley (1979) *The World Viewed: Reflections on the Ontology of Film*, 2nd edn (Cambridge MA, Harvard University Press).

Fellini, Federico (1980) *Fare un film* (Turin, Einaudi).

Forgacs, David, Sarah Lutton and Geoffrey Nowell-Smith (eds) (2000) *Roberto Rossellini: Magician of the Real* (London, BFI).

Klein, Richard (1993) *Cigarettes Are Sublime* (Durham, Duke University Press).

Kracauer, Siegfried (1960) *Theory of Film: The Redemption of Physical Reality* (Oxford and New York, Oxford University Press).

Morin, Edgar (1956) *Le Cinéma ou l'homme imaginaire: essai d'anthropologie sociologique* (Paris, Editions de Minuit); in English as *The Cinema, or the Imaginary Man* (Minneapolis, University of Minnesota Press, 2005).

Mulvey, Laura (2000) 'Vesuvian topographies: the eruption of the past in *Journey to Italy*', in Forgacs et al. (2000), pp.95–111.

Pietrangeli, Antonio (1948) 'Panoramique sur le cinéma italien', *La Revue du cinéma* 13 (May).

Verga, Giovanni (1880) 'Lettera a Salvatore Farina', in *Vita dei Campi* (Milan, Treves).

Žižek, Slavoj (1999) *The Ticklish Subject* (London, Verso).

Notes

1 See, in particular, his essay 'Ontologie de l'image photographique' (1945) in Bazin (1958: 9–17) (in English in Bazin 2009: 3–10), especially the observation (Bazin 2009: 8): 'Seen in this light, cinema appears to be the completion [*achèvement*] in time of photography's objectivity.'

2 For Žižek, see in particular *The Ticklish Subject* (1999), but also his TV programme and DVD *The Pervert's Guide to the Cinema* (2006).

3 Translation in Forgacs et al. (2000), pp.156–7.

4 This translation (by Geoffrey Nowell-Smith) from Forgacs et al. (2000: 157–61).

5 But not universally. In his essay 'Montage interdit' (Bazin 1958: trans. in Bazin 2009 as 'Editing Prohibited'), the principle he asserts is limited to: 'Whenever the essential aspect of an event depends upon the simultaneous presence of two or more agents, editing is prohibited' (Bazin 2009: 81). The fact that Katherine is not always in frame together with what she sees during the driving sequences in *Journey to Italy* does not substantially break this rule.

6 A disquisition on what either Lacan or Žižek means by 'the Real' is potentially endless. Suffice it to say that it is not something you can simply find by stripping away the layers of the imaginary and the symbolic by which it is hidden. Nor is it

just something that hits you in the face when you thought that the symbolic armature surrounding collective or individual subjectivity had precluded its appearance. Rather (if I understand Žižek correctly) it is the radical discomfiture at the point where knowledge fails. It is also (Žižek 1999: 167) that which prevents truth from presenting itself other than as a fiction. Whether it is works of realism (as I assert), or those of mystery and imagination (as Žižek appears to claim), that offer the best possibility of disclosing the abyss must remain an open question.

Chapter Ten

Oshima, Corporeal Realism and the Eroticized Apparatus[1]

Lúcia Nagib

In this chapter, I will look at *The Realm of the Senses* (*Ai no koriida*, Nagisa Oshima, 1976) as a rare and fully accomplished example of how cinema can elicit continuity between terms normally seen as antagonistic in film studies: staged representation and presentation of reality, exhibitionism and voyeurism, critical and cathartic spectatorship. In so doing, I hope to redress perceptions of this film which have systematically resorted to Brecht-inspired body-mind dualisms in order to deny the infectious power of its hard-core eroticism. I will start by reviewing some representative voices in the critical reception of *The Realm of the Senses*, moving on to a meditation on their theoretical fundaments and finally to an interdisciplinary analysis of the film in the light of Japanese erotic prints (*shunga*). By these means, I aim to demonstrate the advantages of a polycentric approach to film studies, drawing on local context and traditions, over the arbitrary application of alien (usually Hollywood-based) paradigms to films produced across the globe.

As a rule, sex in art films, explicit though it might be, is part of a complex network of feelings, moods, psychological states and cultural standards, which infuse it with guilt, frustration and disappointment as a means to cohere with what Freud called the 'reality principle', as opposed to the 'pleasure principle'. *The Realm of the Senses* became the apex of the career of its director, Nagisa Oshima, precisely for contravening this rule; that is, by combining realism with gratifying sex and undisturbed fruition of pleasure, meant to infect cast, crew and audiences alike. It would be easy to describe *The Realm of the Senses* as a film which breaks all sorts of boundaries. But this would obscure the fact that it could only have been made *after* all sorts of boundaries had been broken, not least by the director himself. The film is primarily the fruit of the process of sexual liberation that took place during the 1960s, in both Japan and the rest of the world, but it is also a film of maturity, made by a director whose talent and creativity had been widely acknowledged at home and abroad, and was thus given freedom by the French producer Anatole Dauman to express his wishes without restraints. Above all, the film is the living proof that many so-called boundaries simply do not exist. The aim of my analysis of this film will thus be to revise established theoretical concepts, drawing on such artificial boundaries, in particular those opposing sexual pleasure to intellectual enjoyment, which reflect on questions of identification and critical spectatorship. While questioning their applicability, I will propose new modes of assessment based on an ethical stance which I believe informs this cinematic milestone.

A radical defence of visual and carnal pleasures, as conveyed in the form of an ethical platform for the expression of desire, *The Realm of the Senses* came out in 1976, a year after Laura Mulvey published her groundbreaking feminist attack on visual pleasure derived from American cinema (Mulvey [1975] 1989). These diametrically opposing aims, which were at that time at the forefront of respectively the avant-garde Japanese Cinema and European left-wing film criticism, suggest that Oshima's enthusiastic reception in Europe in the early 1970s may have been based on some important misunderstandings. As I will endeavour to show, these misunderstandings become thoroughly apparent when it comes to the critical appraisal of *The Realm of the Senses*.

'Anti-realism' was the order of the day, and a corresponding theory had been evolving from the late 1960s, particularly in France and the UK, with reflections all over the world, in the form of a prescriptive programme aimed at deconstructing subjective identification, as produced by the 'realist' narrative style of the so-called classical Hollywood cinema. 'Anti-realist' filmmaking was epitomized by the work of Jean-Luc Godard, a counter-cinematic, non-narrative paradigm against which all other films were measured. On the basis of these assumptions, several pioneering concepts in film studies were developed whose usefulness and applicability endure to this day. Among them, the notion of the cinematic 'index', as formulated by Peter Wollen in his famous 1969 essay 'The Semiology of Cinema', which identifies Bazin's ontology with the indexical sign, in Peirce's terms, because it stresses 'the existential bond between sign and object' (Wollen [1969] 1998: 86). Few concepts in film studies have been more widely utilized than Wollen's indexicality, which is also entirely applicable when it comes to Oshima's adherence to the contingent with the performance of real sex in *The Realm*. However, Wollen's intent was certainly not to defend realism as style, as Bazin had done, but to celebrate Godard's Brechtian, self-reflexive cinema as an expression of 'Peirce's perfect sign', insofar as it presented 'an equal amalgam of the symbolic, the iconic and the indexical'; that is to say: 'conceptual meaning, pictorial beauty and documentary truth' (Wollen 1998: 106).

Oshima's first success in Europe, *Death by Hanging* (*Koshikei*, 1968), on a first approach seemed to fit this programme like a glove, and this explains much of the applause he received at the time in Europe. The film is a masterly Brechtian take on racial discrimination in Japan, in which a Korean rapist and murderer is sentenced to death by hanging. The execution proceeds, but the convict fails to die, becoming amnesiac instead. The film then evolves, with the authorities representing his crime to him so as to revive his memory and carry out a new execution in accordance with Japanese law, which requires a convict's full awareness of his crime before being killed. Roles are thus reversed, with the authorities playing the part of criminals and the Korean that of their impassive spectator.

Death by Hanging was prevented from premiering at Cannes in 1968 because the festival was interrupted by the May rebellion, but it caused a considerable stir at parallel showings in France. The *Cahiers du Cinéma*, which had surrendered to cinematic *japonisme* since their discovery of Mizoguchi in the early 1950s, immediately adopted Oshima into their pantheon of celebrated auteurs, while *Death by Hanging* was hailed by one of its most distinguished writers, Pascal Bonitzer, as the quintessence of antiillusionism and denunciation of 'spectatorial "foreclosure" from the film story', and a 'metaphor of the impossibility of the spectator's action' (Bonitzer 1970: 34). Stephen Heath, the main representative of Oshima's devotees on the pages of *Screen*, subsequently joined the chorus by calling attention to 'the radical importance' of *Death by Hanging*, whose self-questioning narrative structure located it in a 'negative hollow' between form and content (Heath [1976, 1981], 1986: 412). This welcoming reception reflects the veritable war then being waged by both French and British critics against narrative cinema, and what was then referred to as 'realism'. Because Japanese cinema was normally at odds with the 'realist' conventions of the so-called Hollywood classical cinema, Japanese directors in general were regarded as 'rebellious' by European critics, regardless of whether they were, like Mizoguchi and (a late Western discovery) Ozu, hegemonic at home (see Nagib 2006: 30–7). And so it happened that Oshima, the rebel *par excellence*, came to crystallize the very kind of countercinema they were craving for.

Turim explores at length the Brecht dimension of this film, starting by noting that:

> Not only is *Death by Hanging* a strategic readjustment of Brechtian devices of distanciation to cinematic form, it invites specific comparison in its treatment of the hanging to that at the end of Brecht's *The Threepenny Opera* (1928). It also invites comparison to his *Caucasian Chalk Circle* (1948). Justice is on trial. For this reason and for its dark humor, its theoretical connections to Brecht are significant. (Turim 1998: 63)

As is well known, Brecht's epic theatre was based on the notion of *Verfremdungseffekt* (variously translated as an effect of 'alienation', 'distanciation' or 'estrangement'), whose point was to appeal to reason (*Verstand*), rather than feeling or empathy (*Einfühlung*) (Brecht 2001: 16, 23). Its purpose was to draw the attention of the spectator to the ideological content of conventional, 'bourgeois' theatre which operated through processes of spectatorial 'identification' and 'illusionism'. Revolutionary though this proposal was, it did not break away from well-established Western traditions. On the philosophical front, it embraces a Christian-inflected body-mind dualism which sends back to Kantian metaphysics. 'Distanciation effect' chimes in particular with Kant's notion of 'disinterest', as formulated in his *Critique of Judgement*, which defines a subject's relation to artistic beauty as an attitude of detached contemplation through which the subject remains unaffected by the physical existence of an art object (Gaut 2007: 29).

Brecht's 'neo-Kantianism' had been the subject of heated discussion already in the pages of *Screen*, the most outspokenly Brechtian of film journals in the 1970s. In his defence of Lukacsian realism, Mitchell (1974, contested by Brewster 1974) had aligned Brecht's concept of *Verfremdung* to Shklovsky's formalist concept of *ostranenie*, based on processes of de-routinization and defamiliarization triggered by works of art. Mitchell argued that:

> Formalist aesthetics is Kantian, topped with modern phenomenology (Husserl was an influence: one sees in Shklovsky's formulation how the 'what' of a work of art can be 'bracketed'...) ...Or to put it another way: the 'what' of representation turns into the 'how'. (Mitchell 1974: 75)

Barthes, another highly influential figure on film theory in the 1970s alongside Brecht, further expanded on this 'bracketing of contents' with his idea of 'third' or 'obtuse' meaning, that which is 'discontinuous, indifferent to the story and to the obvious meaning (as signification of the story)', and for this reason has a 'distancing effect with regard to the referent' (Barthes 1977: 61). It is, in essence, the same idea he puts forward in his insightful book about Japan, *L'Empire des signes* (1970), in which the country is defined as an empty centre with meanings dispersed at its fringes – and from which the French title of Oshima's film, *L'Empire des sens*, derives. Heath translated this idea into the notion of 'excess' (1975) to define film elements with no narrative function, but endowed with the power to reveal further meanings of a film, not least the 'arbitrariness' of its narrative structure (Thompson 1986: 140).

The Kantian idea of 'disinterest' has recently returned to the debate in connection with ethics and processes of 'othering', as put forward by Lévinas and discussed by Derrida (Gaston 2005). It has also been compared to notions of beauty as a function of 'disinterested contemplation' and 'artistic detachment', as found in both traditional Zen and modern Japanese philosophy (Odin 2001). However, notions of 'otherness', as derived from Kant and related philosophical sources, or Japanese 'detached contemplation', which is discernible in filmmakers akin to Zen-Buddhism such as Ozu, could not be farther removed from Oshima's and his generation's aesthetic aspirations. True enough, Zen emphasizes in-between spaces and nothingness, as expressed respectively in concepts of *ma* and *mu*, and certainly Ozu – whose grave is simply marked with the *mu* Chinese character, at his own request – shunned any physical contact in his films, except for extremely rare and highly emotional handshakes. But no less linked to Zen philosophy is the concept of *ukiyo*, the floating world, which celebrates life's ephemerality and a corresponding attitude of *carpe diem*. It is the recovery of this atmosphere of liberty which animated Oshima and the filmmakers of his generation. Rather than the elements of modernity capable of matching Western philosophical abstraction, what interested these filmmakers about Japanese arts and philosophy was a tradition of the cult of the body, and the physical environment able to back their daring approach to material reality. As Dominique Buisson argues:

> Differently from the Judaeo-Christian West, where sex is always associated with evil, Japan does not condemn pleasure as such; sex does not imply any personal guilt, having as its sole limit, according to the Confucian moral, not to disturb the public order and not to stain one's name with an indelible shame. Japanese sexuality is connected with immediate joy, rather than with the Western conception of love. (Buisson 2001: 63)

This is what Anatole Dauman, the French producer of *The Realm of the Senses*, so perceptively intuited in Oshima's previous work when he commissioned from him an outright erotic film. Oshima showed how well he understood the message by focusing on Sada Abe, a modern character whose mindset dated back to the Edo period, or even farther to Heian (AD 794–1185), when exceptional female writers such as Murasaki Shikibu (*The Tales of Genji*) and Sei Shonagon (*The Pillow Book*) spent their lives refining their sexual knowledge and practical experience.

Sada Abe was a geisha and prostitute who, in 1936, became a waitress at a restaurant owned by Kichizo Ishida, who immediately became her lover. After several days of uninterrupted sex with Ishida in a Tokyo inn, she finally strangled and emasculated him. The most striking aspect of her story is her devotion to pleasure above everything else in life. The anti-metadiscourse *par excellence*, Sada's literalness is exemplarily illustrated by the way she put into practice what Freud had famously defined as the female 'penis envy', by simply taking possession of her lover's penis and testicles in their materiality. Not only did she continue to carry this token inside her garments wherever she went, before her arrest, but she cuddled, sucked and tried to insert it into her body (Abe 2005: 205). Repulsive though this mere idea may be, the sensual understanding she had of a woman's love for a man is at times intensely moving:

> People have made an incredible fuss since they found out what I did, but there are lots of women who fall hopelessly in love with a man. Even if a wife doesn't like sashimi, if her husband likes it she will naturally start to like it, too. And there are lots of wives who sleep with their husband's pillow in their arms while he is away. For some women the smell of the quilted kimono of the man they love might make them feel ill. But there are lots of women who think that the tea left behind by the man they love or the food that he has already had in his mouth are delicious. (Abe 2005: 208)

Such statements resulted in moments of rare beauty in the film; for example, when Sada locks herself in a train lavatory to unpack and bury her face into Kichizo's kimono which she is carrying with her. Or when he dips slices of mushroom and other vegetables in her juices before taking them to his mouth and sharing them with her, a scene which comes straight from Sada's own account (Abe 2005: 194). Vivian Sobchack derives an ethics from the aesthetics based on the 'experience we have of ourselves and others as material objects' (Sobchack 2004: 296). This she calls 'interobjectivity', which 'lies in the *subjective* realization of our own *objectivity*, in the passion of our *own* material' (Sobchack 2004: 310). In Oshima's film, a similar process of 'interobjectivity' can be observed in the emphasis placed on the, ultimately utopian, continuity through which a subject aspires to incorporate and become the beloved object.

Sada was furthermore the living proof of the continuity between art and reality. The knife she bought when she first thought of murdering Kichizo was suggested by a theatre play she had watched at the Meijiza in between encounters with him (Abe 2005: 192, 194). Upon her release from prison, she herself became part of a theatre troupe, directed by Mikihiko Nagata (who would later turn to screen writing), performing a one-act play called A Woman of the Showa Period (Showa ichidai onna), based on her own story. Abe even appeared in a documentary film by Ishii Teruo, Love and Crime or History of Bizarre Crimes by Women in the Meiji, Taisho and Showa Eras (Meiji-Taisho-Showa, ryoki onna hanzaishi, 1969) (Johnston 2005: 161).

Donald Richie has a marvellous piece on his encounter with Sada Abe, in the bar she had been working in since 1952, which shows how she had come to fuse performance and real life:

After the war, released from prison, she got herself a job in Inari-cho, in downtown Tokyo: at the Hoshi-Kiku-Sui – the Star-Chrysanthemum-Water – a pub. There, every night workers of the neighbourhood … would gather to drink saké and shochu and nibble grilled squid and pickled radish. And every night around ten, Sada Abe would make her entrance. It was grand … Always in bright kimono, one redolent of the time of her crime, early Showa, 1936, Sada Abe would appear at the head of the stairs, stop, survey the crowd below, and then slowly descend … The descent was dramatic, with many pauses as she stared at her guests below, turning a brief gaze on this one and that. And as she did so, progressing slowly, indignation was expressed … The men invariably placed their hands over their privates. Fingers squeezed tight, they would then turn and snicker. Above, the descending Sada Abe would mime fury, casting burning glances at those below who squeezed and giggled the more. She slapped the banister in her wrath, and merriment rippled. (Richie 1991: 33)

As well as contiguity between art and life, this account testifies to a participative audience, which is precisely the kind Oshima was aiming at with *The Realm of the Senses*.

The Participative Voyeur

While Mulvey denounces the position of the spectators in the cinema as 'one of repression of their exhibitionism and projection of the repressed desire onto the performer' (1989: 17), *The Realm* replaces voyeurism with exhibitionism, so as to encourage scopophilia and identification to the point of pushing the passive voyeur, both within the film fable and on the level of spectatorship, into physically and actively joining the erotic play. A lot has been said and written about voyeurism in the film, and indeed, in its 20 scenes of sexual situations, there is practically none which is not being either secretly or openly spied upon by someone. This has been drawn literally from Sada's own account, in which she reiterates that, in the inns she frequented with her lover, 'whether the maid or anybody else came to the room I wouldn't let go of Ishida' (Abe 2005: 194). Japanese erotic art, an invaluable aesthetic source for Oshima and Toda, is also rife with voyeurism, and I will look at how it relates to the film, as far as voyeurism is concerned, in a moment.

Worthy of note at this stage is that, in *The Realm*, the voyeur is there to be noticed and invited, or even forced, by an all-powerful Sada to participate in the sexual act. Rather than being punished for their intrusion, as happens with the sliced eyes of Bataille (*Story of the Eye*) or Buñuel (*Un Chien andalou/An*

Andalusian Dog, 1929), both of whom are directing their aggression against a repressive system grounded on Catholicism, in *The Realm* the voyeur is often rewarded with sex with Kichi, as in the case of the elderly geisha, Kikuryu, who collapses in ecstasy when penetrated by him. Sada and Kichi find, reveal or even create voyeurs wherever they go, forcing them to confess to their current status with regard to sex, like the virgin servant who is keeping herself for a future husband, or the impotent restaurant cook, who remains unmoved at the sight of Sada's exposed pubis. Bataille's eyes (including the eyes of a bull and a priest) and other round-shape avatars, such as the bull testicles which Simone, in *Story of the Eye*, inserts in her vagina, are here replaced by a boiled egg, which Kichi inserts into Sada's vagina, and she has to return squatting and pushing like a hen – and the egg comes out intact. Rather than any repressive religious or social force, it is the empire of desire which is here at work, leading all characters to attest to their physical, all too human, condition.

Recently, there have been perceptive readings of this scopophilic mechanism; for example, by Sharp, who, in his exhaustively researched and beautifully illustrated book on the Japanese erotic film industry, remarks that *The Realm*:

> rejects the standard voyeuristic *nozoki* position, or rather it subverts it so that most of the scenes are witnessed by women, as opposed to men ... Sada later not only asserts dominance in the bedroom; she more or less 'performs' with Kichi for the benefit of the various female third parties .... (Sharp 2008: 192)

More often, however, voyeurism in *The Realm* has been seen as the introduction of an intermediary instance, as a means to generate a distancing effect. 'The movie prohibits all immediate contagion, all sexual emotion. Rarely has voyeurism been so discouraged', writes Pascal Bonitzer, Oshima's most devoted critic at the *Cahiers*. This is because, as he puts it: 'the spectators see themselves in the film ... The third person's eyes are constantly included in the scene to be challenged' (Bonitzer 1976: 51). Such denial of sexual contagion continues to reverberate in Mellen, who states 'the film permits little vicarious arousal by a spectator' (2004: 36) and, in another passage: 'Deliberately, Oshima refuses the easy palliative of audience identification' (2004: 72). How would these critics then explain the ubiquitous presence of voyeurs in porn films, in which they are obviously meant to *cause* spectatorial identification and arousal? That this is also the voyeur's function in *The Realm* is evident, among other things, in the didactic nature of the camera movements, in charge of Nikkatsu soft-porn cinematographer Hideo Itoh, who guides the viewer/voyeur's gaze towards arousing sights, and the careful positioning of actors' legs, torsos and arms, in such a way as not to block a detailed view of sex organs, penetrations and fellatios, including what in the porn genre would be called 'the money shot', all of which are performed with utter realism so as to expose the state of sexual excitement that cast (and consequently crew) themselves were in during the shoot. It is hard to imagine how any viewer can (or should) remain immune to 'vicarious arousal' at the sight of this.[2]

In this respect, *The Realm of the Senses* is no different from *shunga* (Japanese erotic woodblock prints), which inspired so many of its pictorial compositions and whose function is no other than to provoke sexual arousal and satisfaction, in the fashion of contemporary porn films. An image found in Timon Screech's excellent *shunga* book ingeniously illustrates the inextricable continuity between artistic contemplation and physical enjoyment in the Japanese art Oshima and Toda were clearly looking at when making *The Realm*. The print shows a man who has rolled up a picture of a 'beautiful person' (a prostitute) until only her face remains visible; he then shapes a body out of clothing and ties to it a so-called 'Edo Shape' (*azumagata*), or artificial vagina, made from leather or velvet and stuffed with boiled *konnyaku* (a jelly made of a special kind of potato), with which he can perform sex (Screech 1999: 20) (Figure 1). Abstract thinking thus finds continuity in real intercourse.

This aversion, on the part of some critics, to sexual contagion relates to, and often derives from, Brecht and his body-mind dualism. In an early book which he would probably not subscribe to entirely nowadays, Robert Stam explains

Figure 1   The azumagata *allows the picture viewer to perform sex: abstract thinking finds continuity in real intercourse*

that 'as well as rejecting compassion and fear, Brecht's non-Aristotelian theatre also rejects any possibility of erotic involvement' (Stam 1981: 154).[3] Typically, Stam singles out Godard as an example of how cinema can 'eschew the dangers of sexual images' and 'sabotage the eroticism of the image', as well as avoid 'the traps of art as an ersatz for libidinal satisfaction', 'the spectator's voyeuristic involvement' and 'scopophilic concupiscence' (Stam 1981: 155–6). It is indeed a fact that, in Godard, intellectual activity inevitably collides with and interrupts the sexual act. In his first feature film, *Breathless* (À *Bout de souffle*, 1960), for example, reading disrupts the sexual involvement between the protagonists in a famously long bed scene, in which intercourse is only suggested under the bed covers (Figure 2). In stark contrast to this, a *shunga* print by Harunobu Suzuki (1725–70), on which a scene of *The Realm* was based, shows singing and reading (a poetry book lies open next to the male lover); that is, intellectual activity, as not only not disrupting sex, but enhancing it, with artistic beauty, poetry and music being conducive to sexual arousal. Sitting on her lover's penis in exactly the same position as seen in the *shunga* picture, Sada, in the film, sings to the shamisen for Kichi, to disguise their sexual activity, in case his wife should overhear them through the thin paper door. Her singing then gradually changes into moans as she climaxes, which supplies her artistic/intellectual performance with a physical ending (Figures 3 and 4). Another Harunobu *shunga* print makes this point even more strongly. Here, calligraphy and love poems (intellectual pleasure) are the very motor of sexual activity (carnal pleasure), as a teacher leads the hand of his pupil on the writing of a love poem while he penetrates her (Figure 5).

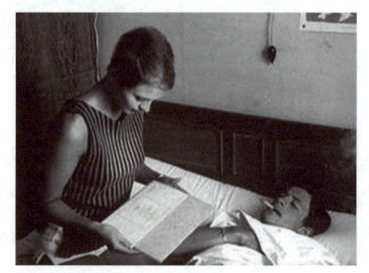

Figure 2   Reading disrupts sex in Breathless

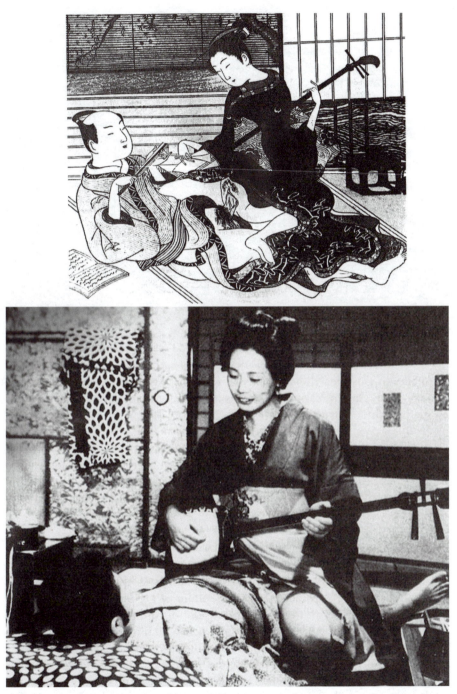

Figures 3–4   As in Harunobu's shunga, Sada's artistic performance has a physical ending

Figure 5   A calligraphy lesson leads to sex

Averse to this idea though many of Oshima's admirers might be, the fact remains that *The Realm of the Senses* is an authentic antithesis to Godard, as Williams rightly remarks:

> Though Oshima's politics and avant-gardism could sometimes make him seem like a Japanese Godard – a filmmaker whose metacinematic qualities he indeed did emulate in some of his earlier films – the narrative of this particular film, which is straightforward, is very un-Godardian. (2008: 186)

As much as any other filmmaker, Godard was obsessed with sex in the liberating 1970s, and a film such as *Number Two* (*Numéro Deux*, 1975) abounds with fellatios, anal sex and female masturbation. However, these images are constantly and purposely dislocated from their aim of producing pleasure, which makes them 'obscene' in the Sartrean sense of disruption between consciousness and the body, or a body 'caught up in acts which reveal the inertia of the flesh' (Sartre 1943: 452). Body-mind continuity is what, in *The Realm*, avoids this sense of obscenity of the unconscious flesh, by candidly exposing bodies entirely and consciously drenched in sexual lust. Lacan reportedly said of *The Realm* that it was 'the most chaste film I have ever seen' (Mandiargues 1989:

237). This curiously echoes Sada, who said of Kichi that: 'Emotionally he was a very simple man. Even little things would make him happy. He tended to show his emotions and was as innocent as a little baby' (Abe 2005: 193). Sada seems to have touched a point: the direct expression of emotion and desire averts all sense of obscenity, dirt, sin and guilt. And this is why the lovers can relish their own smell, even if it disgusts a non-participant voyeur, and delight in each other's juices, including Sada's menstrual blood. The latter example, incidentally, is also directly drawn from Sada's account, which is even more poignant than its screen version: while in the film Kichi licks his blood-sprinkled fingers after playing with Sada, in the real story he goes down on her, despite her uninviting condition. This is not just the film breaking one of Japan's severest taboos, but an example of the non-existence of taboos in the pleasure world Oshima was focusing upon.

But even when Oshima was openly embracing Brecht, as was the case in *Death by Hanging*, the result was far from pure alienation effects. This is precisely what *The Realm*, as the apex of Oshima's career, summing up his most daring experiments, shows: how questionable the very idea of alienation effect is. Cognitivists, such as Murray Smith, have long dismissed 'the commonplace, with very ancient roots in Western culture, concerning the purportedly antagonistic relationship between reason and emotion', and 'the idea that undergoing empathy deadens our rational faculties' (Smith 1996: 132). Instead, he says, 'emotion is integrated with perception, attention, and cognition, not implacably opposed to any of them' (Smith 1996: 132–3).

Interestingly, Brecht was under the influence of the Chinese theatre when he first formulated his idea of 'alienation effects'. According to his translator John Willett, Brecht used the famous expression *Verfremdungseffekt* for the first time with reference to the Chinese actor Mei Lan-fang and his theatre company, when they performed in Moscow in 1935 (Brecht 2001: 99n.). *Verfremdung* is a neologism intended to replace in an art context the concept of *Entfremdung* in the Marxist sense of a worker's alienation from the product of his/her labour. In his article 'Alienation Effects in Chinese Acting', Brecht lists a series of devices he deems 'antiillusionistic' in the Chinese theatre, all of which he would later employ in his own epic theatre, including the rejection of realistic mimesis, the use of symbols, the actors' emotional control, the absence of a fourth wall and the construction of the sets before the eyes of the audience (Brecht 2001: 91ff.). All these devices had the aim of making visible the theatrical 'apparatus'. This is pertinent here insofar as most Japanese art forms derive from the Chinese, and include all these supposedly 'distancing' devices, as can also be observed in *The Realm of the Senses*, close as it is to Japanese traditional arts.

As far as cinema is concerned, since the 1970s the so-called *dispositif cinématographique*, or the cinematic apparatus, has become a central concept, for it describes the ways in which identification and illusionism are produced in order to create an 'impression of reality' (Baudry [1970, 1975] 1986). Psychoanalytic and semiotic theories embraced the concept of cinematic apparatus as the phenomenon of the spectator's regression to the mirror phase, as defined by Lacan. The revelation of this apparatus in the scene, as carried out by Godard, would consequently prevent identification and enable the formation of critical spectatorship in Brechtian terms. Japanese theatre is famous for this kind of recourse, as seen, for example, in the bunraku puppet theatre, where the puppet manipulators are fully visible alongside their puppets. Most critics who believe *The Realm* prevents sexual contagion are, in fact, identifying the visible voyeurs in the film with this kind of purportedly 'disruptive' figure. Let me resort once again to Harunobu's *shunga* prints as a means to demonstrate that the visible apparatus in the Japanese traditional arts, rather than preventing erotic contagion, is itself eroticized; that is, it is a mechanism through which reason and emotion remain intertwined, as is also the case in Oshima's film.

Despite the beauty and obvious artistic value of so many *shunga* prints, their primary function, as I have pointed out above, was sexual arousal and satisfaction. For this reason, they were also called *makura-e* or pillow pictures, and *warai-e* or laughing pictures ('to laugh', signifying 'to masturbate') (Screech 1999: 14). However, the self-reflexive elements abounding in them could easily suggest detachment and distanciation in the very same way Brecht had understood the workings of the Chinese theatre. In order to test this assumption, let us have a look at this Harunobu print (Figure 6). In it, the lovers not only do not look at each other (do not look for excitement in one another), but look in opposite directions. At a first glance, this could suggest distraction, detachment, lack of attention, or even indifference towards sex. A closer look, however, reveals that the two apparently independent activities are in fact inextricable, because the woman is actually drawing sexual inspiration from the sight of pedestrians (possible voyeurs) walking in the rain (water is seen as an erotic element), while the man is expecting the same from an object off-frame (possibly other voyeurs). What they see flows through their eyes and minds, so as to inspire the activity of their lower bodies. As in onanistic activities, sexual desire is aroused by the sight of a third element.

In this print, several of the 'alienation effects', described by Brecht with reference to the Chinese theatre, can be identified:

- Symbolism: the woman's toes are contracted, expressing sexual arousal (Klompmakers 2001: 17), although nothing else in her body indicates that.
- Emotional control: as in Brecht's description (2001: 93), the characters are not in trances, there is no exaltation or eruption.
- The absence of mimetic realism: facial expressions are only slightly indicated with single strokes, male and female faces are very similar,

Figure 6 Two apparently independent activities are, in fact, inextricable

Figure 7 The voyeur's activity mirrors and suggests that of the viewer

resulting in mimesis of the idea rather than of the form; the unnatural position, even contortionism of the bodies, simultaneously conveys the characters' sexual and intellectual activities to the viewer.

This other Harunobu print (figure 7) perfectly illustrates the idea of an 'eroticized' apparatus, in the form of the participative voyeur, who maintains a self-reflexive, ironic attitude, while expressing his own sexual arousal. I am referring to the miniature man, Maneemon, the protagonist of a series devoted to his adventures, as reproduced in Kompmakers (2001). Maneemon is the alter-ego of Harunobu himself, reduced to miniature size thanks to a magic potion he has taken in order to be able to spy on his own characters. Here, a man makes love to an adolescent, who in turn masturbates. The boy's gaze is turned towards the sleeve of his kimono, which has a masculine pattern, the iris, whose leaves are associated with the blade of a sword. The man's gaze is turned toward the boy's organ while he masturbates. The patterns on the futon also indicate sexual love, with the motif of the stylized chrysanthemum which resembles the anus. Maneemon, the 'eroticized apparatus', descends to the tea house's second floor, flying in on a kite, which he still holds in his left hand. The written comments reveal that the scene excites him so much that he needs to fan himself – his samurai outfit, including the sword, indicates the condition of the man, and homoeroticism as a common practice among samurais (Klompmakers 2001: 62–3). What becomes obvious here is the general sexual contagion, including the painter himself, who is not only the excited voyeur within the image, but also the artist indulging his erotic imagination. His activity mirrors and suggests that of the viewer, who is also supposed to engage in onanistic or other sexual practices while looking at the print.

The same can be observed throughout *The Realm of the Senses*, most strikingly in the scene with the elderly geisha Kikuryu mentioned above. She arrives as Kichi and Sada are naked making love, politely congratulates them on their energy, and is hardly able to hide her own excitement as she starts playing the shamisen and singing. A frontal shot captures her through the half-opened shoji in centre frame, with Sada on top of Kichi to the left. Sada then starts to interrogate Kikuryu in a dialogue which actually suggests Sada's envy of the voyeur position. She finally offers Kichi to the geisha. The camera then reverses to show Sada through the half-opened shoji while Kichi makes love to Kikuryu in the hallway. Alternate reverse shots show both that Sada is becoming excited with this sight and that Kichi is looking at her for arousal in his own act. In the role of this eroticized voyeur, Sada is given tighter and tighter close-ups, with her thick, red, trembling lips occupying the whole screen; at this point, Kikuryu gives her climactic sigh, which seems to come from Sada's own lips as she dubs her (Figures 8–12).

*Figures 8–9   Reversing and merging active and passive voyeurism: Sada dubs the geisha's
ecstasy*

The revelation of the voyeur's lust takes place here through literal unmasking: Kikuryu loses her wig and exposes her actually dark skin below the
whitened face and neck, her wilted body revealed under the shiny, elegant red
and white kimono, redolent of the *hinomaru*, the sun disc of the Japanese
flag obsessively referred to in the film as symbolic of Japan's sexual core.
Revelation and general contamination of desire – that is to say, the unmasking

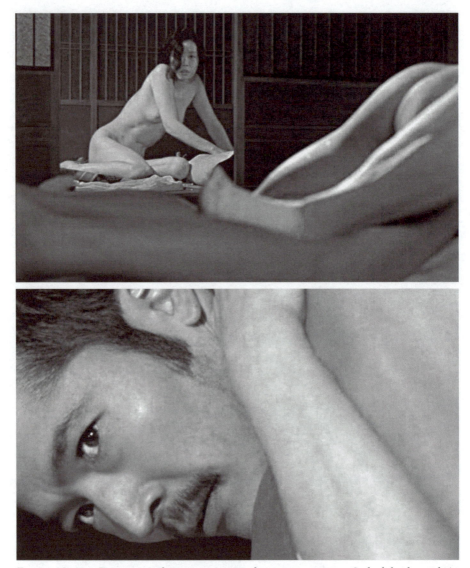

*Figures 10–11   Reversing and merging active and passive voyeurism: Sada dubs the geisha's
ecstasy*

and celebration of total identification, which cause the reversibility and
equivalence of spectators and participants at all levels – is shown to be the rule
in this world of passion, and are propounded as a unifying, ethical principle
connecting art, intellect, the film medium and the body.

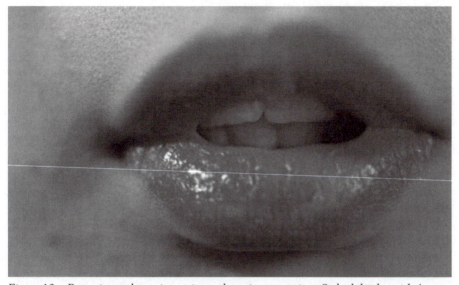

Figure 12   Reversing and merging active and passive voyeurism: Sada dubs the geisha's ecstasy

References

Abe, Sada (2005) 'Notes from the police interrogation of Abe Sada', in Johnston (2005: 163–208).

Barthes, Roland (1970) *L'Empire des signes* (Paris, Champs/Flammarion).

Barthes, Roland (1977) *Image-Music-Text*, ed. and trans. Stephen Heath (London, Fontana).

Bataille, Georges (1967) 'La Notion de dépense', in *La Part maudite* (Paris, Les Éditions de Minuit).

Bataille, Georges (1970) *Œuvres complètes I – Premiers Écrits 1922–1940* (Paris, Gallimard).

Bataille, Georges (1985) *Visions of Excess: Selected Writings, 1927–1939*, ed. and trans. Allan Stoekl (Minneapolis, University of Minnesota Press).

Bataille, Georges (1986) *Erotism: Death & Sensuality*, ed. and trans. Mary Dalwood (San Francisco, City Lights Books).

Baudry, Jean-Louis (1986) 'Ideological effects of the basic cinematographic apparatus'; 'The apparatus: metapsychological approaches to the impression of reality in cinema', in Philip Rosen (ed.) *Narrative, Apparatus, Ideology: A Film Theory Reader* (New York, Columbia University Press), pp.286–318.

Bonitzer, Pascal (1976) 'L'Essence du pire (*L'Empire des sens*)', in *Cahiers du Cinéma* 270, September–October, pp.48–52.

Brecht, Bertolt (2001) *Brecht on Theatre: The Development of an Aesthetic*, ed. and trans. John Willett (London, Methuen).

Brewster, Ben (1974) 'From Shklovsky to Brecht: A Reply', in *Screen* 15:2, pp.82–101.

Buisson, Dominique (2001) *Le Corps japonais* (Paris, Hazan).

Dauman, Anatole (1989) *Souvenir-Ecran* (Paris, Centre Georges Pompidou).

Gaston, Sean (2005) *Derrida and Disinterest* (London/New York, Continuum).

Gaut, Berys (2007) *Art, Emotion and Ethics* (New York, Oxford University Press).

Heath, Stephen (1986) 'Narrative space', in Philip Rosen (ed.) *Narrative, Apparatus, Ideology: A Film Theory Reader* (New York, Columbia University Press), pp.379–420.

Johnston, William (ed.) (2005) *Geisha-Harlot-Strangler-Star: A Woman, Sex, & Morality in Modern Japan* (New York, Columbia University Press).

Klompmakers, Inge (2001) *Japanese Erotic Prints: Shunga by Harunobu & Hokusai* (Leiden, Hotei).

Mandiargues, Pieyre de (1989) 'Propos recueillis par Ornella Volta', in Anatole Dauman, *Souvenir-Ecran* (Paris, Centre Georges Pompidou), pp.236–8.

Marran, Christine L. (2007) *Poison Woman: Figuring Female Transgression in Modern Japanese Culture* (Minneapolis, University of Minnesota Press).

Mellen, Joan (2004) *In the Realm of the Senses* (London, BFI).

Mitchell, Stanley (1974) 'From Shklovsky to Brecht: some preliminary remarks towards a history of the politicization of Russian Formalism', *Screen* 15:2, pp.74–81.

Mulvey, Laura (1989) *Visual and Other Pleasures* (London, Macmillan).

Nagib, Lúcia (1995) *Nascido das cinzas: autor e sujeito nos filmes de Oshima* (São Paulo, Edusp).

Nagib, Lúcia (2006) 'Towards a positive definition of World Cinema', in Song Hwee Lim and Stephanie Dennison (eds), *Remapping World Cinema: Identity, Culture and Politics in Film* (London, Wallflower), pp.30–7.

Odin, Steve (2001) *Artistic Detachment in Japan and the West* (Honolulu, University of Hawaii Press).

Richie, Donald (1996) *Public People, Private People: Portraits of Some Japanese* (Tokyo/New York/London, Kodansha).

Sartre, Jean-Paul (1943) *L'Être et le néant* (Paris, Gallimard).

Screech, Timon (1999) *Sex and the Floating World: Erotic Images in Japan 1700–1820* (London, Reaktion).

Sharp, Jasper (2008) *Behind the Pink Curtain – The Complete History of Japanese Sex Cinema* (Godalming, FAB).

Smith, Murray (1996) 'The logic and legacy of Brechtianism', in David Bordwell and Noël Carroll (eds) *Post-Theory: Reconstructing Film Studies* (Madison, University of Wisconsin Press), pp.136–54.

Sobchack, Vivian (2004) *Carnal Thoughts: Embodiment and Moving Image Culture* (Berkeley/Los Angeles/London, University of California Press).

Stam, Robert (1981) *O espetáculo interrompido: literatura e cinema de desmistificação*, trans. José Eduardo Moretzsohn (Rio de Janeiro, Paz e Terra).

Stam, Robert (1992) *Reflexivity in Film and Literature: From Don Quixote to Jean-Luc Godard* (New York, Columbia University Press).

Thompson, Kristin (1986) 'The concept of cinematic excess', in Philip Rosen (ed.) *Narrative, Apparatus, Ideology: A Film Theory Reader* (New York, Columbia University Press), pp.130–42.

Turim, Maureen (1998) *The Films of Oshima Nagisa: Images of a Japanese Iconoclast* (Berkeley/Los Angeles/London, University of California Press).

Williams, Linda (2008) *Screening Sex* (Durham/London, Duke University Press).

Wollen, Peter (1998) *Signs and Meaning in the Cinema* (London, BFI).

Notes

1 This chapter is an extract of ch. 5, '*The Realm of the Senses*, the Ethical Imperative and the Politics of Pleasure', of Lúcia Nagib (2011) *World Cinema and the Ethics of Realism* (New York/London, Continuum).

2 Sada Abe's story is itself sexually contagious, and there is an interesting anecdote in Johnston's book in this respect. It refers to the main judge in the trial, who confessed in his memoirs, published 20 years later, to have found himself sexually excited while reading the documents related to the case. In order to make sure the other three judges would be able to lawfully release themselves, should they experience the same feelings, he discreetly investigated the time when their respective wives were having their periods (sex during menstruation being a taboo in Japan in those days), so as to schedule the trial in a convenient moment for the three of them (Johnston 2005: 135–6).

3 A thoroughly revised English version of this book was later published as *Reflexivity in Film and Literature* (Stam 1992, first edition 1985).

Chapter Eleven

Realism of the Senses: A Tendency in Contemporary World Cinema[1]

Tiago de Luca

> There is not one realism, but several realisms. Each period looks for its own, the technique and the aesthetics that will capture, retain, and render best what one wants from reality.
>
> André Bazin

Over the last decade or so, a realist tendency has surfaced on the world cinema map, represented by names such as Abbas Kiarostami (Iran), Apichatpong Weerasethakul (Thailand), Carlos Reygadas (Mexico), Béla Tarr (Hungary), Tsai Ming-liang (Taiwan), Lisandro Alonso (Argentina), Alexander Sokurov (Russia), Jia Zhangke (China), Gus Van Sant (USA), Pedro Costa (Portugal), Nuri Bilge Ceylan (Turkey) and José Luis Guerin (Spain), to cite some of the most famous. Despite the differences between these filmmakers, their work can be grouped together thanks to their resolute adherence to devices traditionally associated with cinematic realism, such as location shooting, non-professional actors, deep-focus cinematography and the long take.

Yet, each new realist peak differs from its predecessor, as eloquently expressed in the above quote from André Bazin. What is the distinctiveness of this new realist aesthetics? As will be my contention here, it is steeped in the hyperbolic application of the long take, which promotes a contemplative viewing experience anchored in materiality and duration. In what follows, I will attempt to theorize the sensory mode of address which I define as typical of this realism, based as it is on a protracted inspection of physical reality. I begin with a reflection on the emergence of digital technology, which has prompted euphoric and nostalgic discourses on the demise of realism in film. I then provide an overview of the ways in which the realist style has been historically theorized as connected to the sensory character of the cinematic experience, moving on to formulate my own take on the subject through an analysis of the main aesthetic principles governing contemporary realist cinema. I conclude by defining its political power.

The Real and the Digital

Debates concerning the demise of realism in cinema have proliferated in film studies in the last two decades. Due to digital's ability to elicit simulation, what is today largely known as the indexicality of photography was deemed lost. As is well known, the term indexicality gained currency in film studies through Peter Wollen's assessment of Bazin's concept of the 'ontology of the photographic image' in the light of Peirce's theory of signs (Wollen 1998: ch. 3). Wollen translated Bazin's ontology into Peirce's definition of the index; that is, the sign that connects to its object through an existential link, as observed in the photographic image. With the emergence of digital technology, indexicality, it appeared, was no longer inherent to the photographic image. As a consequence, cinema as we knew it was declared dead, prompting theorizations that either celebrated or lamented the digital turn.

In 1996, for instance, Stephen Prince observed that the 'perceptual realism' of films such as *Jurassic Park* (Steven Spielberg, 1993) and *Forrest Gump* (Robert Zemeckis, 1994) were 'referentially fictional' – that is to say, created entirely through digital processes – while conserving an isomorphic correspondence to the physical properties and Cartesian coordinates of the real world. Digitization, Prince argued, gave a new flexibility to the cinematic image which in turn invalidated the application of classical film theories to contemporary cinematic phenomena (Prince 1996). This idea was later reinforced by Lev Manovich, who contended that cinema was 'no longer an indexical media technology, but, rather, a subgenre of painting' (Manovich 2001: 295), due to the fact that cinematic images could be digitally manipulated. More recently, Daniel Frampton has struck a similar note, arguing that the increase of virtual images in film or, in his words, the fluidity of 'this new digitally manipulatable film image', prompts a reconceptualization of film away from notions of 'automatic photography' and direct 'reproduction of reality' (Frampton 2006: 4–5).

The idea that realist theories were no longer adequate to account for current film phenomena also took on nostalgic overtones. In the introduction to the new edition of Siegfried Kracauer's *Theory of Film: the Redemption of Physical Reality*, Miriam Bratu Hansen argued that Kracauer's realist theory elucidated an indexically grounded cinema which belonged to 'a period that may well be past', helping us 'understand the experience that cinema once *was*' (Hansen

1997: xxxv, my emphasis). Subsequently, Mary Ann Doane observed that Hansen's nostalgic take on indexicality resonated with Paul Willemen (Doane 2002: 227), for whom cinephilia or 'cinephiliac moments' are intrinsically linked to the film's indexical dimension. As Willemen explains, the surfeit of details recorded by the camera enables the unprogrammed contingent to 'shine through' the image, allowing the spectator 'to glimpse something else that you are not meant to see' (Willemen 1994: 241). In this way, 'the less the image has a Bazinian ontological relation to the real... the less appropriate cinephilia becomes' (1994: 243).

Both in the celebratory and nostalgic keys, indexicality is seen as a thing of 'the past'. Closer inspection of contemporary audiovisual practices, however, suggests that this may not be entirely true. In fact, the digital often makes the recording of the real, as well as its dissemination, much easier and cheaper. Our 'obsession with realism' (Bazin 2005a: 12), as Bazin put it some 50 years ago, rather than diminished by the digital, seems greater than ever. Consider, for instance, the boom of reality shows and documentary-style programmes in television in recent years (as pointed out by Nagib and Mello 2009: xv). Take also video websites such as YouTube, whose emblematic slogan is 'Broadcast Yourself', and which has prompted the massive circulation of domestic videos on the Internet. Concerning cinema, it is symptomatic that the documentary genre has seen its levels of popularity and critical acclaim soar in the last few years.

Frampton argues that 'it is hard to find a film that does not include some images or people that were never in front of the camera' nowadays (Frampton 2006: 5). But what kind of cinema are we talking about? Dudley Andrew, for example, disagrees with this view, arguing that 'amidst digital confections tempting filmmakers and audiences to escape to the land of the virtual, world cinema brings us back...to Earth, on which many worlds are lived and perceived concurrently' (Andrew 2006: 28). Of course, this does not mean that world cinema is immune to simulation. On the contrary, digital manipulation of the plastic qualities of the image have become widespread thanks to the digital, an example being Alexander Sokurov's *Russian Ark* (*Russkiy kovcheg*, 2003), the first feature-length film shot in a single long take thanks to digital technology, which, on the other hand, also allowed its images to be retouched in post-production.

As Nagib and Mello note: 'the digital has been more often than not resorted to as a facilitator of the recording of real locations and characters, as well as a means to expand the application of techniques traditionally identified with realism' (Nagib and Mello 2009: xv). As has historically been the case, such techniques are primarily used to express social concerns. An unscripted film such as Abbas Kiarostami's *Ten* (2002), for example, easily proves this point, as it was entirely shot on two portable cameras mounted on the dashboard of a car in movement, without directorial intervention, a method only made possible by the unobtrusive digital equipment. Drawing on observational time and averse to all didacticism, this method allowed non-professional actors to behave naturally and provided the director with plenty of footage for the editing work, aimed at producing a powerful plea for women's rights. The work of Jia Zhangke is another telling example of social concern expressed through digital technology, and indeed an evidence of the revolution caused by this format in Chinese filmmaking over the last decade, as filmmakers have turned to it in order to sidestep censorship and document the environmental transformation effected by the country's economic boom. Portuguese Pedro Costa also opts for the digital as a means to closely document social inequality; in his case, the slum inhabitants on the periphery of Lisbon, as seen in two of his films, *In Vanda's Room* (*No quarto de Vanda*, 2000) and *Colossal Youth* (*Juventude em marcha*, 2006), which he shot entirely by himself with a portable Panasonic DV.

And yet, though the digital and the indexical are not antithetical terms, a digital camera does not capture information in the same way a non-digital camera does. The defining feature of a photograph is the reflection of rays of light, which cause a chemical reaction on the film emulsion through the camera lens. Hence Bazin's famous metaphor of the photograph as a death mask. In digital capture, however, this physical link is less evident, given that the light that passes through the lens is encoded into numerical data. To a film theorist such as D.W. Rodowick, indexicality is therefore 'weakened' in digital capture when compared to analogical photography, because in the latter 'the process of transcription is continuous in space and time, producing an isomorphic record that is indivisible and counterfactually dependent on its source' (Rodowick 2007: 113). This means that photography captures actual blocks of space and time which are dissipated into immaterial algorithms in the digital image. Other theorists, such as Tom Gunning, however, question the notion of a watershed introduced by the digital technology:

> The translation of photographic information into a number-based system certainly represents a revolutionary moment in photography, but one not unlike the replacement of wet collodion process by the dry plate, or the conquering of exposure time with instantaneous photography, or the introduction of the hand camera. Like these earlier transformations in photographic history, the digital revolution will change the way photographs are made, who makes them, and how they are used – but they will still be photographs. (Gunning 2004: 48)

Philip Rosen has used the term 'digital utopia' to refer to the perception that the emergence of digital technology marks a watershed in audiovisual practices. For him, this wrongly 'defines its novelty in opposition to precedent media, identifies precedent media with indexicality, and makes indexicality into a monolithic unity characterized by fixity of world, of representation, of subject' (Rosen 2001: 348). Moreover, Rosen suggests, indexicality is more flexible than recent arguments hingeing on its disappearance imply, and for this reason the novelty introduced by the digital as a simulation tool is only in degree, not in kind. And, indeed, the digital's transformative power has many precedents. Cinematographers, as well as photographers, have always had at their disposal a plethora of formal devices so as to mould the image according to their whims, such as filters, lenses, exposure time, multiple printing, chemicals, etc. No doubt, digital technology intensifies, accelerates and facilitates simulation and manipulation to an unprecedented degree, but this gives continuation to the natural evolution of photography, rather than entailing its end. Foregrounding reality in film has always been a matter of *choice*; that is to say, the result of deliberate strategies, and this long before the emergence of the digital.

Sensory Realism

I would contend that this new realist peak in world cinema is defined above all by a sensory mode of address. Realist styles, and related theories, have always relied on the world's sensory and phenomenological dimensions. Bazin's pioneering realist theory, launched in the 1950s, stated that photography, and consequently film, had an 'ontological' relation with the real, derived from its automatic nature. Therefore, in his defence of realism, he praised those directors who, rather than manipulating objective reality, as in the Soviet montage tradition or in German expressionism, highlighted it through choices such as location shooting, deep-focus cinematography and non-professional acting. Indebted to a phenomenological approach to the real, Bazin revelled in those moments in which the profilmic contingent disrupted the narrative flow, enhancing instead the materiality of the image and thereby triggering a sensuous response on the part of the viewer. His writings are freighted with celebrations of the tactile, physical reality of objects. Take, for instance, his analysis of the final scene of Jean Renoir's *Boudu Saved from Drowning* (*Boudu sauvé des eaux*, 1932):

> The water is no longer 'water' but more specifically the water of the Marne in August, yellow and glaucous. Michel Simon floats on it, turns over, sprays like a seal; and as he plays we begin to perceive the depth, the quality, even the tepid warmth of that water. When he comes up on the bank, an extraordinarily slow 360-degree pan shows us the countryside before him … At the end of the pan, the camera picks up a bit of grass where, in close-up, one can see distinctly the white dust that the heat and wind have lifted from the past. One can almost feel it between one's fingers. (Bazin 1974: 85–6)

Bazin's rhetoric – the 'tepid warmth of the water', the grass which 'one can almost feel between one's fingers' – emphasizes the image's sensory effects on the spectator. As Rosen has recently noted, Bazin's theorization of objective reality as conveyed by film presupposes a subjective investment in the phenomenological real onscreen (Rosen 2003: 41), a subjectivity which I believe has an embodied character.

The notion that the realist style 'affects primarily the spectator's senses' was also put forward in 1960 by Siegfried Kracauer (1997: 158), who, like Bazin, theorized realism as a property intrinsic to the film medium thanks to its photographic foundations:

> [Film] records physical reality for its own sake. Struck by the reality character of the resultant image, the spectator cannot help reacting to them as he would to the material aspects of nature in the raw which these photographic images reproduce. Hence their appeal to his sensitivity. It is as if they urged him through their sheer presence unthinkingly to assimilate their indeterminate and often amorphous patterns. (Kracauer 1997: 158)

Kracauer argued that film's 'affinity' with the material world elicits a corporeal mode of spectatorship: 'The material elements that present themselves in film directly stimulate the *material layers* of the human being: his nerves, his senses, his entire physiological substance' (Hansen 1997: xxi). In her assessment of Kracauer's theory of realism, Hansen would argue that this corporeal approach could not be further away 'from cognitivist conceptions of film viewing as an operation of "scanning", of processing hypotheses relevant for the construction of a story from the film's representational materials' (1997: xxi).

It is interesting to examine how this resonates (or not) with 'body' theories of cinema, which started to emerge in the early 1990s with reference to modes of reception and spectatorship. This was kick-started by Linda Williams, who focused on the physical responses elicited by the 'bodily excess' on display in '"gross" genres' such as the melodrama, pornography and horror films (Williams 1991: 4). In 1993, Steven Shaviro argued for a film theory based on 'the bodily agitations, the movements of fascination, the reactions of attraction and repulsion, of which they are the extension and the elaboration' (Shaviro 1993: 9). Several theoretical approaches, hingeing on the 'sensuous', 'tactile' and 'visceral' dimensions of film viewing, followed in his footsteps. Laura U. Marks, for example, has theorized on the ways in which materiality can impact the viewer in a tactile manner. This she calls 'haptic visuality'; that is, images which foreground 'material presence' through extreme close-ups and unusual framing strategies, engendering a mode of spectatorship in which 'the eyes themselves function like organs of touch' (Marks 2000: 163).

Under the influence of Gilles Deleuze's philosophical approach to cinema, which will be discussed later, these new takes on spectatorship have, by and large, proposed to replace the ideal, transcendental spectator of psychoanalytic and semiotic approaches with a corporeal one, and the concomitant recognition of the bodily pleasures intrinsic to film viewing. In 2000, Vivian Sobchack, drawing on Maurice Merleau-Ponty's phenomenology, attributed this theoretical turn to a dissatisfaction with the way the 'spectator's identification with the cinema has been constituted almost exclusively as a specular and psychical process abstracted from the body and mediated through language' (2000).

Parallel to this, new theories drawing on Bazin's foundational views on realism continued to thrive. Onscreen death and sex, events whose representation Bazin deemed an 'ontological obscenity' (Bazin 2003: 30), as well as physical exertion and animal cruelty, offered new grounds for theorizations on the physicality of the cinematic experience. Ivone Margulies, for example, expounded on what she called 'corporeal cinema'; that is, films which reproduce the 'original urgency' of an event through 'their close association with the carnality of the body and decay ... realities such as possession rituals, animal sacrifice, torture, or physical disability' (Margulies 2003: 1). Sobchack also elaborated from a spectatorial perspective on this physical excess, which in her view ruptures the spectator's investment in the diegesis. This she calls 'the charge of the real', which she illustrates with the famous scene of the killing of a rabbit in Renoir's The Rules of the Game (La Règle du jeu, 1939). She compares the physical quality of this scene with that of the death of a fiction character in Renoir's film, arguing that the latter cannot 'elicit the same level of subjective and physical shiver we feel as our very bodies "know" the existential difference between the character's and the rabbit's ... death' (Sobchack 2004: 271). In tune with this focus on physicality, but moving away from modes of reception and into those of production and address, Lúcia Nagib has theorized on the notion of 'bodily enactment', performed by cast and crew in the recording of the real in the fiction film. She discusses those films which 'give evidence of an actor's physical engagement with the cinematic event' (Nagib 2011: 19), often under extreme conditions. Nagib cites, among others, Glauber Rocha's Black God, White Devil (Deus e o diabo na terra do sol, 1964), in which Manuel's race at the end of the film, performed in reality by actor Geraldo Del Rey in the arid backlands of the Brazilian Northeast, entails for the actor a 'painful, bodily experience' of 'a harsh, cruel soil, under an unrelenting sun' (2011: 64).

In common with, and indebted to, many aspects of these theories, my take on sensory realism presupposes an embodied spectator 'with skin and hair', to cite Kracauer's famous expression; that is, the spectator's phenomenological investment in the onscreen reality. However, my approach claims no position in the debates on modes of cinematic reception. Rather, my purpose is to identify and analyse sensory modes of production and address in contemporary realist cinema, to which I will now turn.

A Cinema of Contemplation

Outside a decrepit shed, the camera records in an establishing shot a herd of cows pottering about and mooing (Figure 1). As the cattle start moving to the left of the screen, the camera follows them in a slow tracking shot while taking in a muddy, desolate wasteland, dotted with crumbling houses and outbuildings. This unbroken shot, which lasts no less than nine minutes, is accompanied by a haunting, eerie soundtrack. Cut. A limping woman, with a broom in hands, walks into an empty cinema's auditorium framed in a static long shot (Figure 2). She enters the frame from the right, walks up the stairs while sweeping the floor, crosses the upper part of the auditorium, then climbs down the stairs and leaves the auditorium from the left, an action which she takes over three minutes to perform. The camera remains imperturbably immobile, recording the now empty auditorium for another three minutes. Cut. Outside a stately home the camera, seemingly static, focuses on a room whose half-open window reveals several musical instruments (Figure 3). On the upper half of this window, the glass reflects the branches of a robust tree whose leaves flutter with the heavy wind. A long-haired, frail man enters the room, and consequently the frame, and starts playing, one by one, these musical instruments: the bass, the guitar, the drums and so on. The camera starts to unhurriedly recede, taking no less than five minutes to unveil the house's façade, its front area and the tree in front of it.

Figure 1   Prolonged stare: Tarr's Sátántangó

Figure 2 *Tsai's* Goodbye Dragon Inn

Figure 3 *Van Sant's* Last Days

These three sequence shots, drawn respectively from Béla Tarr's *Sátántangó* (1994), Tsai's *Goodbye Dragon Inn* (*Bu san*, 2003) and Van Sant's *Last Days* (2005), exemplify the similar kind of realism embraced by contemporary world cinemas. Despite their widely differing settings and objects of attention, they proceed through a similarly protracted and mute contemplation of reality as enabled by the long take. In them, the narrative is not only rarefied through unbroken shots which quickly exhaust diegetic motivation, if ever there was one, but is blatantly averted. Whether through a camera which is content to endlessly reveal a desolate landscape devoid of human presence; or a stubbornly stationary camera which refuses to follow a character that has left the screen; or a slow-moving camera which ostensibly recedes from the main event while framing a much wider visual field, these are cinemas in which the act of recording takes the upper hand over narrative progression thanks to a camera which seems in awe of its own ability to capture overstretched blocs of space and time.

If, as the quote from Bazin which opens this chapter states, each realism 'looks for the technique and the aesthetics that will capture, retain, and render best what one wants from reality' (1997: 6), this contemporary realist tendency has to be defined above all by its hyperbolic use of the long take. It is my contention that these cinemas foreground reality primarily as a perceptual, sensible and experiential phenomenon. Their phenomenological irreducibility can only be perceived and conveyed through sensory experience. At first glance, this superabundant materiality, as enabled by the long take, might seem to accord with the kind of realism championed by Bazin's phenomenology. If that may be the case in many respects, there is also a crucial difference, relating to the way these new realisms far extrapolate the representational imperatives informing Bazin's view of realist cinema. A brief sample of his writings will help me substantiate this claim.

Bazin's thought is traditionally associated with the long take, and yet his defence of this technique is only tangential to it. More than an end in itself, as is often the case in contemporary realism, the sequence shot in Bazinian terms is the direct consequence of another technique, namely depth of field, which, as Wollen notes, is strictly subordinated to dramaturgic efficiency (Wollen 2004: 252). For example, expounding on William Wyler's *The Best Year of Our Lives* (1948), Bazin justifies its lengthy shots with the fact that they are 'necessary to convey the narrative clearly' (1997: 11). Similar justifications are given in his analyses of *Citizen Kane* (Orson Welles, 1942) and Renoir's films, whose use of deep focus is examined on the basis of their ability to conflate simultaneous events. Even when praising *Umberto D* (1952) for its focus on a character's eventless life, Bazin would speak, as Wollen notes, 'of a "dramaturgy of everyday life"' (2004: 253). His analysis of this film also gives him the opportunity to expound on the Bergsonian tenets of his realist theory. In his famous analysis of the scene in which the maid gets up and potters about in the kitchen, he identifies glimpses 'of what a truly realist cinema of time could be, a cinema of "duration"', or *durée*, in Bergson's term (Bazin 2005b: 77). However, this scene does not unfold in a single shot, which prompts one to conclude, as does Margulies, that for Bazin 'what matters is no longer the actual physical integrity of representation – its lack of cuts – but that it *appears* to be physically integral' (Margulies 1996: 39). But nowhere is this representational prescription more overtly formulated than in his appraisal of Luchino Visconti's *La Terra Trema* (1948), whose 'unusually long' and aestheticized shots 'must be applicable to dramatic ends if it is to be of service in the evolution of cinema' (Bazin 2005b: 45). Quite explicitly, Bazin argues that Visconti's 'disinclination to sacrifice anything to drama has one obvious and serious consequence: *La Terra Trema* bores the public. A film with a limited action, it lasts longer than three hours' (2005b: 45).

In fact, if Bazin was impressed with the fact that *The Best Years of Our Lives* does not have 'more than 190 shots per hour' with 'shots of more than two minutes in duration' (1997: 11), he may have been underwhelmed by a seven-hour film such as *Sátántangó*, composed of approximately 150 shots, a large portion of which is simply limited to following characters, with a steadicam and from behind, as they traverse desolate, rainy landscapes for over five minutes. In this kind of realism, spatial and temporal integrity is preserved to hyperbolic extremes, as the aforementioned shots exemplify. As a result, in spectatorial terms, narrative interaction is dissipated in favour of contemplation and sensory experience. We as viewers are invited to adopt the point of view of the camera and protractedly study images as they appear on the screen in their unexplained literalness. This frontally contradicts the Bazinian rules, as the temporal elongation of the shot surpasses by far the demands of the story, leaving the spectator unguided as to how to read that particular scene hermeneutically.

Take, for instance, Van Sant's *Gerry* (2002), itself inspired by Tarr's work. We follow two characters, played by Matt Damon and Casey Affleck, who quickly realize they are lost in a desert (in reality, the film was shot in three geographically different deserts). The viewer is provided with virtually no narrative information. We do not know who the characters are, their relationship or what has brought them to these landscapes, nor are we further enlightened as the film unhurriedly unfolds. Instead, the viewer is offered extreme long shots of majestic landscapes as these characters aimlessly wander through them, hardly ever exchanging a word between themselves (Figure 4). Consider also the entire second half of Apichatpong's *Blissfully Yours* (*Sud sanaeha*, 2002), which simply shows, in protracted shots, its characters eating, resting, having (real) sex and enjoying moments of contemplation on the banks of a river in a Thai jungle. Or take Reygadas' *Japón* (2002), shot entirely on location in a small rural village in Mexico, which devotes most of its time to following an unnamed man as he perambulates across rugged countryside landscapes and

Figure 4   Majestic landscapes, minute humans: Van Sant's Gerry

Figure 5   Alonso's Liverpool

considers committing suicide for unexplained reasons. The scenes of his solitary wanderings undermine narrative momentum, inviting the viewer to contemplate, in silent long takes, images of the empty landscapes he traverses.
Similar examples abound across the world: Lisandro Alonso's *Liverpool* (2008),
which devotes its entirety to the depiction of a solitary man's journey home as
he crosses the wintry Tierra del Fuego in Argentina (Figure 5); Albert Serra's
Birdsong (*El cant dels ocells*, 2008), which re-enacts the Catholic legend of the
Three Kings on their way to offer presents to Jesus by following these characters traversing both the Icelandic and Canary Islands' majestic landscapes
(Figure 6); and many others.

As well as by landscapes, this cinematic tendency is characterised by a protracted observation of urban spaces. Reygadas' *Battle in Heaven* (*Batalla en el*

Figure 6   *Serra's* Birdsong

cielo, 2005) is a case in point of a film in which Mexico City is not merely a figurative backdrop, but indeed the main character itself, perpetuating an Italian
neo-realist tradition while stretching it to contemplative heights. Nowhere is
this better epitomized than in the bird's-eye view shot of a confluence of
avenues in the city. Or in the scene in which the camera starts by showing the
atypical couple at the centre of this film (a white, young, upper-class woman
and an obese, Indian, middle-aged man having real sex, more of which in the
last section). At first static, the camera turns away from the event and pulls out
of the room through an open window to perform a slow 360° pan, capturing in
the process two men fixing a house aerial, a busy street, kids playing in the
garden of another house, storeys of a luxurious building, a dripping tap, until it
makes its way back into the room and find the couple now resting, after no less
than five minutes. José Luis Guerín's *In the City of Sylvia* (*En la ciudad de Sylvia*,
2007) is similarly a film whose main plot line – a man's incessant chase of a
woman – provides the cue for the foregrounding of the city of Strasburg, offer-
ing a rich urban symphony made up of sounds and images of cars, trains, pedes-
trian feet and bicycles (Figure 7). Likewise, cityscapes in ruins in China are also
autonomous objects of contemplation in Jia's films (*Still Life*, 2006) (Figure 8),
the same being true of the derelict shanty towns of Lisbon in Pedro Costa's
aforementioned films and Turkish cities in Nuri Bilge Ceylan's cinema (*Uzak*,
2002; *Climates*, 2006).

In symmetry with that, this is also a cinema interested in lingering on the
physicality of faces and bodies. A telling example of this impulse is Kiarostami's
Shirin (2008), a 90-minute film entirely composed of protracted close-ups of

Figure 7   Cities in Focus: Guerín's In the City of Sylvia

Figure 8   Jia's Still Life

over 100 Iranian women (with the exception of the French Juliette Binoche) while they watch, enraptured and in silence, the film *Shirin*. We as spectators never see the film on the screen, being instead offered plenty of time to contemplate that which has always been at the core of cinema: faces. A fascination with bodies is also noticeable in contemporary cinematic realism. Consider Reygadas' attention to naked bodies which cinema has rarely focused on with such frankness, such as that of a septuagenarian woman in *Japón* and those of an obese couple in *Battle in Heaven*. The carnality of bodies is also at the heart of Tsai's cinema, which is rooted in performative and paratheatrical practices. Here, characters are denied verbal or psychological explanations, being instead characterized by their physical instincts and gestures, often recorded in static unbroken shots. We often see them crawling and crouching about their apartments, as well as performing weird and exaggerated movements, such as in the scene in *Rebels of the Neon God* (*Qing shao nian nuo zha*, 1992), which finds Hsiao-kang (Lee Kang-sheng) convulsively jumping about on a bed while uttering unintelligible sounds.

Binding together these very disparate cinemas is a desire to highlight the materiality of both animate and inanimate beings through what I define as a contemplative approach. One could say that this is a cinema on the frontier between storytelling and sheer recording, the latter constantly undermining the former. By being delayed, the cut ceases to serve dramatic purposes. In their turn, characters are often devoid of psychological traits: they are laconic, listless, impassive. More than their psychology, it is their physical characteristics and physiology which is on display. Narratives are elusive, sometimes mysterious, often deprived of causal logic, its smooth progression truncated by overstretched images depleted of dramaticity. Time ceases to serve the demands of the story: the duration of each shot, diegetically unjustified, makes itself felt. And here we are compelled to revisit Gilles Deleuze's notion of modern cinema, which he defines as the time-image regime.

Time and Image

Deleuze published *Cinema 1: The Movement-Image* in 1983 and *Cinema 2: The Time-Image* in 1985, before the emergence of the realist trend addressed in this chapter. And yet, as one reads the philosopher's description of a cinema in which action and narrative causality are weakened, and in which the act of seeing takes on the greatest importance for characters and, consequently, spectators, one has the uncanny impression that, more than referring to the dozens of filmmakers of his own pantheon (many of whom are entirely reliant on montage and storytelling, such as Ozu, Rossellini and Buñuel), Deleuze is prophesying a cinema which would take a few years to fully materialize. For him, the time-image cinema requires a new type of character that no longer *acts* in perpetual motion and according to a causal logic, as was the case in classical cinema. The actions carried out within the diegesis tend not to have an aim. They are those of walking, strolling, wandering and eliciting a contemplative stance, which is perfectly illustrated by this contemporary realist world-cinema trend. For Deleuze, in the time-image, the character 'has become a kind of viewer ... the situation he is in outstrips his motor capacities on all sides, and makes him see and hear what is no longer subject to the rule of a response or an action' (Deleuze 2005b: 3). This 'cinema of the seer and no longer of the agent' (2005b: 2) decentres the functional dimension of the image, now appearing as 'pure optical and sound situations', which Deleuze explains thus:

> These are pure optical and sound situations, in which the character does not know how to respond, abandoned spaces in which he ceases to experience and to act so that he enters into flight, goes on a trip, comes and goes, vaguely indifferent to what happens to him, undecided as to what must be done. But he has gained in an ability to see what he has lost in action or reaction: he SEES so that the viewer's problem becomes 'What is there to see in the image?' (and not now 'What are we going to see in the next image?'). (2005b: 261)

Granted, Deleuze emphasizes that his is not a realist film theory, arguing that the special power of the time-image is not its ontological force, as defended by Bazin apropos of Italian neo-realism, but its ability to 'prevent perception being extended into action in order to put it in contact with thought' (2005b: 1). Rather than with realism, he is concerned with the way time is rendered non-chronologically within the diegesis in modern cinema. And yet, underlying his approach, it is easy to identify a realist foundation, given its stress on the objectivity of recording. Elaborating on the 'cinema of delay' of Abbas Kiarostami, Laura Mulvey notes its conformity to the tenets of the time-image, as a film aesthetic which starts by:

> deriving images from whatever the camera observed rather than a narrative aspiration to order and organization. With the decline of action, an evacuated cinematic space fills the gap, registering the empty images of landscape and cityscape...This cinema of record, observation and delay tends to work with elongated shots, enabling the presence of time to appear on the screen. (2006: 129)

As well as the autonomy of time, this de-dramatized cinema, I will now attempt to demonstrate, conveys a sense of *pure material and sensible presence* which translates, at least in principle, into a sensory mode of spectatorship.

Pure Presence

Taking up Roland Barthes' essay 'The Third Meaning', Kristin Thompson has examined the conflict arising from 'the *materiality* of a film and the unifying structures within it' (1986: 132); that is, those moments when the material dimension of the image escapes and exceeds narrative motivation and structural patterns, calling attention to its own perceptual fabric as such. Though not mentioning the long take, Thompson concludes that material excess is particularly prone to erupt when a device remains onscreen for too long, which exhausts its functional purpose within the narrative:

> Motivation is insufficient to determine how long a device needs to be
> on the screen in order to serve its purpose ... We may notice a device
> immediately and understand its function, but it may then continue to
> be visible or audible for some time past this recognition. In this case,
> we may be inclined to study or contemplate it apart from its narrative or
> compositional function; such contemplation necessarily distracts from
> narrative progression. (Thompson 1986: 135)

This material surplus has also been analysed from a spectatorial perspective.
Christian Keathley, for instance, argues that the cinephiliac project stems
from a particular way of watching films, which involves scanning the image
through what he calls 'panoramic perception'. Looking for every detail, the
cinephile studies the image beyond their narrative functionality, thereby
reanimating 'the repressed materiality of the film' (Keathley 2006: 53). The
sequence shot, for Keathley, is the device ideally placed to elicit this kind of
perception (2006: 47).

But how can we theorize cinemas in which materiality is not *in excess* of a
causally chained narrative, but quite simply *what there is*? The above formula-
tions are only in part applicable to new realisms insofar as these theorists characterize materiality as a diegetic surplus: the superabundance of details which,
locked in a dominant dramatic structure, posit the danger of calling attention
to themselves rather than advancing the plot. In contemporary realist cinema,
on the other hand, materiality is not 'repressed' by the film's structure and
subsequently perceived as the epiphanic, fragmentary moment theorized by
cinephiliac discourses, as described by Keathley (2006) and Willemen (1994).
On the contrary, through the hyperbolic application of the long take and other
time-stretching devices, materiality is primarily conveyed as non-conceptual,
sensuous phenomena.

Before Deleuze, Pier Paolo Pasolini had already attempted to establish a connection between cinema's empirical and temporal dimensions, as achieved by
the long take. For Pasolini, the long take is, by definition, 'in the present tense'
(Pasolini 1980: 3). Reality as it is lived, he argues, is always from a single
vantage point and unrepresentable: it 'makes no sense, or if it does, it does so
only subjectively, in an incomplete, uncertain, mysterious way' (1980: 4). For
him, only the long take is able to convey the sensuous indeterminacy of lived
reality:

> The substance of cinema is ... an endless long take, as is reality to our
> senses for as long as we are able to see and feel (a long take that ends
> with the end of our lives); and this long take is nothing but the repro-
> duction of the language of reality. In other words it is the reproduction
> of the present. (1980: 5)

Only when montage intervenes is this present tense transformed into past, for it systematizes what is otherwise non-symbolic, purely experiential, indeterminate; it gives a meaningful trajectory to that which essentially lacks signification, namely reality. In this way, Pasolini concludes, the cut in cinema is the embodiment of death, because it organizes one's life according to sense-making patterns, retroactively providing it with a definite and irrevocable meaning.

Now it is obvious, as Pasolini himself stresses, that no film escapes montage, as no life escapes death. Moreover, if we take montage in a broader sense, it also includes the manipulation and arrangement of elements onscreen, camera movements which change frames in time without the need of editing, lighting, *mise-en-scène*, etc., all of which are intended to produce meaning. In filmmaking practice, however, the long take is understood as far less authoritative in making meaning. More than any representational function it may serve, 'its fundamental and dominant proposition ... is: "All this is"'(Pasolini 2005: 240). In other words, the long take highlights the sheer expressiveness of the sensible, as it presentifies the material world. This is best exemplified by the opening of Reygadas' *Silent Light* (*Stellet Licht*, 2007), a seven-minute shot of a dawn which shows, through time-lapse, the gradual rise of the sun in the horizon. At first pitch-black, the screen gradually lightens, revealing the countryside and the immense sky above. As the sun rises, a myriad of changing colours appear in the sky, evoking brushstrokes of an abstract painting which has seemingly come into life. Here, an image of the world appears as a phenomenological and aesthetic presence; that is to say, as realism of the senses.

Aesthetic Realism

To speak of these cinemas as promoting an aesthetic mode of perception makes further sense in the light of what Jacques Rancière has defined as 'the aesthetic regime of art', which in his view opposes 'the representative model'. Rather than an art 'proper' to the subjects and situations which it depicts, aesthetic art confronts 'the old principle of form fashioning matter with the identity... between the pure power of the idea and the radical impotence of sensible presence and the mute writing of things' (Rancière 2006: 8).

For Rancière, the political significance of aesthetic art consists precisely in the way it turns reality into a purely expressive phenomenon, free from mimetic concerns. In doing so, this art effects a disruption in the ways it is expected to represent subjects and objects in an 'appropriate' manner, creating what he terms a 'dissensus'. It is certainly not coincidental that Rancière chooses to illustrate his thesis with the work of a contemporary realist filmmaker such as Pedro Costa, whose *In Vanda's Room*, shot in a slum undergoing demolition in Lisbon, he deems representative of the aesthetic regime. Rather than explaining the social and economic factors which contributed to this situation of extreme poverty, Costa chooses to highlight the aesthetic effect of such reality, as perceived, for example, in 'the strangely coloured architecture resulting from the demolition itself' (Rancière 2010: 151). Characterized by rigorously composed static silent shots, this film impresses for the artistic imprint of its visual compositions, which reveal at the same time a terrifying reality. At stake here is an art which accepts its 'insufficiency', its limitations as art restricted to sensory experience. It is an art that 'contributes to the constitution of a form of commonsense that is "polemical", to a new landscape of the visible, the sayable and the doable' (2010: 149). This, Rancière concludes, is political.

I would like to cite three works within the realist tendency in contemporary world cinema which provide eloquent illustration of this political aesthetics. The first is Reygadas' *Battle in Heaven*, focused on a highly atypical couple: a young, rich, white girl (Ana) and an obese, Indian, middle-aged man (Marcos), played respectively by the non-professional actors Anapola Mushkadiz and Marcos Hernandez. Engaged in real sex onscreen, they provide a shocking opening to the film, as Marcos and Ana phenotypically encapsulate the social and ethnic segregation of Mexico. They are, I would argue, 'the impossible'. And yet the film refuses to explain this impossibility and the hierarchical disruption it performs. Rather than inserting this relationship within a plausible dramatic structure, the camera contemplates these bodies as aesthetic objects themselves. Extreme close-up shots and overstretched camera movements inspect, dissect and magnify their purely fleshly quality (Figures 9–11). Averse to all victimization and moral didacticism, *Battle in Heaven* exposes an abyssal

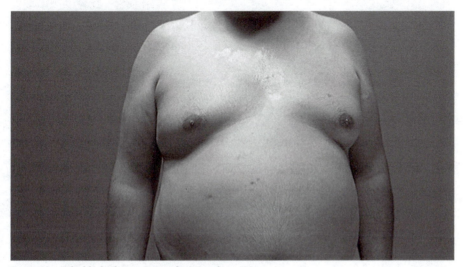

Figure 9   *Fleshly bodies in Reygadas'* Battle in Heaven

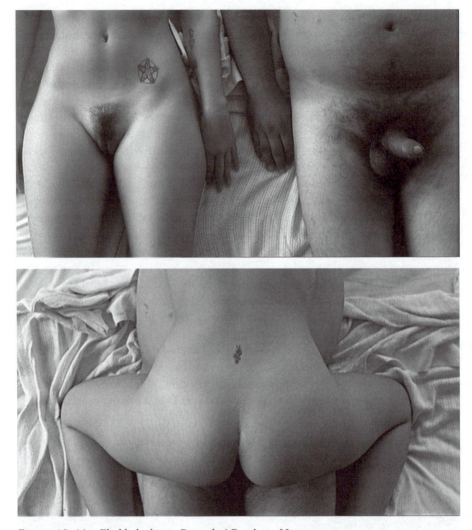

Figures 10–11　Fleshly bodies in Reygadas' Battle in Heaven

social divide by bridging this gap and making this couple possible *in reality*, refusing to acknowledge its incongruity within the social establishment.

Something similar happens in Van Sant's *Elephant* (2003), in which the director faced the task of re-enacting the deeply traumatic event of the Columbine massacre. Rejecting a representational carapace which would justify his choice of subject matter as in service of a moral message, Van Sant chose to depict this event in its sheer elusiveness, shattering its linearity and depriving it of a causal logic. In the film, there is no demonization and no heroism. Indeed, there is hardly any narrative. Featuring actual students from the school in which the film was shot, *Elephant* spends most of its time following these real adolescents simply traversing the school's corridors through smooth, elegant, minutely choreographed tracking shots. We observe their bodies, their gestures, their way of walking, often in slow motion and to the sound of Beethoven's 'Moonlight Sonata', which lends the film a languid, soporific quality. Here, too, these teenagers are framed as purely aesthetic objects for the camera's gaze, which seems enraptured by its object of attention. Amidst numerous possible ways to approach this event, Van Sant chose to frame it through a contemplative sensibility whose political significance consists in the way it enables us to look at this event anew, making us confront it in its bewildering complexity and harrowing terror.

The last work is *The River* (*He liu*, 1997), the third film by Taiwan-based Tsai Ming-liang. The film focuses on a working-class family living on the fringes of society in rapidly industrializing Taipei, and its most notorious scene shows an incestuous homosexual act. Unknowingly, father and son meet in a gay sauna in a dark room and have non-penetrative sex. How to depict this shocking event? *The River* opts to give us a highly aestheticized scene. Framed in a static medium shot lasting over four minutes, the event is presented in almost complete darkness, the silhouettes of bodies only dimly visible. Positioned at the centre of the image, we occasionally get glimpses of the characters' skin as their bodies mutate into changing forms overflowing the borders of the figurative. The loaded representational character of this event – that is, the way in which it immediately questions all sorts of historical discourses and constructions – is not acknowledged as such, but transformed into a purely aesthetic spectacle of contours, light and forms. What this film affirms is that cultural conventions are inventions, and therefore always available to be dismantled and reshaped by the sensuous power of art.

References

Andrew, Dudley (2006) 'An atlas of world cinema', in Stephanie Dennison and Song Hwee Lim (eds) *Remapping World Cinema: Identity, Culture and Politics in Film* (London and New York, Wallflower Press).

Bazin, André (1974) *Jean Renoir* (New York, Dell).

Bazin, André (1997) *Bazin at Work: Major Essays from the Forties & Fifties* (New York/London, Routledge).

Bazin, André (2003) 'Death every afternoon', in Ivone Margulies (ed.) *Rites of Realism: Essays on Corporeal Cinema* (Durham and London, Duke University Press).

Bazin, André (2005a) *What is Cinema? – Volume 1* (London and Berkeley, University of California Press).

Bazin, André (2005b) *What is Cinema – Volume 2* (London and Berkeley, University of California Press).

Deleuze, Gilles (2005a) *Cinema 1: The Movement-Image* (London, Continuum).

Deleuze, Gilles (2005b) *Cinema 2: The Time-Image* (London, Continuum).

Doane, Mary Ann (2002) *The Emergence of Cinematic Time: Modernity, Contingency, The Archive* (Cambridge and London, Harvard University Press).

Frampton, Daniel (2006) *Filmosophy* (London and New York, Wallflower Press).

Gunning, Tom (2004) 'What's the point of an index? Or, faking photographs', *NORDICOM Review* 5:1/2 (September), pp.39–49.

Hansen, Miriam Bratu (1997) 'Introduction', in Kracauer (1997).

Keathley, Christian (2006) *Cinephilia and History, or The Wind in the Trees* (Bloomington and Indianapolis, Indiana University Press).

Kracauer, Siegfried (1997) *Theory of Film: The Redemption of Physical Reality* (Princeton, Princeton University Press).

Manovich, Lev (2001) *The Language of New Media* (Cambridge and London, The MIT Press).

Margulies, Ivone (1996) *Nothing Happens: Chantal Akerman's Hyperrealist Everyday* (Durham and London, Duke University Press).

Margulies, Ivone (2003) 'Bodies too much', in Ivone Margulies (ed.) *Rites of Realism: Essays on Corporeal Cinema* (Durham and London, Duke University Press).

Marks, Laura U. (2000) *The Skin of the Film: Intercultural Cinema, Embodiment and The Senses* (Durham and London, Duke University Press).

Mulvey, Laura (2006) *Death 24x a Second: Stillness and the Moving Image* (London, Reaktion).

Nagib, Lúcia (2011) *World Cinema and the Ethics of Realism* (London, Continuum).

Nagib, Lúcia and Mello, Cecília (eds) (2009) 'Introduction', in *Realism and the Audiovisual Media* (Basingstoke, Palgrave Macmillan).

Pasolini, Pier Paolo (1980) 'Observations on the long take', *October* 13, pp.3–6.

Pasolini, Pier Paolo (2005) *Heretical Empiricism* (Washington, New Academia Publishing).

Prince, Stephen (1996) 'True lies: perceptual realism, digital images, and film theory', *Film Quarterly* 49:3, pp.27–37.

Rancière, Jacques (2006) *Film Fables* (Oxford and New York, Berg).

Rancière, Jacques (2010) *Dissensus: On Politics and Aesthetics* (London and New York, Continuum).

Rodowick, D.N. (2007) *The Virtual Life of Film* (London, Harvard University Press).

Rosen, Philip (2001) *Change Mummified: Cinema, Historicity, Theory* (Minneapolis and London, University of Minnesota Press).

Shaviro, Steven (1993) *The Cinematic Body* (Minneapolis and London, University of Minnesota Press)

Sobchack, Vivian (2000) 'What my fingers knew: the cinesthetic subject, or vision in the flesh', in *Senses of Cinema*. Online at: http://archive.sensesofcinema.com/contents/00/5/fingers.html. Accessed August 2010.

Sobchack, Vivian (2004) *Carnal Thoughts: Embodiment and Moving Image Culture* (Berkeley and London, University of California Press).

Thompson, Kristin (1986) 'The concept of cinematic excess', in Philip Rosen (ed.) *Narrative, Apparatus, Ideology: a Film Theory Reader* (New York and Guildford, Columbia University Press).

Willemen, Paul (1994) *Looks and Frictions: Essays in Cultural Studies and Film Theory* (Bloomington and Indianapolis, Indiana University Press).

Williams, Linda (1991) 'Film bodies: gender, genre and excess', *Film Quarterly* 44:4, pp.2–13.

Wollen, Peter (1998) *Signs and Meaning in the Cinema* (London, BFI).

Wollen, Peter (2004) 'Citizen Kane', in James Naremore (ed.) *Orson Welles's Citizen Kane: A Casebook* (Oxford and New York, Oxford University Press).

Note

1 I wish to thank all the directors whose films' frames illustrate this chapter. I thank, in particular, Carlos Reygadas for allowing me to conduct research at his production company (Mantarraya Produciones), as well as interview him in Mexico in 2009. He also provided me with the complete storyboards of his films and precious material, for which I am grateful. This research trip was partly funded by the group Santander, which I also thank. Thanks are also due to Tsai Ming-liang, who took time to give me a long interview during his busy visit to the University of Leeds in 2010. I finally thank the editors of this book for their insightful comments and suggestions to this chapter.

Chapter Twelve

Rear-Projection and the Paradoxes of Hollywood Realism

Laura Mulvey

Although rear-projection technology had existed for some time, it was adopted widely in response to a three-fold problem that the arrival of synchronized sound (in the late 1920s and early 1930s) posed for industrial film production: how to combine star presence and narrative setting with audible dialogue. Recording on location was not possible in the early days of synchronized sound; even as the technology improved, the advantages of studio recording presented irresistible technological, practical and financial attractions for the studios. To combine all elements (star, dialogue and fictional location), the film scene had to be split into two separate parts. For an average movie, first the narrative setting would be filmed on the appropriate location (often by a second unit). This transparency or plate would then be taken to a specialized studio adapted for the rear-projection process. As the stars, or relevant actors, were placed in the confined studio space, their fictional setting would be projected behind them onto a translucent screen, and they would then act out the scene. This technique allowed stars to remain in privileged close-up, their words clearly audible and their emotions clearly visible, while the dramatic setting, landscape scenery or urban streets rolled behind them.

In this chapter, I will discuss rear-projection (my reference will be to Hollywood, although it was, of course, used elsewhere) as a device that offered solutions to some practical problems of star-system filming, but also, if only incidentally, produced images that were at odds with the principles of transparency and associated realism to which Hollywood cinema generally aspired. As it was almost impossible to conceal completely the mechanics of the device, the discordance between studio and setting tended to become visible, affecting narrative coherence and threatening the transparency of the classical cinema. Consciously or unconsciously, rear-projection inserted into movies another cinematic realism, one that foregrounded the 'reality' of process and material. In order to reflect on this paradox, I want to consider, first of all, the contradictory perspectives of modernity and modernism in the cinema.

Throughout its history the cinema has been divided between an aesthetic commitment to making visible its materiality, and, on the other hand, a belief that only the medium's transparency will entrance the mass of movie-goers needed by a successful film industry. The two terms may be translated, or reconfigured, as follows: the materiality of film relates to the *reality* of the mechanism; transparency relates to the *illusion of reality*. By and large, this opposition conjures up a division between, first of all, cinema as a mass, industrial medium, supremely adapted to story-telling and spectacle – *the* privileged site for a flourishing popular culture throughout the twentieth century. Secondly, cinema as an integral part of twentieth-century modernism in which baring the device of this medium of illusion, bringing its material attributes into visibility have been an essential strategy in keeping with the aesthetics of 'medium specificity'. (Needless to say, the tradition of art cinema has juggled these extremes to varying degrees across its own history.) Rear-projection's clumsy visibility seems to smuggle something of modernism into the mass medium of modernity, creating an unusual paradox, almost a clash of cultures, within a single sequence.

As in all other branches of art, the cinema's modernist aesthetic has aspired to foreground its material specificity; but these strategies have further implications for film, one shared with the photograph and particular to their common attributes. In photography, as light hits the photosensitive material, it leaves an actual inscription of the objects, people, place and space registered by the lens. While this 'indexical' aspect of the photographic image may lie equally at the heart of popular cinema, another layer of time, that of fiction, is superimposed over it, which not only demands the suppression of any awareness of the cinema's mechanics, but also needs to maintain its own diegetic cohesion and temporal credibility. These conventions are crucial to Hollywood's realism.

These points are, of course, extremely familiar to all film theorists and, indeed, to anyone at all interested in the cinema. I rehearse them only as an introduction to the paradox created by the rear-projection device that I mentioned at the beginning of this chapter. Although the device has been mocked for generations precisely for its clumsy visibility, I want to suggest that the passing of time has given rear-projection a kind of archaic aesthetic preciousness and a retrospective theoretical interest.

In order to discuss this point, I will be introducing the work of an artist, Mark Lewis, who has recently been using rear-projection in his installations. His 'recycling' of the now archaic technology introduces another temporal dimension into the overall picture, as his use of rear-projection becomes a citation, a shift in context that confuses its original, industrial, use, but draws attention to its paradoxical qualities. Lewis' interest in the device led him to compose a work around it, *Rear Projection Molly Parker 2006–7*, and in order to film the device accurately he used the Hansard studios in Hollywood. As the Hansard family operated the last rear-projection studio and were rapidly going out of business, Lewis went back the following year to make a documentary, *Back Story*, that recorded their history and their account of the process itself.

The shift in aesthetic sensibility represented by Lewis' return to an archaic industrial device as one of concealed modernism may be due, in the first instance, to passing time, but recent radical technological changes are a contributing factor, aggravating the sense of distance between now and the heyday of cinema. Over the last 20 years, 'cinema' has become increasingly detached from its filmic mechanisms. While continuing as an institution (social and economic), technological change has been transforming its material base. In the industry, celluloid held its own for some time as a superior means of registration (increasingly less so as digital cameras improve exponentially), it has disappeared completely in the editing process, and is now threatened as a medium for public exhibition, while, more radically, private consumption of DVDs has altered the way films are seen. The change in the sphere of the avant-garde or experimental film is even more marked. One aspect of aesthetic reference, key in each of the 'avant-garde waves' from the 1920s onwards, has undergone a major conceptual and practical shift; that is, the inscription into film of its medium specificity and its materiality. Now, experimental film has lost touch with many of its traditional sites of exhibition, and has moved closer and closer to the sphere of art, is exhibited by digital projection in galleries, leaving, as it is commonly said, the black box for the white cube.

Nothing divides the history of the cinema into pre- and post-digital more clearly than the world of special effects, and nowhere is this division clearer than in the total disappearance of rear- or back-projection. Unlike those special effects that exhibited their expense and excess, rear-projection, by and large, aimed at an invisibility that was all too often visible, so that critics and audiences were routinely contemptuous of its clumsiness. As so often happens with passing time, its definitive disappearance has given this once despised technology new interest. Now, watching Hollywood films made after the coming of sound, the eruption of rear-projection seems to be not only emblematic of a given aesthetic, but also of a studio system that disappeared in the industrial shake-ups of the late twentieth century. Passing time further effects rear-projection's temporal discordances, its archaic mechanism drawing attention to the changing nature of cinema.

These recent changes have created a gap between the here and now of cinema (still in an evolutionary phase, uncertain as to its future) and the past of its film-based history, rendering it increasingly archaic, increasingly associated with the machine age, the twentieth century, and its particular cultures of modernism and modernity. As I argued in my book *Death 24 X a Second* (2005), due to, and out of, this gap, cinema's intrinsic relation to the photographic real has risen, as it were, from the shadows of illusion into a more pronounced consciousness, thus foregrounding more acutely the cinema's relation to time, affecting perception even of the products of the Hollywood studio system. Rear-projection's paradoxes have a particular relevance to this heightened, retrospective, consciousness of both cinematic time and realism.

The opening shot of Lewis' documentary *Back Story* shows Mr Hansard Senior demonstrating how the rear-projection process works: sitting in the studio – that is, in the space of the actors, in front of a plate showing a swimming pool scene with swimmers and divers – he carefully coordinates the balance between the background and foreground lighting, and the focus of the two scenes (Figure 1). He also enacts the temporal dislocation between the two: the time of the background literally predates the studio scene, so that the sense of photographic time suspended at the moment of registration is doubled into an uneasy but fascinating mismatch within the single screen image. However skilfully the effect was composed, and the Hansards were masters of their technology, the rear-projection effect introduced a dislocation to the conventions that preserved the unity of the fictional time and space essential to Hollywood realism.

In the first instance, the split between foreground and background threatens the coherence, and thus the realism, of fictional time. The artificiality of the studio as fictional space and the artificiality of the star as a fictional character are heightened as star presence, almost literally, come to the fore. In the constrained space in front of the translucent screen, the actor's gestures become overly considered, almost laboured or acted out, exaggerating the essential

Figure 1   Back Story: *Mr Hansard demonstrates the rear-projection process*

dualism of star and character. As the device highlights star presence, so also its artificiality heightens the dual persona that a star inhabits: always recognizable and nameable while adopting a fictional name and persona for a particular role. Bertolt Brecht commented on the double role of the actor. In A *Short Organum for the Theatre*, he writes: 'the actor appears on the stage in a double role, as Laughton and as Galileo ... the showman Laughton does not disappear in the Galileo he is showing' (Brecht 1964: 194). In the context of rear-projection, the split, dual and hybrid nature of the image, and the denaturalized close-up, exaggerate the oscillation between star and character. Furthermore, due to the absolute necessity for the actors to stay exactly in the spaces allocated to them, their limited range of performance sometimes evokes the tableau effect that Brecht considered essential to the epic theatre. In this sense, rear-projection also resonates with the Brechtian concept of estrangement or distanciation, as well as the traditions of modernist film.

In addition to the dualism encapsulated by the star in the studio, rear-projection technology further confuses fictional realism as it puts onto the screen, within a single image, two distinct points of time and space. Through its very nature, rear-projection folds one time/space level into another, as that of the 'setting' is asynchronous with that of the figures in the studio foreground. Fictional time should transcend the essential photographic time that I referred to earlier as indexical; the spectator should be sufficiently absorbed into the story and its events to overlook the presence of that 'present' time at which they were actually inscribed onto celluloid. However, rear-projection renders this transcendence fragile, once again bringing these contradictory realities in the cinema into visibility: should the difference between the illusion of reality and the real of its mechanical infrastructure become apparent, if only for a few moments, the mechanism threatens to intrude into, and puncture, the world of the fiction. The splitting of the scene into hybrid time and space introduces not only awareness of the original moment of cinematic inscription, the real time of the index, but the indexical time is also doubled. And the clumsy absurdity of the device gives way to a kind of trompe-l'oeil effect, as cinema's (and indeed the photograph's) already paradoxical relation between the then of registration and time suspended into the now of watching is overlaid: the 'then' of the background lying behind the 'then' of the studio scene. The paradoxical time of the photographic index is complicated by the paradoxical doubled time of rear-projection. This not only further enhances the estrangement, or distanciation effect, latent in the rear-projection mechanism, but it also draws attention to a further tension between the figure, its events and actions, and its landscape setting, to which I will return later in this chapter.

Although over the years the illusion improved, it was always vulnerable, always verging on visibility and a certain absurdity, even in its heyday. Furthermore, the device, in order to fake mobility, reverses the natural order of things: the figures supposedly speeding in a car or train remain static in the studio, animated by a 'mobilized' landscape unwinding behind a window, or simply framing the scene like a theatrical backdrop. This aspect of rear-projection has a direct genealogical descent from the pre-cinematic panoramas and dioramas, used either as a special effect in the theatre or as popular entertainment. (An aside: when he made *Heller in Pink Tights* (1960), George Cukor paid tribute to the theatrical illusion. In the film, a little theatre company travelling the West puts on a performance in which a live horse, with Sophia Loren strapped to its back, gallops on a treadmill placed on the stage while a panorama of the steppes unfolds in the background. The treadmill remained an essential part of rear-projection technology, allowing stars to seem to walk towards the camera, along a street or any other location unfolding behind them, while remaining within the confined space allotted by the background plate.)

There is a further incompatibility, a further paradox, inherent to the rear-projection process. The location footage can seem especially 'realistic', almost like documentary film footage, when it intrudes into otherwise wholly-staged narrative dramas. The juxtaposition produces a unique and strangely beautiful montage effect. Highly artificial looking, these scenes of studio and location, of fiction and documentary, quickly became the orthodox means by which actors and audiences were both 'taken' into a simulated real, while also being distanced from it. An early example of rear-projection illustrates this point: *Her Man* (Tay Garnett 1931) shows stars Helen Twelvetrees (Frankie) and Philip Holmes (Danny) in conversation as they are 'driven' in a little carriage through the streets of a Caribbean port such as Havana (Figure 2). Perhaps partly due to its date, the studio and the background are particularly poignantly dislocated: the background has a distinctly documentary feel, as the street scenes include an unusual amount of detail. However, as Frankie admits not knowing her birthday, a cut in the background scene temporarily excludes the street activities and her studio close-up is framed simply against a 'passing' wall, to avoid distraction from the emotion of the moment.

Many directors despised rear-projection. Max Ophuls would never use it – notwithstanding his tribute to its pre-history in *Letter from an Unknown Woman* (1948). Alfred Hitchcock, on the other hand, returned to it persistently, not only to the railway carriage as a favourite site of drama, from the 1930s (*The Lady Vanishes*, 1938) to the 1950s (*North by Northwest*, 1959), but in many other settings. In fact, Hitchcock's near obsession with this special effect went beyond convenience, and he continued to use it even after it seemed antiquated to his technicians, not to mention critics and audiences. For instance, when *Marnie* came out in 1963, critics condemned its 'processed shots', most particularly one when Marnie is first shown riding her horse. For Hitchcock, it was essential to combine close-up with action. In a pre-production meeting, he said:

Figure 2   Rear-projection process: Her Man

Now we show her riding … and then we go to Close-ups which will mean plates and things for her Close-ups showing her enjoying it and her hair blowing and it's very important that we establish here one big Close-up of the hair blowing as she's riding…. (*Take One* 1976: 36)

As the intensity of movement is reduced to repetitive gesture in the studio and displaced onto the passing background, the star appears in a strange, disorienting space. Her emotion replaces the actual motion of the action. The character's loss of all sense of time and place, due to her pleasure in riding, fuses with the discordance of time and place characteristic of rear-projection. And this shot dissolves into the stylized overhead shot of Baltimore Street where her mother lives.

In his essay for the exhibition catalogue, *Hitchcock and Art: Fatal Coincidences,* Dominique Païni argues that Hitchcock used rear-projection for its dreamlike qualities, the uncertainty that double filming brought to the cinema and ultimately for its modernity. He says the effect 'creates a semblance of reality without erasing the illusory device that goes with it' (Païni 2000: 58). In a comment on the dance sequence in *Saboteur* (Alfred Hitchcock, 1941), a sequence that has had particular influence on Lewis, Païni points out that the different aspects of Hitchcock's use of rear-projection come together in the interests of an overarching emotional effect, as he:

isolates his dancing couple from the surrounding action and spirits them away from the other characters. This cinematic sleight-of-hand lends the situation an air of enchantment. The scene is a perfect example of the dramatic, poetic and visual power of Hitchcock's transparencies at this point in the 1940s. (2000: 63)

He goes on to draw attention to the way that this scene also coincides with Hitchcock's more obviously self-reflexive moments, when characters emerge against an actual film projection as, for instance, later on in the denouement of *Saboteur*. This paradoxical, impossible space, detached from either an approximation to reality or the verisimilitude of fiction, allows the audience to see the dream space of the cinema. But rear-projection renders the dream uncertain: the image of a cinematic sublime depends on a mechanism that is fascinating because of, not in spite of, its clumsy visibility. Païni describes rear-projection's characteristic montage of time and space in terms of strata of scenery, in which nature may become 'portable', and the ultimate space results from an *aggregate* in which film studio and the actual location sequence, filmed in the 'real world', remain uneasily separate.

Mark Lewis' original interest in the old, celluloid-based rear-projection arose out of the aesthetic discordances that I have been discussing. He wrote at the time that 'the two elements march to different beats':

> Back projection, certainly early back projection, brings together so inefficiently two completely different types of film experience that we can hardly not notice their montage effect: we experience the two visual regimes as separate and unwoven, literally as collage. Therefore, that which is designed to make the transition scenes relatively seamless … in fact makes transition truly palpable. On the face of it, this is a paradoxical condition, achieved against the putative intentions of the scene itself. (Lewis 2003)

His new rear-projection film, *Nathan Phillips Square, A Winter's Night, Skating* (2009), was shown in the Canadian Pavilion at the Venice Biennale 2009, and, as I mentioned earlier, he has made a documentary (also shown in Venice), *Backstory: Hansard Rear Projection* (2009), about the Hansard family's work with this technology in Hollywood over three generations (Figures 3–4). Lewis first encountered the Hansards when he made his 2006–07 film *Rear Projection: Molly Parker*, and his aesthetic interest in using an old technology in a contemporary context then extended to the actual story of its rise and decline. In the documentary, the surviving father and son team, located in front of backdrops typical of the device, tell of the success of their family business over a number of decades, until it was overtaken and displaced by electronic effects (green and blue screen) and, finally, computer-generated imagery. Here, in a compressed and poignant form, is a first-hand account of the modern object's trajectory to

Figure 3   Back Story: *Mr Hansard: 'Business is so bad I sometimes call myself on the phone to make sure it's working'*

Figure 4   Back Story: *Billy Hansard: 'They'll make a nice diving reef for the fishes'*

the 'outmoded' that so fascinated Walter Benjamin: a mechanism, once incorporated into the everyday of its own historical moment, falls into disuse and finally becomes archaic. But recycled obliquely back into history, it can acquire new unexpected interest and aesthetic significance. As well as drawing attention to the complexity of the original effect, Lewis has used it as a means to return to consider the modern, and to reflect on ways in which its aesthetics and its politics, now past, might still speak across these technological divides to the present.

I want to use Mark Lewis' citation/quotation of rear-projection for his portrait of the Canadian actress Molly Parker (best known for her role as Alma Garret in the HBO series *Deadwood*, 2004) as a means to reflect further on its implications. The landscape background to *Rear Projection: Molly Parker* (the 'plate' projected behind her in the studio), shot on location in Ontario, begins in autumn with characteristically lush colours until, after a few minutes, the scene mutates to the deep snow of a Canadian mid-winter. Here the effect is doubled, as the background is not only separated from the time and space of the figure, but the background was itself filmed at different seasons, linked by a dissolve that is, itself, reminiscent of a magic-lantern effect. Molly's dress seems reasonably compatible with the autumn setting, but exaggerates the discordance between studio and plate when the scene turns into winter. The landscape background includes an abandoned road-side gas station and café, with its sign Howlin' Wolf still prominently displayed, not only in keeping with Lewis' return in earlier (and later) films to abandoned buildings, but also carrying the idea of the disused and the obsolete across from the technology to the image itself. Molly is filmed with a complex camera movement that combines a track with a zoom, further flattening and making strange her figure's relation to the background screen.

In his early reflections on rear-projection, Lewis related its aggregated space to an aesthetic device that comes from a very different point in the history of representation. In a certain kind of Renaissance painting, the figure or figures occupy the surface of the picture, celebrated, as it were, in 'close-up', and 'superimposed' on a far-away landscape that stretches into the distance. Lewis drew particular attention to this Renaissance topography in the catalogue for his 2006 exhibition at the FACT Centre, Liverpool, where the Molly Parker work was first exhibited. He included particular images – Jan van Eyck's 'The Virgin of Chancellor Rolin' (1435–36) and various portraits (by Memling, Velázquez and others) – in which the foreground, occupied by the central figure, is detached from its background in an arrangement that recalls the aggregated spaces of rear-projection. The paintings in which the figure is located in an interior use windows and arches to separate the foreground from the background, and suggest rear-projection's frames within frames, as in the motor-car or railway train effect. The paintings in which the figure is in an exterior space have more difficulty with the transition between foreground and background, so that the effect is more pronounced and often even more beautiful. Landscape painting aspired to integrate the figure into the landscape, creating a more naturalistic representation of space and ultimately also escaping from the hierarchy of significance demanded, for instance, by Christian iconography. While cinema was obviously able, effortlessly, to produce a natural representation of the figure and landscape relation, rear-projection 'regresses' and breaks with realist expectations of seamless and integrated representation of space. In *Rear Projection: Molly Parker*, Lewis was referring particularly to the stratification of exterior space, with its opposition between the flattened foreground occupied by the figure in the Renaissance portrait, situated in 'close-up', and the distant landscape background.

This opposition returns to the question of the star and his/her particularly elevated place in Hollywood (not only the key rationale for rear-projection, but also the source of its flawed realism), and to the topography of the Renaissance space. The Hollywood film industry was axiomatically built around stars. Their characteristic attributes and legendary place in genres raised these iconic figures to a privileged position for the spectator's eroticized gaze, possible edification and even adoration. The studio space could highlight their beauty, literally enhanced by the controlled studio technology, and their most highly dramatic moments and characteristic poses were exaggerated by the stasis enforced by the technical device. Here again there is a link to the spatial and conceptual organization of the Renaissance portraits that superimpose highly emblematic figures against symbolic and natural worlds. The elevated importance of the figures and their iconographies suggests a parallel with the Hollywood stars. Whereas the holy figures – Christ, saints or donors – had to be raised out of ordinary surroundings, brought close to the spectator for reverence, contemplation or supplication, they were also embellished with extraordinary beauty, and dramatized by characteristic gestures or poses. Furthermore, the actual, material, spatial dislocation takes the flattened foreground outside time in a way that also enhances the special nature of the figures (whether those of Renaissance iconography or the Hollywood stars). From this perspective an ambiguity affects the studio space: on the one hand, the performers are enacting their narrative roles, even advancing the narrative action; on the other, they are overtaken by their iconicity and the isolated, timeless nature of the space.

Passing time is an essential element in this reassessment of the aesthetics of rear-projection. It is from this perspective that it conforms to Walter Benjamin's sense that new life may be found in seemingly outdated objects, as he discusses in his essay on surrealism:

> Breton was the first to perceive the revolutionary energies that appeared in the 'outmoded' in the first iron constructions, the first factory building, the first photos, the objects that have begun to be extinct, grand pianos, dresses of five years ago, fashionable restaurants when the vogue has begun to ebb from them. (Benjamin 1979: 229)

In his Arcades project, Benjamin looked back at nineteenth-century Paris from the perspective of the 1930s, and suggested that obsolescence brings with it a kind of utopian detachment from use which releases an outmoded building or technology for an altered aesthetic.

Lewis' work with rear-projection should be understood within the context of Benjamin's comment on the return of the outmoded; the shift from use value to cultural value as, with its citation, the object becomes a point of reference back across time. At the end of *Back Story*, the Hansards father and son announce the end of the rear-projection era. The son, Billy, is now employed by Sony as a projectionist, showing films to people who were once his clients. Both vividly evoke the present uselessness of their once productive equipment. Mr Hansard senior says: 'I don't see a couple of years in the future, it will be a couple of months before I take this stuff down to Catalina and use them as sea anchors....' And Billy adds: 'They'll make a nice diving reef for the fishes.'

To bring back the paradoxes of a forgotten, widely despised, technology suggests a parallel, non-teleological approach to cinema history, one that zigzags and can leap-frog across time to make unexpected links between a 'then' of the film industry and a 'now' of art that quotes it. The quotation draws attention to the hidden complexities of the original device and also confuses the linear relation between past and present. I want now to return to the 'aesthetics' of rear-projection in itself, rather than as a source of quotation. I have argued that the device brought with it an estrangement effect, which Viktor Shklovsky (1965) (in his original use of the term) understood as enforcing a disruptive pause in the continuum of whatever human habit was in play at the time. In the case of cinema, the 'habit' might be understood in terms of the spectator's absorption into the coherence and homogeneity of a fiction and its temporal credibility. Thus consciousness of a film's original moment of registration, or a spectator's sudden awareness of the present moment, could threaten fictional time. In this sense, the artificiality, and the given temporal dualism, of rear-projection, always hovered uneasily within its surrounding temporal conventions.

All too often, the absurdity or artificiality inherent in the device risked exposing the mechanism's fragility. It may, indeed, be anachronistic to apply the concept of 'estrangement' retrospectively in this way and to a special effect that belongs to mainstream commercial cinema, but as the history of cinema is re-examined, as films produced industrially are re-watched and reinterpreted in the light of passing time, their complexities emerge more clearly into view. The classical realism of Hollywood cinema seems now to be more heterogeneous than critics and theorists have claimed, as its aesthetics (of which rear-projection is only one example) and the iconography of its stars fragment its supposed realism. However slight the estrangement effect might be, it has allowed Mark Lewis to celebrate a device, widespread within the film industry of modernity, as an unwitting parallel to its contemporary modernisms.

References

'Alfred Hitchcock: A Friendly Salute' (1976) *Take One* 50.

Benjamin, Walter (1979) 'On surrealism', in *One Way Street, and Other Writings*, trans. Edmund Jephcott and Kingsley Shorter (London, Verso).

Brecht, Bertolt (1964) 'A short organum for the theatre', in John Willett (ed. and trans.) *Brecht on the Theatre: The Development of an Aesthetic* (London, Methuen).

Lewis, Mark (2003) 'Foreword', *Afterall* 8.

Païni, Dominique (2000) 'The wandering gaze: Hitchcock's use of transparencies', in *Hitchcock and Art: Fatal Coincidences* (Montreal, Montreal Museum of Fine Art, and Milan, Mazzotta).

Shklovsky, Victor (1965) 'Art as technique', in *Russian Formalist Criticism: Four Essays*, translated and with an introduction by Lee T. Lemon and Marion J. Reis (Lincoln, University of Nebraska Press), pp.3–24.

Index